POLITICAL THEOLOGY:
DEMYSTIFYING THE UNIVERSAL

ENCOUNTERS IN LAW AND PHILOSOPHY
SERIES EDITORS: Thanos Zartaloudis and Anton Schütz

This series interrogates, historically and theoretically, the encounters between philosophy and law. Each volume published takes a unique approach and challenges traditional systemic approaches to law and philosophy. The series is designed to expand the environment for law and thought.

Titles available in the series
STASIS: Civil War as a Political Paradigm
Giorgio Agamben
On the Idea of Potency: Juridical and Theological Roots of the Western Cultural Tradition
Emanuele Castrucci
Political Theology: Demystifying the Universal
Marinos Diamantides and Anton Schütz

General Advisor
Giorgio Agamben

Advisory Board
Clemens Pornschlegel, Institut für Germanistik, Universität München, Germany
Emmanuele Coccia, Ecole des Hautes Etudes en Sciences Sociales, France
Jessica Whyte, University of Western Sydney, School of Humanities and Communication Arts, Australia
Peter Goodrich, Cardozo Law School, Yeshiva University, New York, USA
Alain Pottage, London School of Economics, Law School, UK
Justin Clemens, University of Melbourne, Faculty of Arts, Australia
Robert Young, NYU, English, USA
Nathan Moore, Birkbeck College, Law School, University of London, UK
Alexander Murray, English, University of Exeter, UK
Piyel Haldar, Birkbeck College, Law School, University of London, UK
Anne Bottomley, Law School, University of Kent, UK
Oren Ben-Dor, Law School, University of Southampton, UK

Translator: **Nicholas Heron** is a Postdoctoral Research Fellow in the Centre for the History of European Discourses at the University of Queensland. He is the editor, with Justin Clemens and Alex Murray, of *The Work of Giorgio Agamben: Law, Literature, Life* (Edinburgh University Press, 2008) and the author of a forthcoming monograph entitled *Liturgical Power: Between Economic and Political Theology*.

www.edinburghuniversitypress.com/series/enlp

POLITICAL THEOLOGY: DEMYSTIFYING THE UNIVERSAL

Marinos Diamantides and Anton Schütz

EDINBURGH
University Press

Edinburgh University Press is one of the leading university presses in the UK. We publish academic books and journals in our selected subject areas across the humanities and social sciences, combining cutting-edge scholarship with high editorial and production values to produce academic works of lasting importance. For more information visit our website: edinburghuniversitypress.com

© Marinos Diamantides and Anton Schütz, 2017

Edinburgh University Press Ltd
The Tun – Holyrood Road
12 (2f) Jackson's Entry
Edinburgh EH8 8PJ

Typeset in 11/13 Palatino by
Servis Filmsetting Ltd, Stockport, Cheshire,
and printed and bound in Great Britain by
CPI Group (UK) Ltd, Croydon CR0 4YY

A CIP record for this book is available from the British Library

ISBN 978 0 7486 9776 2 (hardback)
ISBN 978 0 7486 9777 9 (paperback)
ISBN 978 0 7486 9778 6 (webready PDF)
ISBN 978 0 7486 9779 3 (epub)

Contents

1

Premises and Arguments

1.1

Our book is inspired by the observation that all attempts to provide a modern Western model for a convincingly non-imperial[1] type of global civilisation have so far failed, just as the many fruits of the modernity it has fostered have spread, or at least are known, everywhere. The West[2] has brought about the kind of society that is complex enough to necessitate those features that most of us cherish: subjective right and freedom of scientific enquiry; yet apart from that, it has also promoted the myth of a sovereign Will imposing a universal moral duty of working for 'progress' (as opposed to the idea that all work is always and essentially work-in-progress), which, often seen as promoting 'emancipation', is nearly as often the site of serial collateral damage, ending up, as most frequently it does, with the waste of yet another specific form of life. Ironically, subjective right and the freedom to enquire have, led us to discover, not to everybody's liking, that Contingency trumps Will, and that epigenetic developments trump causal explanations and require us to manage ever new unintended and unexpected consequences; yet the 'West' continues to distinguish itself 'from the rest', no longer as colonial master, but still as *primus inter pares*, on account of its blind trust in the ideological notion of cumulative progress and its concomitant indifference to the collateral damage produced, often unintentionally, in the course of its many initiatives that seek to lead the world to 'progress'.

Our attempts to establish the reasons why current evolution seems to follow this direction ever more resolutely, have provoked a series of interrogations and investigations that further extend this unhappy result. What is lacking, we found, is not a more precise blueprint or model of a potentially shareable 'institutional vocabulary' that would enable us to trace the ground lines of global 'occidental civilisation' against its Eastern or Southern 'other'. Nor does the solution lie in a new model of pluralism that would encompass multiculturalism. What is needed, we found, is not the restoration of non-occidental cultures, most of which had been in ruins long before some modern agent further destroyed them (say, Lord Elgin in Athens; IS in Palmyra); rather it is to gauge the conditions for effectively functioning and reproducing social entities and cultural units in the emerging world society, whose key feature – namely a high degree of functional differentiation – rests on the religious ruins of the premodern West, with which most of the global population, availing itself of its own ruins, has no affective relationship. Dealing with matters legal, it cannot be stressed enough that, historically, the simultaneous foregrounding of the rule of law and of the critique of 'the law' corresponds exactly with the legacy of Christianism's critique and 'overcoming' of Judaism, resulting in Christian individualism. Likewise, in politics, the postulation of sovereign will that is equidistant from such binaries as immanence and transcendence, natural and positive law, liberty and statism, revolution and law, rights and social justice, etc., as the 'necessary' basis for organised society, is indisputably what identifies occidental Christianism (Catholicism and Protestantism), including in its latest form: secularism.

Today, there is a vast and rapidly growing offer of studies based upon the perception that the classically modern idea of an uninterrupted route from municipal prejudgement and arbitrariness to the realisation of a single and self-transparent humanity, a global melting pot, has come to nothing, with neo-nationalist, isolationist populism on the rise. Our 'global village' increasingly resembles a world-compassing Tower of Babel, except that it is a topsy-turvy one, in whose construction conflict persists despite most of us understanding the same conceptual languages, notably of legal and political constitutionalism. One way of showing this is related to the spread of Western law; as Samera Esmeir shows, referring to nineteenth-century colonial Egypt, the widespread presence of the Western 'positive law versus natural law' debate took up all available space for discussion in the very name of 'modernity'; this, thereby, both presupposes the violent dehumanisation of subjects of alternative, non-occidental, institutional models, and forecloses the evolution (or even the taking into account) of these models; today the 'positive law versus natural law' model is still playing the role of a resilient and uninterrupted consensus worldwide and is thus structuring the ensuing 'juridical humanity', to quote Esmeir's title.[3] The 'global village', in other words, is real and functioning regardless of barriers and walls extant or proposed. Yet there is no hiding that not everyone feels equally at home in it and that the management of the affairs of the global village is too complicated to be a subject of sovereign will.

A first step that needs to be made in understanding this situation is a partial rehabilitation of Samuel Huntington's 1996 *Clash of Civilizations and the Remaking of World Order*, with the immediate provision that, as we will argue, since no viable 'traditional' moral or practical alternative to Western Christian/secular/post-secular modernity is on the horizon, any conceivable 'clash' can only be endo-civilisational – a clash, or perhaps a civil war – and take place between secular Western models. Critics have focused on Huntington's supposed and supposedly scandalous turn from mere politics to the much 'vaguer' (as it was dubbed by the majority of critics) concept of 'civilisation', and his supplying a divisive substratum of geopolitical tension. The most resolute critics, Edward Said and Noam Chomsky among them, also focused on the other word in the title: 'clash', in view of its aggressive connotations. Now the aggressive character of the title of a book that constitutes an official contribution to US foreign policy is barely surprising; but this should not prevent one from noticing the presence in the title of a hint to a far more important, indeed decisive, thesis. What has escaped all but the most perspicacious observers is the discreet yet significant use of the word 'civilisation' in the plural. For the first time in the history of this type of literature, Huntington's much-disputed and bluntly conservative study has introduced the notion that world conflict may be ultimately based neither on promoting/fostering nor on blocking/sabotaging a single humanity-wide model of evolution (say of despotism by bourgeois democracy and of bourgeois democracy by socialism, to note one well-known narrative) by/through the agonistic action of political strategies, systems or classes.

World conflict, according to the view submitted by Huntington, is not about any of the numberless shades between warfare and politicking, nor is it a matter that belongs, as one contemporary school would have it, exclusively to the international system of politics. Rather, the site of conflict is located, Huntington explained, in the evolution of what lies below political decisions, namely in the diversity of ways of instituting humankind, among which the occidental, and by now globally familiar triadic model of 'humanity' centring on the specific ideas of the political animal (the *zoon politikon*, to recall Aristotle), the juridical human (the 'homo juridicus', to quote A. Supiot's title[4]) and the economic human (the 'homo economicus', to cite critics of A. Smith, J. S. Mill, etc.), is but one among many. Huntington's emphasis on 'civilisations' is much more important than his cocky (and dangerously Schmittian), notion of a 'clash', which also negligently implies that a genuine *agon* can exist among different civilisations as such. Yet it can be said that, with these provisos, corrections and rehabilitations, there is one essential point that Huntington's title and theses do not miss: they locate the main international stake in institutionally manifested latent diversity. And this is how they succeed in profiling an irreconcilable counter-position to the equally programmatic, but – from our viewpoint – much less helpful essay *The End of History and the Last Man*, by Francis Fukuyama. Indeed, even though Fukuyama was a pupil of Huntington, their claims point in exactly opposite directions. One needs to carefully identify what is at stake when a member of the Washington political elite uses, as the distinctive term of his title, the word 'civilisation' by casting it in the plural: what is at stake is Huntington's resolute unsubscription from such singular notions as 'history' or its 'end'. Huntington's notion of a 'clash' should not be taken as a hint of impending doom and global conflict but, on the contrary, as a way of channelling as much attention as possible towards the issue that 'civilisation' – a word which looks back at a relatively short, yet explosive career – can be used as a reference to multiplicity, in direct opposition to its singular use, which reasserts and over-stresses (and over-stretches) the humankind-wide claim to the 'universality' of one civilisation.

When, and only when, we think of civilisations in the plural, without considering them either as classes of cases of one common type, or as species of some common over-arching archetype or genus, without assuming anything like family resemblances between two or more civilisations or of something (or someone) who guarantees them, there shows up a whole new landscape of realities and constraints, possibilities and no-go zones. In thinking of 'universalism' it pays to remember that Cicero's neologism 'universus' meant 'tending to turn into oneness that which is multiple', and that this tendency has not been the prerogative of the West even though it is the one that has proved the most successful. Thus, what best distinguishes the 'pluri-civilisational' viewpoint that we endorse is that we opt to take seriously the fate of civilisations' dispersion into historical blocks – to the point of questioning the effective presence of any unifying power. While, to take a contrasting example, Fukuyama and the (Leo) Straussian school chose to align with the Eurocentric Hegelian idea of history by centre-staging secularised politics and economy, for us the universality of secular modern values remains suspect: suspect of being a harbinger of cultural colonialism, insofar as it is predicated upon the paradigmatically occidental supplement of entitlement as it is gained by a long past of worldwide domination or leadership, or, alternatively, and far more discretely, in the 'light' version, the more 'private' relationship known as *primus inter pares*, based upon a merely operative identity. The nexus of *primus inter pares* being the currently best-working occidental 'recipe' serving the postulation of a binary distinction between the domains of law/politics and 'religion', as based upon a mere 'as-it-happens' sovereignty, a post-sovereign 'sovereignty light', located far below any unpalatable claims to superiority and perfectly compatible with the notion that sovereign power is essentially something that remains permanently in the making.

There is no disputing the large shadow that Western institutions, complete with the unending and continuously radicalising processes of differentiation that characterise them, cast upon planetary evolution, ever modifying and fine-tuning Western humanity's long-standing historical choices of differentiation. Such choices are increasingly hard to unsubscribe from, and hence they determine social evolution, mostly because they are always heavy with collateral consequences; in order to experience the resulting disorder with a sense of certainty, however, humans tend not to abandon their original paradigm but on the contrary stick to it, with some investing in self-similar repetition and others in increasingly refining the distinctions on which this paradigm is based, such as that between law/politics and religion. So far, only in the field of the so-called hard sciences of the laboratory have modern humans been able to endure abrupt 'paradigm shifts'. The increasing instances of xenophobia, which would be ridiculous if they were not terrifying, confirm this – for example, the fear of the burkini on Europe's beaches, which recently witnessed the obverse policing of swimwear, is all the more terrifying because this clothing item, invented only a few years ago by an entrepreneurial female Lebanese–Australian fashion designer, is a perfect example of what had been christened 'glocal-isation' (a term first used in the *Harvard Business Review* in the late 1980s, popularised a decade later by sociologist Roland Robertson, and is now generally taken to refer to the simultaneity or the co-presence of both universalising and particularising tendencies). If the West, the *global space* where the simultaneous presence of binarily organised differences, is a key feature and where commodification, for all its faults, requires cultural flexibility, and 'commercial' peace reverts back to the *particular place* called Europe before the burkini, this is a truly horrifying thing. The burkini exemplifies perfectly how the non-Western subject can be peacefully inserted into the *oikonomik*/managerial mode of social existence pioneered by Christianity and, consequently, into the global space of Westernised/Westernising world society that became accessible with decolonisation; this is a space whose key ideological feature is the simultaneous presence of binarily organised differences – e.g. religion and the secular - under the ideological aegis of sovereignty; its main actual feature, however, is the constant management of differences by a wide range of loosely interconnected actors – from burkini designers to security experts. Insofar as contemporary incidents of Western xenophobia, chauvinism and nationalism suggest a desire to insulate, by means of sovereign will, the West's 'particular ways of life' from the necessary adaptations that come with the globalisation that these very same particularities initially made possible, this amounts to a desire to revert back to the particular place called 'the West' from which to oversee the management of the global space of Westernised/ Westernising world society. The violence of such chauvinism can be and is met with even more violent forms on the part of those Westernised/Westernising non-Christian others whom it angers. All this amounts to bad *oikonomia*, that is, a situation where bio-political power is expected to serve ideological power rather than then other way round; in view of the Westernisation of the whole world, this leads not to a genuine 'clash of civilisations' but to an endo-civilisational 'civil war'.

In this sense, the continuously radicalising processes of social differentiation that the West pioneered have remained predicated on its particular ideological and identitarian paradigm of continuously distinguishing between law/politics and religion while centre-staging questions about the nature of the sovereign who encompasses and guarantees these distinctions. Where and how these adaptive processes are/are not happening determines which are/will be the most successful and competitive sections of humankind, garnering evolutionary advantages at the expense of less competitive sections, in a process that obviously deepens the distance separating both sides. It would however be an error, and incidentally one that is to be found equally frequently in liberal and in Marxist interpretations, to believe that the distances and differences incurred between fast-differentiating societies and others will necessarily give rise to a melt-down of plural civilisations into one ever more self-identical single civilisation. We suggest that ignoring, as a matter of indifference (in the sense of an absence of any relationship whatsoever, agonistic or not), the contribution of civilisational collusions and collisions in the emerging, in modernity, of well-defined and exclusive zones of functionally differentiated sections of humankind, and the consequent increasing gaps in matters of success, growth, and opportunities that lead to crises (which in turn require policing and management), is symptomatic of a foundational Western schizophrenia. Specifically, this outward display of indifference correlates to an internal, constitutional, identitarian, indifference of Western civilisation towards its own split between, on the one hand, the processes of increasing functional differentiation and the techniques of management and social government that allow and invite these splits to develop, and, on the other hand, the actual presence or absence of conditions for truly liveable forms of social coexistence, with the constraints these tend to impose upon institutional conditions, and with the risks they entail of decelerating the tempo of evolution. What the horrifyingly ridiculous burkini saga shows is that whereas the tendency towards increasingly functional differentiation favours an ever increasing density of interdependency relations, plasticity and 'glocalism', the parallel tendency towards imposing identity-related constraints reduces interdependency, even governability (while potentially increasing authoritarianism) and takes, over the long-term, culturally and often religiously shaped forms.

1.2

We contend that, by perpetuating the myth that management serves sovereignty in the name of equitable progress, the West tends to ignore the very features that allow it to simultaneously pioneer and undermine universal interdependency. In doing this the West remains indifferent to the collateral effects on others of its own constitutive, trade-mark European, indifference towards the gap between, on the one hand, its managemental and decision-making arts and the recipes of social government, and, on the other hand, the actual presence or absence of conditions for liveable forms of social coexistence. In doing so we build upon Agamben's account of Western legal and political imagination as incorporating Christian economic-political theology.[5] By now the post-sovereign, biopolitical model of administration of persons and things alike – wherein some precious human 'resources' are treasured and others wasted or discarded – is a visible, worldwide reality. Secular modernity constitutes itself as the constant management of interminable crises, while the late modern global 'empire of management' can be rendered as multicultural domination[6] and 'administration without sovereignty'[7] in a disenchanted, post-hierocratic, post-sovereign, polycentric, 'flat' world society. It is a truism that states lose their role as comprehensive welfare providers and are even side-lined in the competition to play the role of *maestro* by such transnational organisations as the European Union (EU) or the World Trade Organization (WTO). States are reduced to the role of police (immigration control and tax collection) – a role a handful of them play on a global scale on account of their military might; they no longer appear to be the holders of that fantastic super-power that we call 'sovereignty' and that lies at the centre of the occidental legal and political imagination: that is the power to constitute and defend, either by means of juridical fiction or political decisiveness, organised human communities the aggregate of which is globalised as 'humanity' in both its Kantian and Marxian varieties. This situation exacerbates a modern crisis of legitimacy/authority[8] so that overall the sovereign is exposed as both *illegitimate* and *impotent*. Yet across the Westernised and Westernising world less authority has not only meant more normalising power but *also* an increased desire for a potent sovereign. This can be seen in the UK, where Brexiteers were sold the idea of 'taking back control', as much as in Egypt, where scholars speak of a '*loop*'[9] between the suspicion of all past and extant couplings of law and politics and a desire for either improved legislation or legal interpretation, and/or a new, 'revolutionary' shift by means of constituent power (be it as part of class struggle or the pseudo 'clash of civilisations)'. This 'loop', we submit, is part of the *originally Western cybernetics-of glorious-sovereignty-cum-inglorious-administration* that affects the unhappy Briton, who claims that Brexit means 'making Britain great again', as much as the unhappy Muslim British man who goes to Syria to kill and be killed for the glory of an 'Islamic state'. So-called 're-religioning' forces: IS, religious Zionist settlers, genocidal Eastern Christian Serbian bishops, Sri Lankan Buddhist monks blessing genocidal politics, and so on, are best seen *not* as signs of a clash of civilisations in the plural, but as mere fragments of the indefinite and multifaceted 'crisis' that is by now globally conceived as taking place *inside* humanity's 'common household'.

One can speak with Agamben, of all contemporary conflict as instances of 'civil war',[10] which requires management in deed, but sovereign decision in name only. Inoperative, vulnerable life is thus exposed throughout the world at once to the efficiency-based logic of post-sovereign, neo-liberal managers, but also to their technologically savvy activist/ hacktivist opponents *and* a whole spectre of crusaders and anti-crusaders who are enamoured with the conceptual message of Western *political theology*, ignorant, as mostly they are, that this message is embedded in the image of the *impotent-yet-triumphant* God on the cross, and abstracted out of it in a secular context: God/the sovereign state – liberal or 'Islamic' – is to be glorified even if evidently weak and *failing*. The suggestion, by contrast, that what we are confronted with is an epic, genuine, inter-civilisational battle for sovereignty between the 'secular' and the 'religious', which is bound to end only with the sovereign triumph of either side, is not only conceptually misleading, but also unfair: it privileges the subject whose imagination and affects are structured according to the Western Christian/post-Christian tradition of flexible (economic) political theology, as opposed to, say, a subject structurally enamoured with the idea of crusade to recover the holy land from the infidels, who has no strong affective attachment to the idea of *glory in impotence* and *oiko-nomia* and the correlative institutional history. If the war goes awfully wrong, the former will launch an 'enquiry' to 'learn lessons' *to be used in the next war* (e.g. the 'Chilcot' Iraq War inquiry in the UK); the latter might detonate a suicide bomb. If (and only if) one asks who, if anyone, could be at ease with the present situation, whereby popular sovereignty simulta-neously implodes *and* is glorified as immortal, there may not be another answer than the Christian/post-Christian occi-dental subject, as the only human who has been exposed long enough to the theo-political notion of an *oikonomia* com-prising both sovereign will and management – the idea that the king reigns but does not govern. Think, for example, of how – in Greece, 'saved' from bankruptcy at least formally after the relevant EU laws were suspended as an instance of European 'solidarity' (although in reality it looks as if what was saved in fact was only certain banks) – the popular Will was entrusted in a category of actors who are defined by the fact that they started as would-be glorious sovereigns but ended up as mere administrators, acting unwillingly or with 'malevolent neutrality'.

1.3

The situation today presents us with two distinct, decisive realities, each of which poses different epistemological problems. First, the long-standing 'crisis of legitimacy' of modern liberal democracies that so many theorists have been writing about is compounded by a crisis of sovereignty triggered by the implosion of Western-style sovereign nation states' power to provide citizens, and growing numbers of immigrants, with dignity, welfare and security. With nation states dramatically weakened, the continuance (or rather, the gradual abandonment) of the basic functions they are meant to discharge now falls to loose transnational networks of unaccountable (also often very largely *hated*) bureaucracies and experts, whose rationality is neither political nor legal, but rather administrative/managerial. Confronted with this administrative/managerial reality, we hold that the priority is to turn to tools allowing us to understand this situation in appropriately non-dramatic, non-apocalyptic terms; we note social systems theory for its virtue of showing the most navigable path out of the Old European politico-legal labyrinth made of sovereignty, authorship, control and a few others, by downgrading them from seething but grandiose problems to mere administrative routines. Second, however, we highlight another reality, parallel to the implosion of sovereignty, which, we shall argue, cannot *not* be subject to dramatisation, discontent, even hysteria and violence: everyone today speaks of a generalised *crisis of trust* in institutions of government but also in all other pillars of modernity (except science), including business. This *subjective* crisis, we argue, is one to which systems theory has little to offer (other than, ironically, becoming itself the object of mistrust). The capital point to make here is that this crisis of trust in the institutions and processes of modernity that most of us want to enjoy is unevenly and differently felt and provokes different reactions, with some people (individuals or groups) finding it easier to cope with the ensuing uncertainty than others. But in this sense, the very real divide between those who benefit from globalisation and those who don't, is not sufficient to explain where, when and how the crisis of trust manifests itself. While we fully accept the relevance of this divide we think it is far from sufficient because it is centred too much on the common humanity-wide denominator of secular modernity: the idea that the human is primarily defined by material needs and by the work that is necessary to meet them. Our contrary view on this point is, briefly, that the speaking animal is never – and perhaps never can be – quite as *ideologically naked* as the non-speaking animal.

Throughout history, social relations have required – and cultural groups have invented, traditions have organised, etc. – the dimension of *sense* on which inter-subjective trust is based, and which bears *little or no relation to reality*. This brings us to the topic of different *religions*, which we understand not as matters of private faith coexisting with universalisable, secular, public reason – as the Enlightenment believed – but as the domain of subjectivity's institution via *affective* identification with particular metaphysical postulates to which the subject can remain indebted even after their deconstruction. Engaging in secular public reason, we hold, also *presupposes* such blind trust as is generated among those who still believe in the truth of such metaphysical postulates or/and those who simply validate them as true social facts in a performative manner. Hence we shall isolate and discuss certain such key postulates, mostly those of Western Christianity, which – or so we shall argue – still bind together 'in blind trust' Christians and post-Christians and, *ipso facto*, separate them as the 'West' from the 'rest' – even as we are all, by now, inevitably working to give rise to a global society.

Sovereignty plays here a paradigmatic role. Not only does it function as a *sine qua non* of state-based geo-sociality, it also epitomises the identitary bond and as such must be 'glorified', even – indeed especially – when humiliated: an image remarkably evocative of Jesus on the cross. Other interlinking postulates – or perhaps facets of the same postulate – are the idea of the world as an *oikos* ('household'), whose management is distinguished from its ownership, and the idea of continual moral progress. We do not suggest that these, or any, postulates are static and thus we shall not argue that society remains hierocratic or subject to political theology in Carl Schmitt's sense of this term. Using various resources from diverse fields, we shall demonstrate the dynamic process of *epigenesis*, which has led these initially religious postulates to be reconfirmed via ever more secular developments in the world of ideas that have better served the needs of their times. Hence, for example, we do not suggest that belief in moral progress today is merely a superficially secularised version of eschatology; rather, today it is largely an old fashioned expression of the *anti-eschatological* attitude shown by modern humans who are determined to proceed towards the future constantly 'learning from their mistakes', at once acknowledging contingency and seeing the unintended consequences, or non-consequences, of their actions/decisions as crucial ingredients of a non-ending 'learning curve' (while accepting their negative impact as collateral damage, as if saying 'stuff happens', or some equivalent formulation of indifference). Similarly, we show how the old Christian notion of an absolute power that is 'economically' related to its shortcomings has given rise to a political and legal imagination; the democratic Greek *polis*, prone to *stasis* (civil warfare) and faction, has been absorbed, in the history of the Christianised Roman (later Byzantine) Empire, by the much more solid Roman *dominium*; once the latter was Christianised it was once again reconceived as an *oikos* whose ultimate master, God, could pass on the keys to whoever could act as his vice-master, lieutenant, or vicar. The first candidates for this office were the Christianised (Byzantine) emperors themselves, who were at once seen and respected as *dominus mundi*, in the Roman fashion, and as priests (priests outside the Church). In this quality, the imperial master was equally required to be an *oikonomos* of his realm, stripping laws of their absoluteness whenever it was convenient.

The universal modern idea of 'humanity' that lives in the world *qua* global household, at once as its own master and servant, would be unthinkable without Saint Paul, but not only him; this cosmopolitan character made full use of the opportunities of globalisation in his time by spreading the old message of the Covenant in a revised form; reshaping the decreasing difference between Jews and gentiles with the substitution of the circumcision ritual by the 'circumcision of the heart') and turning conversion to Christianity into a personal choice – thus instituting a revolutionary shift from being born into a religious identity to *choosing* one. This focus on individual desire and the openness to conversion

– aided massively by the perks and patronage it attracted in Byzantium – is certainly a part of the genealogy of what we call modern subjective right. It not only facilitated the spread of Christianism; it also provided the ground for late medieval Catholic lawyers and intellectual friars who, by holding that the world as house of God was no longer a specific place of domination but an abstract *dominium mundi* (a 'dominion' without domination or mastery) that included the unexplored parts of the earth and, beyond, the whole cosmos, thus laid the ground for later expansionist European 'discoveries'.

Finally, in the occidental high Middle Ages, the idea of an impotent yet glorious God gave rise to the idea that absolute power (that of popes and emperors) must also be limited at the same time: without this move, modern constitutionalism would never have found the materials to conceive of sovereignty as all-powerful ('constituent power') and also limited ('constituted power'). The ultimate inheritor of this double power is of course the modern individual and 'humanity'.

1.4

In Part I of this book, we expound – referring to a wide range of writers in law, politics, sociology and philosophy – the suggestion that our global situation now verges on anomic administration without government, obscured by our ideological fixation with the 'rules' of democracy or of law; we argue particularly in favour of those for whom the very notion of sovereignty produces this mixture of hierarchy and anarchy. Yet already in Chapter 2, we are pressed to observe that, notwithstanding the implosion of sovereignty, Western and Westernised political theorists and public lawyers, with rare exceptions, take sovereignty, understood either as a purely political or as purely legal construct, as an indispensable feature of political life, and concentrate on the secondary issue of the crisis of legitimacy, emphasising lapses in states' commitment to both political and legal Right (e.g. growing social injustice and protracted uses of state of emergency). In order to explain this disparity between imploding sovereignty and a growing concern for legitimacy, we proceed by turning to the issues of religion and political theology, each of which is here given a fresh interpretation. In Chapter 2 we also begin by exploring

Giorgio Agamben's genealogical investigations of Christian/ post-Christian *economic-political theology*, which, as he argues, still gives modern secular Western legal and political imagination its basic structure, whereby an ever-acclaimed yet weak sovereign is combined with unglamorous yet effective administrative rationality. In Chapters 3 to 5 we tackle head-on the accusation of determinism and essentialism that one can level against this – and indeed any – genealogical view. Starting with determinism in Chapter 4, we turn to systems theory and explore how its ultra-modern, definitively non-genealogical use of the word 'sense' as something that concerns only impersonal communications that occur now, free from the past, is quite intelligible and yet fails to explain the ideological hold of the notion of sovereignty. In sum, we argue that while systems theory makes perfect universal conceptual sense in describing our highly complex, functionally differentiated, globalised society dispassionately in terms of the impersonal dynamics of continuing function systems (e.g. law, politics, science, the economy, art, religion) on the one hand and of elementary 'communicative systems' on the other hand, at the level of subjective and particular *sense-as-human-consciousness* – where humans construct identities – systems theory and the reality it describes need to be *re-dramatised* (if not re-humanised) as part and parcel of the history of Western dominance and decay.

To explain this, in our discussion on 'the religion of progress' in Chapter 4 we do not discuss 'religion' as private faith with a universalisable kernel of conceptual truth (as is its dominant, Enlightenment-based understanding notably, but not only, in German Idealism): instead we follow a line of thought that suggests that conceptual meaning – the domain in which modern humans are freer than ever before to produce sense, to escape from the lies of their traditions, to suggest science-based alternatives – is not the most fundamental level of meaning as far as the institution of the linguistic animal in society is concerned. Rather, the most fundamental levels of meaning are affective (iconomic and experiential); throughout human history it has been blind trust in, and love of, particular metaphysical postulates that has allowed humans to experience contingency and the perpetual contemporary change and disorder it entails with a false if comforting sense of order and continuity. We suggest that neither modern ideas of civil religion, nor a 'public reason' that all can equally engage in regardless of faith in order to produce consensus, can overcome (and indeed both presuppose) such blind trust. In Chapter 5, on political theology, we turn our attention to the justified rejection of any essentialism; we begin by explaining the effective function of the *ruins* of mediaeval Western political theology, especially in its occidental late mediaeval version. After showing how Carl Schmitt succeeded in reminding us that the mediaeval theo-political tradition is not quite overcome by secularisation only at the cost of reanimating it, we show how our modern, secular, legal and political imagination, including his, is the unwilled, *epigenetic*, distinctive product of a long-dead mediaeval tradition. Traditions, we argue from an evolutionary standpoint, do not survive unless they transform and adapt, and in this regard it is true that Christianism was neither truly nor superficially displaced by secularisation; rather, as surprising as this sounds, secularisation is found among Christianism's core values. Yet the contemporary fascination with the question of the 'return' of religion and political theology, mirroring perfectly the mediaeval fascination with such binaries as the 'the sacred' and 'the temporal', suggest that the Christian/post-Christian subject desires intensely to experience the turbulent post-religious present with a sense of order and identity. Likewise, in constitutionalism, the intense desire either to juridify or to repoliticise our managerial world suggests a desire to experience the disorder that comes with the demise of the rule of law and of democracy with a continuing sense of blind trust in the old image of a sovereign who structures the tension between the transcendent and the temporal. In this sense both the attempt to dismiss and to overplay the role of political theology are signs of Western and Westernised consciousness making fictional, identity-enhancing, continuity-promising, glorious *surplus sense* out of the non-fictional, purely present-related sense offered to us by systems theory, whereby the impersonal self-management of inglorious inter-systemic communications *is all there is*.

In Chapter 6 (Part II), we highlight the need for a historicised comparative political theology. If modernity, including constitutionalism, has been the collateral, epigenetic product of a particular religion, Christianism, and if our fascination with the idea of a sovereignty that strides the immanent and the transcendental, the pragmatic and the right suggests a need to experience the present from the comforting position of inheritors of the ruins of Christian economic-political theology, then the current crisis is experienced differently across civilisations, with only the Western Christian/post-Christian subject availing of the blind, affective trust in sovereign will as an all-encompassing 'circle' in which everything somehow falls into place. To put it differently, while the whole world has by now bought into Christianity's loop of progress narrative, which rests on the image of a see-saw between sovereign will and management, causality and contingency, when the chips are down only *some* of us can remain perfectly stoic – as if we still believed that, at the end of the day, whatever happens must be part of a mysterious *oikonomia* that has always played out as *a see-saw* between willing and managing. We look at modern Israel as an example of a Westernised political and juridical culture where, in order for permanent crisis management to be dressed up as democracy and rule of law, an *oikonomic*/economic symbiosis had to emerge between Westernised secularist and 'religious' Zionists who worship the ruins of *Western* political theology. Subsequently, in order to gain perspective, we look at the ruins of two different, non-occidental, premodern religions and political theologies, a love of which, even an interest in which, in the categories of Western modernity, can only count as a disadvantage: Biblical Israel and the Eastern Roman Empire (Byzantium). Wrongly presented in occidental historiography respectively as theocratic and caesaro-papist, two supposed 'problems' that occidental political theology managed to 'correct', these theo-political imaginations were rather distinguished by their weak notions of sovereignty: by putting the sacred and the temporal; the transcendent and the immanent; absolute and limited public power; the glorious if impotent sovereign will and the mundane if effective management of populations, in a perpetual, unfalsifiable dialectic 'relation', occidental political theology did not so much democratise the exercise of the 'power to steer' social life and 'cause' results, as it perpetuated the myth of such causal power and obfuscated its effective helplessness in a sea of unmasterable, at best only manageable, contingency. In Chapter 7 we speak of secularisation as one of the many works-in-progress that characterise modernity; we consider the views of such thinkers as M. Gauchet and J. L. Nancy, who see Christianism as the flagship among the 'great religions' whose trajectory is, they assure us, assuredly headed towards secularisation. What we suggest, *pace* Gauchet and Nancy, is that the occidental phase of Western political theology might represent a 'stalling' of the historical process of the 'disenchantment' of the great religions and the 'auto-deconstruction' of monotheism respectively. This explains the endless fascination with the relation of religion to law/politics at a time when a large share of those fascinated declare themselves atheists. The key issue we identify in this regard is the Christian inflection of history not quite as work-*in*-progress but as the result of taking up the moral duty to work *for* progress; for centuries occidental political and juridical culture has invested unduly in the metaphysical idea that there is a cumulative surplus of value in the necessary work humans undertake to survive in their ever changing environments: this is the key ingredient of occidental civilisation's success and self-confidence; yet it is also what condemns it to the well-known charges of negligence, indifference and hypocrisy in relation to the multiple 'collateral damages' triggered when the duty of working for universal progress is carried out.

On the one hand, if the human person, instituted according to the occidental mode, is the result of the polarity between two ideal-typical positions existing alongside each other and in mutual presupposition, the legislator and the legal subject (the *powerful sovereign* and the *autonomous human*), then the key of this relationship is, in historical terms, the Western theme and deed of *revolution* justified as the harbinger of *progress*, endowing occidental modernity with the ideas of limited government, subjective right, liberty, revolutions accomplished *by means and in the name of authority*, not challenges to it. At the same time, however, the modern occidental Christian/post-Christian subject hangs on, beknownst or unbeknownst, to its privilege of being still attached to, be it only to the ruins of, its erstwhile religion and its economic-political theology, and it is this fading remainder that enables it to blindly trust the all-encompassing quality of the sovereignty imagined as the never-ending 'dialectic' of power and legitimacy, while simultaneously blinding it to the catastrophic, collaterally damaged aspect of its dedication to the pursuit of 'progress'. The idea, for example, that bourgeois democracy and capitalism, first, and socialism and communism, second, merit all kinds of sacrifices as superior stages of moral advancement, an idea discredited in the light of the immense collateral damage it caused alongside with some more beneficial aspects, continues to be commended, sometimes discreetly, sometimes with full propagandistic thrust, by its activist advocates who feel as morally bound to announce to the world the 'Good News' of moral progress as had been the whole train of their role models – currently spearheaded by Saint Paul.

In Chapter 8 we pursue this theme further, in relation to a range of both key Enlightenment writers and contemporary 'post-secular' writers who recognise the role of ideology and faith but wish to channel them towards progressive goals. Both sets of writers appear to 'iconomically' and experientially *identify* with the metaphysical postulate embedded in images and rituals that the Greeks and Romans – at least pre-Constantine – ignored: notably the sign of the cross as one of *failure AND glory*! Thus, as far as the speaking beings and their state of coexistence is concerned, a long Western tradition of rationality has been *entrusted* to the shaky, non-rational, programmatic, unquestionable postulate: progress! In the gesture of contradicting and rejecting the Universalist–Christian, Christological, theo-political mediaeval tradition, in the very gesture of disavowing and re-appropriating this tradition, which throughout two millennia has affectively seduced the Western subject through its symbols (starting with the cross, the symbol of universal salvation through martyrdom and resurrection) and rituals (e.g. those that celebrate the Pentecostal miracle – which allows the 'Good News' to be known equally by all), the thinkers of the Enlightenment, and today's neo-Paulists as well, take up and revalidate this very tradition whereby the announcement of the 'Good News' is deemed more important than any negative consequence it may generate; in contemporary politics, this charge applies to both neo-liberals and neo-Marxists. The right and the left are two sides of the same Christian/post-Christian civilisational coin that is incessantly cast, with scant regard for the effects on others, on pluralism and, hence, on democracy. This prompts us to ask whether we have not reached the point in which the Western mode of world making would be best advised to clarify its specific relationship to *universalism* and its inherent tendencies determining how *universal* human problems are *experienced*. If so, the grand promise that a better world is possible, itself predicated upon an interplay of political sovereignty/constituting power/revolution and legal sovereignty/constituted power/constitutional settlement, sounds just as convincing (or as hollow) as does the throne of the god of the onto-theological imagery that it replaces once the god of revelation has been killed. We conclude Chapter 8 with a summary of our positions and situate accordingly the *words-cum-deeds* of today's public intellectuals vying to either re-juridify or, alternatively, repoliticise a world that is, very largely, subject to mere management. Let us be clear: Our point here is not to unsubscribe from the critique of bio-politics. We do want to raise the bar for such critique, however, because we think that ritually reasserting a critical stance is simply not good enough. That ideologies, fantasies, even shared values and consensuses, can continue their hold on the subject even after what has been, perhaps in some respects prematurely, hailed as their 'deconstruction', is a possibility that we believe needs to be taken seriously.

Part I
Religions R Us

2

From Sovereignty to Negeschatology

Today, as Wendy Brown laments, 'with rare exceptions, political theorists take sovereignty to be a *necessary* feature of political life' (added emphasis). Her charge relates to the fact that, in her words:

> Sovereignty produces both internal hierarchy (sovereignty is always sovereignty over something) and external anarchy (by definition, there can be nothing governing a sovereign entity, so if there is more than one sovereign entity in the universe, there is necessarily an anarchy among them). Importantly, both hierarchy and anarchy are at odds with democracy, if the latter is understood as a modestly egalitarian sharing of power.[1]

Yes, the notion of sovereignty allows us to think of a political unit as being necessarily both hierarchical and anarchic; yet it has a long (pre-)history that, importantly, does not have all its roots in the ancient Greek democratic polis, which had a tendency to disunion, faction, stasis; there, the binary relation of internal hierarchy and external anarchy lacked, as it were, the solid, omni-resistant anchor that is offered by our concept of sovereignty. The concept of sovereignty is unthinkable, we submit, following Agamben and some others, other than within a Western (Greek–Roman–Christian) paradigm that presupposes unity as, and entrusts it to, a flexible economic–anarchic 'relationship' of relative indifference between hierarchy and anarchy, which ultimately finds its model in the Trinitarian God. For said notion of unity as 'relationship' – which we call, following Agamben, *oikonomia* – is, we argue,

23

epigenetically responsible for the fruits of modernity. Also, (1) it condemns lives and 'forms-of-lives' in ways that are iniquitous, and (sometimes) can be understood as 'collateral damage' or as the costs of modernity, if by the latter we mean something more glorious, more overwhelmingly attractive, than it is suggested by modernity's sternly self-restrained understanding as held by Max Weber or Michel Foucault; (2) it obfuscates the anomia behind the imaginary notion of sovereign will. Thus, we claim, the 'human waste' that goes with modernity is seen as un/worthy sacrifice on the altar of 'progress' under the auspices of a sovereign, which some 'want' and others 'oppose', thus giving us plenty to fight about and generating crises that call for yet more *oikonomia*, and so on. Here, what is most important to retain from Agamben's complex narrative is, first, that in the scheme he presents all differences are imagined as contained in the idea of a relational unity (according to the image of the Triune, which is one and yet consists of the relations of its constituent hypostases); and second, that the classical Greek distinction between *oikos*/household and polis/politics was enveloped in the Christian imagination by the notion of *oikonomia*.

Under Western-Christian skies human life-time used to be suspended upon eternity through many centuries; eternity, however, had not been the Christian contribution to occidental time-architecture. This was eschatology, the horizon of the last things to come. Accordingly, the new micro-biopolitical reduction to instant decision-making efficiency should be qualified as *negeschatology*. Heralding the beginning of bio-politics and managerialism, the rise of the Trinitarian God and the vision of the social as household gave rise to an imagination whereby all binary distinctions require not synthesis or resolution but flexible management and administrative (rather than legal, political or ethical) rationality. In fact, this (Trinitarian) economic-political theology eventually made possible, in the sixth- or seventh-century canon law of the Byzantine Church, a new meaning of 'exception' (to a rule or principle), referred to as *oikonomia*. *Oikonomia*, which in classical Greece had meant the apolitical administration of a household, had by then become the mysterious divine praxis undertaken for the salvation of humankind.[2] The second lesson from Agamben's thesis is that the Christian theological idea of exception-as-*oikonomia* came to coalesce with, respectively, the Greek and Roman legal concepts of *epieikeia* and *aequitas*, fairness and justice, and ultimately to justify the anomic dispensation (*dispensa*) that relieves one from too rigid an application of the canons in imitation of divine compassion for humanity.[3] This process marked a shift in the exercise of power in the Byzantine political and legal system: dispensation from the law gradually replaced legislation as the main expression of sovereignty. Byzantine rulers found it equally expedient to gain legitimacy by appearing as merciful Christians, e.g. by annulling onerous contracts binding the meek but also pardoning their corrupt officials.

Agamben is not a historian, but his view on the mediaeval Trinitarian dogma gives us precious help in understanding certain contemporary problems. Among the growing number of critics of contemporary liberal democracy who refer to political theology, he supports his criticism with a historicised perspective to today's crisis of legitimacy; whereas democracy theorists as well as constitutional lawyers speak of modern government as based on free, rational public deliberation, for Agamben there has not been effective democracy since classical Athens. Deliberation, he claims, has long been substituted, at first by carefully orchestrated ritualistic acclamations of the 'charitable' sovereign in the mediaeval era (with the decisive input of religious authorities) and, today, by the media-manipulated construction of 'public opinion', regarding the public good (with the decisive input of 'experts' – say, on the economy, or security). The crucial point then and now is that the 'sovereign', be it the Christian monarch or the 'people', do not really rule through their decisions; rather, their decisions follow the dictates of those who know, or purport to know, how 'to manage' the situation. Thus, real power resides with the civil and clerical bureaucracy of the Christian Byzantine emperor, the majordomus of the occidental anointed king and, in modern times, with increasingly differentiated professions (lawyers, politicians, social scientists, etc.) and impersonal bureaucracies and organised interest groups, who derive their legitimacy neither from democracy nor from law but from their expertise, and whose input into political and legal decision making is more decisive than we like to think. Today, this critique is becoming increasingly relevant with the constant talk of crises of trust in government; moreover, as many now talk of imploding political sovereignty (say, in Greece) and protracted legal exceptionalism (e.g. wherever open-ended states of emergency have been declared), it is easier to be persuaded by the critics that ours is not a culture of legal and/ or political *krisis* (Greek for 'decision') but of perpetual crisis requiring, not principled decision/judgement but management. Said differently, Agamben's challenge is that for over two millennia of Western history, behind the façade of (legally or politically defined) sovereignty there is anomic administration without government.[4]

2.2

The suggestion that some 'higher' instance and/or its vicarious agents on earth can actually or potentially 'steer' human associations and their fate is an old dream shared by all pious monotheists (including some 'mono-pantheonists', for if there is only one pantheon, the unity effect is arguably the same). Now, it so happens that these religions, as we are told by Marcel Gauchet, brought with them a threefold 'dynamics of transcendence'.[5] First, the idea of the 'sacred', previously dispersed and coextensive with 'something like nature', mutated into one omnipotent creator God who was still sustaining the world, yet now from a position that was increasingly withdrawn from it. Second, the notion of God's transcendence led man to abandon magical explanations in relation to the phenomena that surrounded him (realising a potential that, according to Nancy, we find exclusively within monotheism[6]), and third, the idea of human universality under one God and His human vicar both legitimated and spread with political empires – for the new God was to be God of all men. Per Gauchet, these three dynamics of transcendence result in a fascinating paradox: the more powerful God becomes, 'the more man is free' in the sense that man begins to question the divine law once it is brought to bear on earth, and so to reason for himself, to embrace his freedom. Similarly, Nancy writes of the 'auto-deconstructive' tendencies of monotheisms,[7] which gradually marginalise their myths in favour of narratives that relate directly to the needs and interests of man, including in relation to law and politics. It is difficult to fault such paradoxological theories for focusing on the 'great religions' and the imperialist politics that they find themselves associated with, at the expense of 'lesser' religions: for, at least in Gauchet's case, there is a conscious understanding that 'progress' is, in any case, an incorrect description of what happened in the historic sequences concerned. Yet for both Gauchet and Nancy, Christianism and the Roman statist-juridical legacy, as it was acculturated in the aftermath of Christianisation and secularisation, represent the epitome of a somehow greater world-changing process, which 'leads us out of religion' into law/politics proper. That the 'way out of religion' passes through the turbulent process of putting law and state increasingly into the place formerly held by religion is a theme retained by both Gauchet and Nancy, even as neither of them shows interest in the particularities of this religion, especially in its mystical economic theology. Gauchet and Nancy expose themselves to the reproach that by still allowing, if uneasily, the fantasy of a modern-style unitary (political or legal) sovereignty to persist (as part of the historic tendency of finding a way 'out of religion'), they still subscribe to the above-described Janus-faced, see-saw image of sovereignty as the economic relation between (1) absolute decision-making power and (2) a need for legitimacy. They thereby inadvertently sub-introduce a rather questionable genealogical connection according to which the current turn to management, managerialism, 'managementality', represents a stage in the evolution of modern, post-religious politics.[8] It is this argument that, in the light of some of the more recent and most innovative contributions of Agamben, deserves a closer look.[9] Agamben forestages the inseparable links between the history of *oikonomia*/management and the Trinitarian constitution of Christianism, including its post-history. If indeed it is by virtue of this economic-political theology that the Christian/post-Christian West distinguishes itself from other civilisations, then the merit of the belief in transcending/exiting parochial religious creeds by sticking to the reference to universal reason appears in a different and less exciting light.

Any attempt to grasp its two-layered model of governing – one millennium Greek–Roman, one millennium 'reformed' Roman–Christian – requires the student of Western institutions to look for its two conditions: the factual indifference with respect to the outcomes, collateral victims, etc., of its own action, that allows it to keep going; and the deep concern about them that allows it to consider itself as superior to any merely imperial type of global civilisation. This, we claim, involves: (1) thinking within a landscape of binary distinctions, some of which are inherited from classical philosophical meta-physics (e.g. body/mind, *zoe/bios*, private/public, emotion/reason, *dynamis/energeia*, *auctoritas/potestas*, autonomy/heteronomy); some of later provenance such as the distinction between God and Caesar, or the modern secular trilogy law/politics/religion. *Ipso facto*, as Agamben's *Homo Sacer* series shows abundantly, we tend to disregard ('abandon') any 'form-of-life'[10] that cannot be neatly placed on either side of these distinctions. And (2) postulating a third element capable of encompassing such binary-relational encryptions of reality, without dissolving them, thereby stabilising their 'tension'. In this regard, recall how the Stoics introduced for this purpose the ideas of *Logos* and *Pneuma* (Greek for 'spirit'), to be replaced in the mediaeval period by the Christian postulates of God and the Holy Spirit. Further important ingredients are the postulate of an incarnated Son of God/Son of Man and the idea that the world is organised as a huge household (Greek: *oikos*) originally 'owned' by God and, later, with secularisation, by this God's universal church-cum-'humanity'. Although this divinity is no longer referred to in public discourse today, our thinking still remains 'deficiently immanent' (and heir to the Western/Christian tradition) insofar as we still think in terms of unfalsifiable dialectical relations constituting a unity in ways that mirror the Christian imagery according to which all differences – including the modern distinction between 'public reason' and 'religion as private faith' – boil down to binary relations within one household, the house of God, of the people, of humanity, organised in a way that prevents them from ever merging or separating, and whose tension requires no resolution, but ongoing management and housekeeping.

By speaking of Trinitarianism we wish to refer to a Western Christian trump card whose range extends far beyond the sphere of religion – that is, if by 'religion' we mean, following widespread usage, a matter of mere belief. Trinitarian theo-technology neutralises the objections of those who find

Agamben's formulation reprehensible, arguing that what is dealt with under the heading of 'Christianism' must be 'about religion', or one would incur a 'contradiction'. The point here is neither religion maintained nor religion diluted by secularisation: it is, rather, the non-religious career of Christianism, in particular of occidental Christianism. We must leave for another occasion the question how far certain ideas about Western Christianism and its theology suffer from a 'religionist fallacy', but to 'naturally' subject Trinitarian theology to the solely religious sphere clearly indicates a lack of appropriate categories. The Trinitarian innovation features God as a strip with the two surfaces 'one' and 'three' disposed in such a way that the two do not rule each other out, but are in constant and continuous connection – a genuine pre-topological advance of the Moebius loop. We limit ourselves to two steps. One happened in the fourth century CE in the Christian East. We know that the Christian faith, after ages of external persecutions and internal disputes, was finally chosen by an emperor who simultaneously emigrated from Rome to the Eastern city he founded, naming it after himself, to be henceforth the Roman Empire's official religion. But in order to prove its superiority the new faith needed to stick to a coherent creed – a difficult task, given its components: the extreme theological transcendence of the divine one, and the equally extreme immanence of the crucified. No elegant solution, none at least that could exclude other solutions, would fall into place on its own. The Gospel says little about their relations. Neither would faith have been able to exclude dogmatic discord by providing the community of believers with a sustainable structure; any imaginative and communicative Christian would have come up with their own version. Instead of one Church, Christianity would have become a mosaic of geographically differentiated religions, resembling the colourful disorder of local city-gods and city-goddesses characteristic of the religious situation under the older polytheist deal. The capital in oneness gained by the new Christian deal would have been lost. Thus, in order to give the Holy Trinity 'standing', 'identity', a name under which it could be legitimately governed, heavy construction work was needed. The series of Eastern Synods, initiated and presided over by emperors starting with Constantine, managed to deliver this admirable piece of work of theological engineering.[11] In order for the two poles – creation, redemption; Father, Son; God, Man – to convincingly cohabitate, discouraging the otherwise omnipresent perspective of an endless resettling of unclear accounts, there was only one answer: to find an equidistant third pole, a component/supplement in charge of relating the two. But such bilateral arrangements tend to be fair-weather arrangements, predicated upon a lasting will to conjugality, unable to reliably prevent their descent into conflict. This is why, in order to provide an anchoring point, an equator between the poles, conferring a new type of being-in-time on what would otherwise remain a mere relationship, only a trilateral setting will do, with the third element sharing the same level as the two others that it supplements. The construction of the Holy Trinity from the first synod (Nicaea 325) onward, of one God in three hypostases or persons, succeeded in creating a God who, without ceasing to be a person, was also a triad of persons, even three persons.[12] This step was recognised and integrated by all but the rarest, most extravagant and courageous dissident groups. Let us not forget that, in the West, individual theologians taking issue with the transformation of God into a trinity suffered heavy trans-confessional persecution as late as the sixteenth and seventeenth centuries. Only the eighteenth century opened itself to ideal non-Trinitarian Christianisms such as that of the Unitarians.[13]

2.3

We follow Agamben in saying that the roots of this new, late modern, all-wrapping household management, which today inspires the campaigns of politicians, revolutionary leaders, militant activists, etc., would be unthinkable without roots reaching right into what appears to be one of the most profound 'themes' of Christianity: the doctrine of an *oikonomical* intelligence that is constantly at work; in fourth-century religious history in Greek-speaking New Rome, this gave rise to the theologico-institutional edifice of the Trinity, the image of the 'world-as-*oikos*', and the Christian version of the *oikonomos* martyr who takes to heart the duty of saving the household, to the point of giving his life. It is confirmed by the parable of the tax penny (Matthew 17:24) with its differentiation between religion and the state and its unambiguous message as to the simultaneous and equivalent claim each of them wields, suggesting that any perspective implying the absorption of either by the other is in contradiction to the Gospel. Thus, from the outset, one needs to resist the notion that the economic Trinitarian, Christian theology is only 'about God or about divinity'; rather, it is immediately about the economy and providence, in other words, it is an activity of self-revelation and government, of self-revelation in the service of government, and that means, in turn, of care for the world. The deity articulates itself in a trinity; it does so, however, not in a way that might be understood as a form of 'theogony' or 'mythology'; rather, what it offers is an *oikonomia*, and this not in the weak, negative – although perfectly 'economic' – sense of dispensation or government by so-called 'one-off' or 'exceptional' cases, but also in the strong economic sense of a 'household' articulation and administration device, a way of making sense of what it is for a community to live under the divine command of a Trinitarian God, which includes a sustainability-oriented conception of life, and thereby of the government of creatures. Divine freedom and providence support creaturely freedom precisely in founding and governing 'an immanent praxis of government'.[14] Agamben proposes that in order to gain access, let alone understand the structures and functioning of power, we must set aside the 'pseudo-philosophical analyses of popular sovereignty, the rule of law, or the communicative procedures that regulate the formation of public opinion and political will', turning instead to the analysis of an unbroken Roman–Christian tradition of doxology, with its hymns and acclamations, which 'seemed to have disappeared in modernity', but in reality reaches its climax in what Debord calls the 'contemporary society of the spectacle',[15] wherein, per Agamben, 'power in its "glorious" aspect becomes indiscernible from *oikonomia* and government'.[16]

> To have completely integrated Glory with oikonomia in the acclamative form of consensus is . . . the specific task carried out by contemporary democracies and their government by consent, whose original paradigm is not written in Thucydides' Greek but in the dry Latin of mediaeval and baroque treaties on the divine government of the world.[17]

In short, Agamben claims that modern democracy – government by consent – pertains to a tradition in which we endlessly and thoughtlessly (or: performatively) glorify the economic administration of the world. Administration by governments that promise optimal conditions for advantageously reproducing the chances that some new kinds of activity – new 'forms' (Agamben) or 'exercises' (Foucault) of life – instrumentalise persons and things while being deeply indifferent to our own uselessness and inoperativity as living things. However, this administration, these governments, tend to abandon us, typically and unavoidably, to political irrelevance, and a growing share of us to unemployment as well. This acclamative biopolitical tradition – where God, or the sovereign Will, are glorified regardless of their truth or falsity – was never really in jeopardy from such key modern constitutionalist ideas as legislative sovereignty, natural right and the separation of powers, all of which rather reify the tradition by presupposing a 'unitary yet divided' political subject along the lines of the Trinitarian God. First: God, or pope/emperor; then, under the sign of secular nature, Leviathan, or the people (people/nation). Nor, arguably, is this tradition notably inflected in a further step, and by a more recent set of 'post-modern' ideas, those foregrounded by 'reflexive constitutionalism'.[18] As we know, this set of ideas is based upon a further notion of people/the people understood as 'pure communication'. Here belongs the consensual position of a Jürgen Habermas, which Gunther Teubner and others try to develop into a reformed/informed updated version.[19]

Now, to say that liturgical theo-political traditions, such as acclaiming the Christian sovereign regardless of his impotence, survive modernity is a big claim and requires clarification. The first thing to note is that whereas for most human history authority was contingent upon its sanctification (i.e. its involvement in the liturgies through which non-coerced people validated 'ultimate sacred postulates'), in more technologically and socially complex societies the relation of authority to sanctity may be inverted, as both coercive force and more subtle disciplinary mechanisms can ensure that people who no longer accept as true an erstwhile 'sacred postulate' – for example in the USA, the idea that citizens form 'one nation under God' or that they share the faith in a God in whom we 'trust' (as the dollar note declares it) – must participate in secularised rituals that transmit to them, and subject them to, its message. Thus, whereas the economic management of populations and resources was once authorised by a sovereign who in turn was sanctified by God, today's sovereign is ostensibly authorised only by the People who took over from God: in reality a divinised 'hand of the market' forces the hand of the sovereign, who then forces his people to become subject to an instance whose commands are certainly no less absolute than those to which earlier populations had been subjected (while, ironically, there is a good chance that they are less subject to a controlling architecture of command-limiting checks and balances). The act of ritual acceptance of authority, which had once been the site of a numinous experience of 'wholeness' more profound than belief, becomes a proverbial form of bottomless and, what is worse, also inescapable hypocrisy. For:

> in refusing to participate hypocritically no less than in hypocritical participation, the conscious minds of men and women become divorced from those deep and hidden portions of themselves to which ritual participation introduced and bound them. The sense of holy grace [i.e. the numinous experience of integrity/wholeness attained by participating in rituals] is increasingly difficult to attain, for the self becomes fragmented and some of the fragments may be lost, or are sent into long-term exile. The consciousness that remains is likely to be trapped in its own radical separation. For those not deluded or oppressed into subordination in the name of salvation there may be alienation from the deepest parts of the self.[20]

Whereas rituals used to sanctify authority by speaking to the part of the self that engages in direct or experiential (including numinous) meaning, now they merely serve falsifiable conceptual meaning, or indeed of false conceptual meaning such as 'sovereignty' under 'one God in whom we trust', whereas the true sacred postulate is: 'The business of America is business' or, 'what's good for business is good for America'.

2.4

That said, we note that despite being all-encompassing, the dogma has not been as solid as Agamben allows. Agamben silences the momentous fact that only in occidental Christianism was the Holy Spirit 'confiscated' on behalf of Jesus and his 'vicars' on earth, that popes anointing German kings as 'Holy Roman Emperors', kings with 'divine right' and, eventually, the self-divinised people (nation) or individual is an exclusively Western phenomenon – something altogether absent from the first thousand years of the Christian Empire: so is the idea, moreover the immense promise of an (interchangeably) legally Right/politically just government. This can be shown through a comparative discussion of Greek and Latin (post-Augustinian) theology culminating in the Filioque controversy in the eleventh century, but the difference between Christocentric West and pneumatocentric East is easily gauged in Domenikos Theotocopoulos' *The Dormition of the Virgin*, which was painted before the artist migrated to the West: there it is the Holy Spirit, not Jesus, who takes centre stage and waits to transpose Mary to heaven. What in *The Kingdom and Glory* passes as the canonical version of the Trinitarian Credo – the view of God as the sum total of the relations between His constituent persons – is in reality occidental, not part of Nicaean Trinitarianism, but a later variation, alien to the Eastern tradition. The variation was formalised when the clause known to specialists as the 'Filioque' was eventually inserted into the Roman rite in 1014 CE at the request of a German king (Henry II) who was eager to cause a rift with Constantinople, by a Pope (Benedict VIII) who was grateful for the king's help in restoring him to the papal throne. Opposing this, Eastern Patriarch Photius complained, in arguments he presented to the Latin pope, that the insertion of the Filioque to the Creed destroyed '[t]he monarchy of the Father', relativising 'the reality of the personal, or hypostatic existence, in the Trinity'.[21] In other words, contrary to the concept that prevailed in the post-Augustinian West and in Latin scholasticism, Greek theology attributes the origin of hypostatic 'subsistence' to the hypostasis of the Father – not to the 'common essence' qua relationality, in which Western man partakes, via Jesus, the pope, the divinely ordained king, or the secular government, and to which individuals entrust their absolute 'natural' right. In the East, the Father remains the sole cause (*aitia*) and the principle (*arche*) of the divine nature of the Son and the Spirit.[22] Contingency, therefore, is not understandable in the East, in terms of relation but of divine will. These two versions of Trinitarianism, we submit, correspond to two versions of Christian government that coexist as layers in a palimpsest: (1) More visibly, the later occidental version was made possible by the alteration of the Credo via the Filioque clause that represents the complete equalisation in glory, of God and the Son of Man, and, therefore, of His Vicar and the Emperor or King he anoints and, therefore, constitutes as legitimate; contingency is explicable in terms of binary 'relationality;' By extension the Filioque perfectly captures the political dualism that characterises occidental political/legal thought and which Byzantium never had; already in the Merovingian dynasty a glorious king reigned while his majordomus governed, while from the ninth century there is the additional dualism of pope–emperor, etc. (2) The earlier, Eastern, version, however, was one in which the biblical notion of the divine origin of autocracy[23] was retained in parallel with the added idea of the divine origin of the Church. Justinian's famous sixth novella makes clear that the monarchy was believed to have been instituted – like the Church, but independently of her – by God alone. It did not, therefore, need to be reinstituted by the Church.

Thus, a deep, open, dogmatically hardened and almost sectarian east–west division exists right within the central Trinitarian creed dating back to the ninth-century modification of the dogma in the Occident through the insertion of just one word: Filioque, which is Latin for: 'and from the Son', thus resulting in 'and He [the Holy Ghost] proceeds from the Father and from the Son'. In its occidental version the Trinity is thus characterised by the fact that the Spirit 'proceeds' from both Father and Son – and not alone from the Father as monarch (or from the Father through the Son, another Eastern suggestion). What 'to proceed' actually means in Trinitarian lingo is much too voluminous a question to be entered here; but what can be said is that, when confronted with a triangle, say on a page, most people tend to introduce, be it

35

unbeknownst, a notion of verticality. Between the two conceptions of the Spirit's 'procession' (Greek: *ekporeusis*), the top is represented either by one of the three angles (in the Eastern version, the Father as absolute monarch is the sole source of Spirit), or by a horizontal line connecting two angles (the Western solution: the Spirit proceeds from both Father and Son). Whereas in the East the Spirit testifies to the primacy of God the Father, in the West the Spirit is conceived of as an instrument (a test, witness, measure) of the equality of Son and Father. Theologically, this correlates to a key difference between Eastern and Western political theology and the corresponding secular legal and institutional political imaginations and preferences, as well as its epigenetic chain-reactions. In the Eastern (Byzantine) paradigm, God as Father and, by analogy, the sovereign as monarch are sources of legitimacy as long as their power is felt; in the East, God, if suddenly unable to perform miracles, is simply no longer God. Likewise, a Byzantine sovereign is first and foremost a source of potestas, and ceases to be sovereign as soon as some usurper wins or a popular rebellion succeeds. Each Eastern emperor was understood as embodying the 'substance' of a Christian polity, unless and until, for whatever reason, he lost this backing; there was, between each reign, interregnum, standstill, often upheaval. By contrast, in the West, where God and Son are equal, the theo-political model that prevailed was the model of an unfalsifiable unending dialectic between 'two powers'. To be sure, the notion, in occidental Trinitarianism and its epigenetic products, of a split or double top, a top disposed in twin peaks, is suggestive. Here, we shall limit ourselves to one aspect: the politico-theological proximity linking Western institutional preferences – the Filioque Trinity and its choice of 'from the one, but also from the other' – to the paradigm of an unending industrialised competition, an ideal image of the public space in the West as a contest, trial, game, or race. Consider the Scottish botanist Robert Brown (1773–1858) who paradoxically earned his greatest success for a non-botanical discovery: with the help of one of the better microscopes of his time he found that any type of non-organic matter, if observed through the microscope, is home to the turbulent movement named after him, 'Brownian motion'. A century later, Max Planck described it as follows:

The state of a liquid at rest in uniform temperature should be perfectly free of any change. No difference, no tension, thus no change. Yet whoever has a look under the micro at what is going on inside a liquid such as water sees a thing it is unlikely that he will ever forget [. . .] Instead of the tomb-like immobility that it was natural to imagine, the observer witnesses the most turbulent racket [. . .]. One is reminded of an ants' hive, except that, at night-time, the insects stop being excited, while the particles, as long as the temperature remains constant, show no sign of tiring. What we see is, strictly, perfectly, a 'perpetuum mobile'.[24]

We think that an appropriate analysis of the Filioque includes its interpretation in terms of an anticipated theological repetition of the perpetuum mobile that Planck saw in the Brownian movement. The Spirit that proceeds as much from the Son as it does from the Father dissolves all structure without return. The Filioque arrangement replaces structure with action, an action without telos, but with mastered performance, monitored management and all the dimensions of strict and extended (modern) *oikonomia*. It asserts the possibility that the Spirit cannot ever come to rest but instead must remain open, in an endless oscillation, ever preparing for the next round, staging 'negeschatology', a game with no last round, a match that cannot ever be won or lost, or simply be over, but must go on precisely as a perpetuum mobile moving back and forth between Father and Son, never actually reaching the unity of differences, but remaining hostage to a differentiation that it introduces but never transcends. The model of the dance of the particles discovered by Robert Brown in 1827, himself so close to his speculative predecessor Giordano Bruno who, 250 years earlier, observed the 'vicissitude of all things'; the countless occurrences of the twentieth-century topic 'game', in philosophy and in so many other disciplines, with particular density in the English-speaking world, suddenly stop looking like a mere coincidence. This, however, is only the second half of the Western prehistory of the discovery of the agon of the particles as portraying the ultimate condition of matter; in fact, the disquieting notion that what needs to be portrayed as the unsurpassable yet manageable condition of being, matter, life, are unrest and bipolar tension, has been at work right at the core of occidental theology since around 1300 when, in the word of a commentator who lucidly summarises what might be called the post-lapsarian actionism of John Duns Scotus: 'For Scotus, being is constituted by intrinsic, self-differentiating activity'.[25] Whether the actionism that undergirds the passage from the model 'substance' to the evolutionary model 'game', or 'competition never ever to be resolved', or endless protean 'challenge' and ultimately non-transcendable duel, is genealogically rooted in the Filioque, remains a point of discussion. The isomorphism is harder to deny: life, condemned to a state of perpetual operativity without restful shabbat – this is also present in the physics of particles in unending motion.

3
Social Systems on the Cross

3.1

In its pre-Nietzschean coinage 'genealogy' refers to the self-subjection of a present living subject under a previous, by now past or absent, state that presents itself as knowledge, an instruction, a narrative; this allows for the introduction of an element of verticality or hierarchy and thereby of a claim to be able to govern/steer what 'happens now', in the name of what had happened before. In this sense, Old European societies, and not only them, appear committed to the politico-centric wager of providing themselves with an *arche* (Greek for source of action) – an unquestioned ability to determine that society shall be in control of its fate according to its own decisions. It will prevail, in other words, against anything not located within some actor's control – evolution, for example. Upholding the wager of the absolute relevance of performative utterances under the conditions of an ultimately helpless exposure of the human flock to contingent happening means accepting that humankind replies to the onslaught of upcoming and unpredicted facts by mobilising its 'capacity' of being sovereign and subject, of governing and of being governed, something that Kant understood but also dignified as imperative. While our main argument in this study is directed against the overstatement of anthropological transformations separating the modern social regime from its predecessors, we also reject any denial or downplaying of the powerful innovative forces unfolding within the evolution of society.

Today, many observers of matters social and societal opt, for reasons either procedural or consensual (in fact, mostly both), to cleanse the inquiry into the present horizon by rejecting genealogy in favour of a purely presentist approach:

this attitude can be cast, at least parodied, as a preference for, say, genetics over genealogy. That there exist good and valid arguments to be made in favour of this rejection is difficult to deny; it corresponds to research in biology showing a transition from evolutionary origins to evolutionary patterns, such as the study of 'independent repetitions'[1] – i.e. of the fact that different forms of life have responded in identical or similar ways when exposed to identical or similar circumstances. This relativises the primary interest in initial states or initially given forms by emphasising their later environmental exposure. When this way of thinking is applied to the evolution of society, as in the theory of Niklas Luhmann, who can be seen as the eminent representative of the preference allotted to such an 'advanced calculus',[2] the conclusion is: '[E]verything that happens, happens simultaneously'.[3] This uncompromising paradigm is admirable in its audacity for admitting the helplessness of any attempt to reduce the hypercomplex networks of interdependency relationships that constitute today's society to simple cause–effect relations. By contrast, in earlier social or societal conditions, because one was renegotiating one's identity anew at every point, one's identity could very well have been defined causally. Today, schematically speaking, too many things are happening at the same time for causal accounts to be able to deliver more than a parody of what they seem to promise. But the step into a post-causal, functional, differentiation-based account of society is also pioneering in another respect, applied as it is to society rather than life. It synthesises, for the uses of the social scientist, the epistemic consequences of Darwin's step of introducing the postulated existence of something called 'environment' into the evolutionist account of life, at the expense of the earlier conception – Lamarck's for instance – of individual living beings as inheritors of acquired properties. Game-changing as the introduction of the concept of the environment has been for the study of biological evolution, that same principle is even more relevant in matters social and most specifically matters legal since it is closely related, mutatis mutandis, to the general procedural principle of review and reviewability of legal decisions. Legal decisions – the 'products' of legal systems – are accountable to general law-internal instances of judicial reviewability (or again, to a horizon of expectations constituted by an always-possible judicial review to which the legal order in its entirety is continuously subject or, rather, to which it subjects itself), which is not incomparable to the 'biological environment' to which the products of life ('species' in Darwin's wording) are subject, and within which they are candidates to 'fit', candidates to inhabit a niche. The predecessors of Darwinian evolution theory, construing species as 'un-reviewed', so to say, by any 'environment' in the form of internally represented finitude – needed to suggest some other type of relationship between being (or life) and time; the solution had generally been a simple learning theory: every animal species makes, collects, stores and forwards (transmits) the experience of what its component animals go through. An epistemic correlative of this pre-Darwinian bet upon free, unrestrained self-perfection consists of arguments that any understanding or explanation is, in itself, sufficient for mastering (transforming, for instance) that which it understands and explains; consider Lenin's claim: 'The teaching of Marx is all-powerful because it is true', or: truth is victorious against the ideological delusions it understands or explains (the weakness of this stance is admitted by a post-Lacanian neo-Marxist such as Slajov Žižek, when he assumes that ideology survives its deconstruction as fantasy[4]). By contrast, in the Darwinian social-systemic conception, what is happening is presented without a dimension that transcends the present tense, cutting causality out of the meaningful directions of inquiry; this then supposes not a process of 'progress' – of cumulative self-perfection through the inheritance of acquired characteristics, for example – but of contingent selection of what is fittest with respect to the contingent 'bite' of the ever contingent environment.

The identification of the environment, or, simply, the inclusion of an entity of that name and with those attributions within its dramatis personae is, as it is well known, the seal of Darwin's genius in suggesting his solution of the riddle of the evolution of species. A problem of the same Darwinian order also haunts human society, largely unbeknownst to the diverse form or schools of 'social Darwinism', however it does so in an even more intense or exacerbated, perhaps 'second-level' form. That human society is itself subject to evolution appears more sulphurous and perplexing an idea than when it was first suggested in relation to the origin of species, but is unsurprising since, after all, human society has instituted in itself the foolhardiest and, at the same time, the most fragile of all possible or imaginable ventures: to impose its own resolutions upon its own being. In order to succeed in this endeavour, in the institution of self-subjection to the fictional mastery that human collectives successfully claim to exercise over themselves, *utterances* suffice to provide differences that make a difference (Gregory Bateson).[5] Human society, the society of the language-inhabiting animal, demands and obtains submission or obedience from itself as its own master. Modernity has not changed but at best only 'de-ontologised' this[6] by consistently accelerating the frequency of relevant events, giving rise to new social patterns without modifying the structuring two-foldness of subjection and sovereignty, submission and mastery, hearing/obedience and speech-acting. The anomaly of social as opposed to biological evolution is predicated upon the human power of utterance.

In this regard an unquestionable feature of Western legal and political imagination, since the Catholic Middle Ages continuously to this day, is the image of sovereignty as a binary relation of 'absolute' and 'limited' power. This premise, we suggest, generates the very conditions in which the spectacular show of promises by absolute sovereignty always remain deficient, amounting to less than had been expected in the process of its stage management and acclamation by the public. Even so, we too find it impossible – to place a little 'spoiler' right here – to extract ourselves, in the twenty-first century, from these mixed imperialist–Universalist campaigns with their provincial or indeed parochial occidental attributes rooted in the legal/political imagination that featured such institutional analogues of the Western Christian's God's scissile power as the set-up of a whole arsenal of polarities: pope/council, king/parliament, people/parliament, constitutive power/constituted power, etc. When early modern European lawyers, writers and politicians of the period known as 'the autumn of the Middle Ages' came up with the notion of sovereignty (an immortal, corporate, always-already legitimate, abstract power) they inaugurated a series of centuries unfolding in the sign of a grasp for world power in the guise of a grasp for world-rationality,[7] eventually giving rise to the modern, socially differentiated society and its 'offers', notably subjective right. How could such a programme be successful? The programme worked, it might be suggested, by means of the usurpation, first by the occidental king/prince, later by the occidental 'individual' heir – first nobleman, then bourgeois – of God's double politico-legal faculty in natural theology: His *potentia ordinata* plus His *potentia absoluta*.[8] The scholastics had attributed these powers to God; it is essential to resist the temptation of identifying the mediaeval theological predecessor of the arch-modern secular notion of sovereignty in only one of the two. The conventional understanding of the polarity as a 'distinction' between two powers in God makes the point needlessly complicated: what we are confronted with is a case of two carefully articulated faculties arranged so as to bolster each other. The binomial formula simultaneously announces and excludes any limit to legitimacy and to power. The image of the see-saw proves instructive here, as does the figure of Janus, the Roman God of boundaries, whose two faces look in opposite directions. Just as the scholastics, only a few decades after having been handed the largest part of Aristotle's work via the Muslim Averroes, re-construed the God of Christianism as at the same time insuperably powerful and insuperably irreproachable, the universality of the Western social order, first achieved in and then exported by the early modern secular state, is Janus-faced or based upon two conjoined elements: a named superpower element, i.e. the power of occidental empire (*imperium mundi*) plus an impersonal, legitimacy element (*dominium mundi*). For the occidental Christian/post-Christian subject, we suggest, this dualism makes perfect sense both at the level of what is happening and at the level of consciousness and continuous identity: 'Yes, we Europeans did lay the foundations for modernity, but this is now irrelevant since this dualism derives from the dualism of power of our, now dead, God.' It is more unlikely in a non-occidentalised subject that serving this legitimate universal modernity is worth setting aside their identitarian needs for than it is in the Western one. To say 'Yes, we Europeans did lay the foundations for modernity, but this is now irrelevant since this dualism derives from the dualism of power of our, now dead, God' is consistent with this; for the *occidental* Christian-post-Christian subject, we suggest that this dualism makes perfect sense at both the level of what is happening *and* at the level of consciousness of a continuous identity. By contrast, to the non-occidentalised subject, the injunction to set aside their identitarian needs can make sense only on the conceptual level of a prudent choice; at the level where sense means identity, however, such a statement is as irrelevant as the claim of European colonisers who addressed native Americans by reading to them a Papal letter *in Latin*, that they must rejoice at the good news of their 'inclusion' in the civilised world qua common household of 'humanity' or *dominium mundi* without a *dominus*.

It has often been observed that utterances have, under certain circumstances, the 'magical' power of exercising an effect on, if not directing or shaping, other people's action. Inbuilt in this instituted split between obligation on the one hand, and the sovereignty that expresses itself in successful utterances on the other, there is something like a daring counter-factual claim: statements, if found valid, come complete with an entitlement to exercise an impact, to trigger consequences. Despite what is constantly being taught by the trivial everyday experience of collective powerlessness, blind trust in the relation between sovereignty and responsibility, between *potentia absoluta* and *potentia ordinata* in mediaeval theological terminology, has never stopped organising the political scene – not before and even less after the great mediaeval/late mediaeval front-staging of this duality. The most breathtakingly moving feature of human history and existence is precisely located in this alliance of sovereign and responsibilised subject. It matters little whether emphasis is put on the strength of sovereign mastery or the weakness of its subject; they do their work as a pair; this explains how the capacity of self-alienation is such that the appearance of the couple mastery/responsibility is omnipresent, despite the apparently unmistakable evidence of powerlessness as the most common feature of collective human existence.

3.2

If it is the case that, in disenchanted modernity, the reign of genealogical fiction and of the no less fictional causal accounts underlying it are out of use, then the social world needs to be understood and perceived accordingly by the relevant disciplines. In dealing with the processes that constitute the ever-emerging process-reality of modern society, rather than claim to stick or return to the ontological glory of no-longer-applicable Old European institutions and their majestic vocabulary, one needs to look for models that can understand modern society according to its everyday constitutive–reproductive processes; otherwise we would be programming a parasitical and illegitimate method that shields political analysis from its legitimate exercise, which is, as with any other analysis, a cognitive exercise: recognising the recognisable. Social systems theorists have learnt to be particularly careful at preventing their knowledge of the conditions that preside over the process-enterprise society and decide about its continuation from unhelpfully sweeping outside their strict domain of competence. In order to do so, systemists consider society not as being composed by a group or collective of people, but as the continuously changing results of an affluence of 'communications' – a linear process of a very large number of 'serially' accomplished mini-events. Society, in a systemist's understanding, is made up by the continuous, ever-renewed brouhaha of these continuous communicated choices, wagers, even hesitations.

The inaugural commitment of Luhmannian systems theory is precisely that of staying clear of the comforting duo of genealogical and causal accounts. According to this agenealogical method, radicalised by the supplementary claim that, while modernity can perfectly turn against itself (it has incontestably done so over decades now, staging a sequence of exemplary *exodoi* from modernity in matters of mind-frames, subjectivities, commitments), there is, in matters of society, no conceivable such step out of it, no return to premodern forms or ways of existence. The (Bill) Clintonian campaign director who invented, in 1992, in slightly different wording, the proposition 'it's the economy, stupid!' has provided the appropriate vocabulary – even the fitting syntax – to hint at the political system that it needs to take into account that politics in modern society is eminently not in the position of a superpower against any unexpected evolution happening in the economy – and not only in the economy, but in a number of other functionally differentiated systems. 'Functionally differentiated' for our purposes, means that we are no longer living under the conditions of stratificatory differentiation, no longer in a world in which the political system is endowed with a monarchical–hierarchical superiority in power enabling it to 'steer' any and every non-political happening; the Schmittian veneration of politics, as being gifted with the outstanding and singular honour of speaking in the name of the 'highest degree of intensity', does just that: it assigns to politics a monarchical–hierarchical superiority. In this context, the address 'Stupid!' has its importance as a warning against the very appealing perspective of falling back into the unreal world where glorious politics can do – and is seen to do – everything. Of course, modern, functionally differentiated society is by no means a mere *pas-de-deux* of a political and economic system, neither part of which can substitute for the other.

There are, operating under similar conditions of operational closure,[9] other function systems around law, for instance, but also science, religion, education, art and some others.[10] Historically, or if one wishes critically, though this would not reflect Luhmann's proceeding, the salient contribution of systems theory layout is the downgrading of the political system to the post-glorious political level, which is that of providing a condition for the functioning of the social totality, a provider status that it shares with each of the other social systems.[11] In the event-governed and, therefore, rapidly changing build-up of social evolution, conditions or events are present as part of the social world that constitutes itself at every moment as the outcome of its own ongoing operations and, to this extent, they might possibly offer relevant 'information'; if, however, the 'information' they offer concerns exclusively 'initial conditions' – and genealogy, in the older sense, takes its information exclusively from initial conditions – this means that no information about the actual situation is gained, even if a sense of identity, continuity and certainty are enjoyed. Critics of systems theory, moved by the desire to find and expose some cunningly disguised attribution of causality for the predicament or 'the state in which we are' – a frontrunner is currently 'neo-liberalism' – suspect that this outline of society as a matter of countless communications boils down to a mere extension of the paradigm of economic decisions, especially by investors.[12] Effectively, the face of society is composed by very important choices made and communicated: the investor, as much as the lawyer, the scientist, the teacher, the pupil, the medical doctor, the parent and the politician, all share with the politician the perfect awareness that, tomorrow, when the dice have fallen, one is bound to either regret or be happy about the choice one has made today. Even so, it is misleading to identify this position as 'neo-liberal';[13] rather, it merely reflects one elementary feature of contemporary society in the making. The drive to hold Luhmann to account for his 'neo-liberalism', remote-controlled by a consensus of what deserves and what does not deserve to be forestaged as the central feature of social-ised existence, misses the essential point; in modern society decision making (and also betting) is not only a matter of investment as in finance or the economy (even if it does play this role there as well): the force of the systemic model resides in the fact that there is almost no one who is not contributing, unintentionally and unbeknownst, to society's continuous 'self-defining'work, adding their choices to the myriads of choices that constitute the only self-delivered orientation that modern society can find. Each single communicated choice, each single element of the uncountable plankton of communications that constitutes modern society, emerges facing the verdict of the contingent future.

Today, in the immediate aftermath of the 'triumphant' Brexit, approaches to modern society fall into two camps; while the reactionary camp feels happy to continue the sense-making programmes based on identity or integrity (to which the exorcism of those suspected not to be full members of the inclusive whole is added as a supplement), others resist the spell of totalities; while the first group fears/desires a monster the others rather discern the omnipresent, dispersed, insignificant but ever-decisive plankton that the monster is composed of. The ontological way of proceeding, identifying singular causes and hunting down the causal culprits, does not produce the type of knowledge that proves relevant and valuable in current processes today, even if it nourishes heated political debates. Availing more information than ever before –'too much!', some lament – and being just as unable to foresee our future as before, we ceaselessly communicate and choose under conditions of limited knowledge while being perfectly aware of the excessively powerful position of the dice once fallen. Our time is rich in examples not only of unexpected news, but of unexpected happenings. Needless to insist that information shapes the existing and choice-sculpting expectations about the future, or, rather, about present futures (which are among the genres of human production that are gifted with the highest amount of plasticity,[14] to use a fashionable term of contemporary philosophy, or certain schools thereof), including further communications. Nonetheless, while communications give rise to further communications, the fact is that all communication – of which the self-reproduction of society at large consists – takes place within and by the means of the medium Sinn (mostly translated into English as 'sense'). The systemist account of modern society offers an incomparable glimpse at and way of understanding its object without a whole list of ancillary constructions; indeed, one of the decisive advantages of the systemic-evolutionist account of modern society is that it allows us to part ways with an entire list of virtuous transcendences, teleologies and other secular and political, moral, philosophical, identitary revelations, as it refuses to routinely assume their justifying, value-enhancing, or simply integrating function.

Modern society is not a means towards a worthy end, it is an emerging entity. The systems-theoretical *homo faber* offers a picture of modern society that is not, and does not even have to be, up to normative standards, promises or values; it is not something one can (might, should) claim to be the right way to follow. Rather, modern society simply proves possible in evolutionary terms, possible in that it reproduces or better, continuously produces, itself. It has succeeded in producing itself up to the present day, and its future continuation, as unknown as anything in the future, is nonetheless observably being taken for granted, equally continuously, in so many ongoing communications. This extraordinary feat of unpretentiousness and abandonment of political ambition with regard to an Old European tradition understood as an impotent mastery and steering power by means of which society only claims to impose upon itself its own direction, singularises systems theory, distinguishes it by its rejection of illusory self-overstatement; having evolved *pari passu* with modern society without buying into its own culture of politics-as-promise, social systems theory remains undeceived by its glory – the missions and aspirations that contemporary society, or specific institutions within it (including even 'critical' law-schools), offer as justification for their high standing. In this cognitive respect (not, of course – we have repeatedly underscored this – with respect to the underlying appraisal of the role of politics), it can be said that social systems theory today shares decisive aspects with Marxism a century ago. Like Marxism, social systems theory is not a science of moral betterment; instead, it lets itself be guided by the need to offer a faithful description of society-in-progress, of the societal process in the making, rather than by its faith in society's fundamental, legitimising, constituting claims. What helps us to understand the stakes here is to take up – with Agamben, among others – the distinction between leading a city (politics) and running a house (*oikonomia*, Greek: economy) not only as a distinction between larger political and smaller economic units – as in Plato – but in its Aristotelian form between politics as a command structure (a 'state') that involves many, and *oikonomia* as the monarchic/despotic command structure that corresponds to the business of coping with the problems encountered by the management of a house. One can then say, for instance, that Marxism and systems theory have in common the fact that they are looking at society in the making as opposed to society in its representation, at society as household management, *oikonomia*, that consistently follows not a monarch or a dictator (or if so, then only as glory-providing complements of the nameless manager-administrator navigating the house society through the vicissitudes of history), but the thalweg of its own perduring crisis. Society in the making has nothing to do with the niceties of constitutional–procedural rules determining access to power. In this sense systems theory also effectively offers an economic theory of society in close correspondence to the primate conferred by Marxism on the economic infrastructure. This of course does not mean that it attributes to the economic system a unique, exclusive role, superior to law, politics, science, religion, or the media. If systems theory comes close to Marx, this is in view of its general framework being built on a non-deontological overall conception; Marx, too, must be seen as renouncing any general deontological foundation of rule or action, simply because, as long as history is a succession of class struggles, there is no such justifiable rule available; the revolution-to-come, put by Marx and others since, in the role of the only shelter and refuge of political legitimacy, is the unique source of any possible 'rules' based on society's prehistory (or antici-pated post-history). This common element in the thought of Marx and Luhmann, however, can be referred not to the paradigm of an unbroken integrity of a compassing rule, or even as one of constant exception (the distinction of rule and exception ultimately belongs to a positivist account that both authors try to escape), but, rather, of radical contingency, and accordingly, constant oscillation or variation. What both of them questioned, for us, is whether there is such a thing as an unbroken compassing rule – an 'inviolate level' (Hofstadter);[15] only if the answer is positive can one speak either of rules or 'exceptions having become the rule'. Otherwise one must be satisfied with referring to strains of evolutionary luck. The common segment of Marx' and Luhmann's thinking can thus be specified by saying that they depict modern society as deprived of any inviolate integrity or transcendence, in such a way that a consequentialist or 'futurist' type of action – no matter if based upon a landscape of revolutionary or on the contrary 'counter-revolutionary' claims or promises, or exclu-sively and even 'officially' upon crisis management – takes the scene and leaves no space for rules or deontologies.

The main difference is that the absence of transcending rules, which in Marx's case is predicated upon the expectation of the one decisive and revolutionary future event that alone will create undistorted cognitive conditions, is on the contrary pred-icated, for Luhmann, upon an uncountable number of micro-events happening all the time – indeed, in Luhmann, 'society' does not refer, as any writer of the Old European galaxy would refer, to a collective of people but, rather, alludes to the myriads of mostly insignificant and only minimally world-changing events that he calls 'communications'.[16] There is no unitary control of this strange 'being' we refer to as modern world society, with ultimately unjustified taken-for-granted-ness: we have to be content that there is no mastery-holding sovereign 'in charge'. All we are left with, is: (1) a social world not determined or structured by the actions of world-construing agents; instead, it is the overall result or epigenetic outcome of chains of communications further triggering such chains, etc.; (2) a society differentiated no longer hierarchically/vertically but horizontally, into function systems that have emerged in the process of dealing 'serially' each with one type of complexity; (3) said function systems, in order to go on, are predicated upon the functioning of the other function systems.

3.3

There is, however, more that needs to be said about social systems theory as a suggested alternative to the Old European blueprint of imagining either a perfect or, on the contrary, an imperfect society. Contrary to a widespread preconception among non-readers of Luhmann, 'social systems', as he understands them, are neither giant, all-inclusive and irresistible steering regimes, nor heavily equipped German armies destined to grasp, monopolise and eternalise power or kidnap its structure; quite to the contrary, social systems are described as extremely fragile ('improbable') and merely emerging 'quasi-entities', each of which continues its operations as long as it happens to succeed at passing the test of its environment, depending on it as it is. Distinguishing themselves from – and thereby 'coping with' – their respective environments, social systems place themselves, on the map of declivity of power, below their environments. This feature, the radical exposure that flows from each social system's effective reliance upon an environment, is what Luhmann's 'society' has in common (though Luhmann, who often uses Old European terminology, acknowledges this structural affinity only in passing) with the fundamental social notion of pre-classical and classical Greece, the household (Greek: *oikos, oikia*). Now, sense (or 'meaning', as others translate the word 'Sinn' in Luhmann's use) plays an important role in Luhmann's account of impersonal social systems, in which phenomena of difference and indifference, and specifically the differentiation between social systems and their environments, play the leading role, displacing humans (called: consciousnesses, even at times: psychic systems). In fact, far from being protagonists of modern society, humans, for Luhmann, are part of the 'environment' with which social systems have to cope. Be that as it may, the 'socialisation' of the medium sense has never been total and is not today. Social systems were second and late in their discovery and use of the medium sense. Until modernity human consciousnesses alone had been acknowledged as the laboratories, if not the constituencies, of sense. Moreover, it is not only sense-processing that has been what distinguished humans since times immemorial, but also, and up to this day, humans still hold on to their capacity to develop social relations based on sense (cf. memory, identity, affect, sensibility). Communicating social systems and continuously monologuing human consciousnesses thus hold in common an indistinct ability to operate by and through sense: with every communication the medium sense is triggered and used anew by the operations of social systems but also, in its often silent, but always unstoppable 'diktat', by psychic systems. Although and because Luhmann specialises in the former, the indistinction and ambiguity that result from the simultaneous use of sense, from the fact that any element of sense triggers both the psychic and the social systems involved, makes it necessary to introduce both an organising difference and a model of correlation-without-fusion (implying also: without causality), or 'structural coupling'. Psychic systems (or consciousnesses, or persons, etc.) and social communications use the same wavelength. Now, that this must lead to interference is not surprising. The immaterial robots that Luhmann calls social systems need, in order to work smoothly, the consciousness/sense operations of psyche-endowed human beings to respect their limits, their social status: a status of being outsourced to the systems' environments. In view of this, we suggest, it is promising to take a second look at the basic – thoroughly impersonal – dramatis personae of Luhmann's social systems theory in the light of the characters we, as humans, can readily identify with, at least insofar as we make claim to our dual modern Western identity: being ourselves the sovereign masters or administrators, but also the polities-cum-households to which our mastery and administration applies. Thus, we can cast the impersonal social systems in the role of dutiful *oikonomos*-slaves in the Greek *oikos*. Not only is the *oikos* different from the *polis* in that it is governed by only one master (or *archon*), as opposed to the *polis*, which has several *archontes*,[17] but also in that the omnipresent personalities in the house are not the despots, who wield the threefold lordship of a father, husband and master (in the strict sense of the master/slave relationship), but his chief executive or 'vice-master'. In antiquity, the *oikonomos*, or manager of the household, was a figure mostly chosen among the slaves with the explicit task of watching over the successful everyday coping with any business that came along, and feared more by the other slaves of the household than the master himself. Like oikonomising slaves, social systems have no glorious lords, and also no other being, 'no other life', apart from their operations. And the sovereign master of the extended household we call modern humanity? To recall Adolphe Thiers, 'le roi n'administre pas, ne gouverne pas, il règne', which made sense in human minds long before the rise of constitutional monarchies, even longer before the recent and current vicissitudes of legal and political sovereignty; it applies to all instances of conceiving of a god/sovereign whose being is split from his praxis so that the authority that comes with his gloriously absolute power ends up underwriting the mundane management of beings and things, of human and non-human resources. A parallel and mutually dependent co-evolution of glory and routine.

In terms of sense-as-consciousness, we suggest, Luhmann's impersonal social system stands in need of re-dramatisation. Its likeliest casting is to the role of the *oikonomos*, the slave who merely holds or is confided a despotic power that neither is nor could ever become his own. If the social system emerges as a 'fold' (Deleuze's guiding term in understanding Leibniz fits perfectly) within the fabric of its environment, if the decisive site of systems-formation is the boundary – the membrane, as he also calls it – between the system and the environment, the lesson is that social systems, despite their pompous-sounding name, operate in a never-overcome condition of constant perilous exposure. Coping or managing are born from weakness – this predicament of weakness and

the ensuing need of coping with it would be the point where
further research should investigate into Luhmann's conception from the viewpoint of its *théologie cachée* (in the terminology introduced long before Schmitt, in 1851, albeit within
another religion, by the Galician savant Nachman Krochmal,
in his comment on Maimonides' *The Guide for the Perplexed* of
the present era). Luhmann's conception of society, entirely
predicated upon the capacity of 'coping' (called 'reduction
of complexity') would in this perspective appear as an utter,
yet also utterly consequent, secularisation of the central
Christological motive of the powerless yet duty-burdened
slave and house-manager (here: Jesus the Oikonomos of the
house of creation). The system embodies the predicament of
the *oikonomos* (manager/steward) and his duty of 'having-to-
manage', or 'having-to-cope' with any upcoming business at
his own responsibility and peril, thereby structuring a position that is related both to Heidegger's Dasein, understood
as 'being in question' or 'being for which its own being is at
stake',[18] and to the indifference that greets the issue of life
and death of the *homo sacer* according to Agamben.[19] There is
– to use Agamben's terminology – no Kingdom and no Glory
to be spotted either in the ancient charge of an *oikonomos* or
in the modern 'robotic' substitute that system's theory attributes to its eponymous device. The social system has inherited the role of the *oikonomos*-slave, the executive manager,
burdened with borderless responsibility yet deprived of the
relevant means, powers and abilities, which are held only by
the *despotes* or master. Now, since there is no lord or master –
the situation here has changed since the last relevant surveys
(including Hegel) – it follows that the subject is enslaved to
its environment: to an anonymous, acephalous, deperson-
alised, irresponsible but unflinchingly absolute imaginary
master, on which nonetheless depends the social system's
being or not-being.

Where sense-processing takes place both in human consciousness and in impersonal communications among social
systems, we think it appropriate to consider the double
employment of the medium sense and of the resulting competition in a narrative perspective that connects it, 'genealogically', to the rise of social systems. The photograph that
emerges from this superposition distinctly increases the

depth of focus of the over-quoted 'dialectic of lord and bonds-man', in that it reveals a long-term stratagem of bottom-up vengeance imposed by the efficient and risk-taking *oikonomos* against the ineffective, but right-holding *despotes* or titular master.[20] Remakes are galore and include, in high mediaeval Frankish history, the rise of the Carolingians, first managers of the Kingdom (maiordomus) in the service of the legitimate Merovingian dynasty, which they finally replace. Anti-genealogical Luhmann would barely have bought himself into such associations; his interest lay exclusively with the impersonal and systemic sense of observing and coping. Yet this sense, we tried to show, has its location on one but not on the other side – the 'oikonomic' but not the 'despotic' side. But before we look at how the oikonomos upstaged the master we have to ask, first, whose drama is this? Which form of sense-as-consciousness provides an adequate stage or pedestal for glorious mastery, side-by-side with unglamorous *oikonomia*? Second, we also need to ask, in reverse: who lives this 'drama', which at closer looks is at best akin to the theatre of the absurd and at worst to a form of bald hypocrisy ('hypocrisy' is the original Greek word for acting as well as for acting uncritically, by abjectly dutifully following a mere script)? These are first, geopolitical or 'who' questions. Who can more or less make do with a world where 'transcendental' Universalist values and principles, of European origin, from self-determination to human rights, are constantly declared 'supreme' only to be brushed aside, increasingly often, as soon as this is expedient to the self-interest of those in charge of the series' next episodes? Who, inversely, is discontent and likely to feel left behind by the global staging of 'universal' values acclaimed as supreme by populations subjected to anomic administration? Formulated differently, what are the conditions for a subject to accept contingency and enjoy mastery? And what distinguishes it from a subject relegated to the status of a confused, thus vulnerable subject or system, destined to disappear silently as a collateral damage, as payment to contingency, after life-long discreet service? These are the questions that boil down to that of religion and of 'whose religion?' in particular.

4

The Religion of Progress

4.1

Over the past few centuries, diverse political philosophers have succeeded in escaping state-policed religious orthodoxy, thereby discovering the laws that constitute the physical world and 'demystifying' or 'disenchanting' the social world. The way, however, in which this story tells itself and is being told, or rather staged, in front of a public of subjects for centuries, now resembles a repetitive opera buffa: Father Old Europe tries to marry his daughter, alias the upcoming generation, to a scion of the religious establishment. She, however, elopes with a free-thinking young man who believes only in the lessons of his own experience. The split, the rift, which this plot is glossing over is right in the middle between the words 'religious' and 'establishment', which, in line with the Trinitarian paradigm, are being (mis)taken as constituting one inseparable unit, much as if establishment and religion were only facets of the same reality that only a new general civil religion or political theology can give meaning to (i.e. the unbroken conviction of countless generations). Thus, modernity validates Trinitarianism indeed even as belief in God recedes. Here, instead of iterating the idea of a radically new civil religion or political theology that would encompass the old religion/establishment divide, we ask a more fundamental question: can we talk of Christianism as a religion of establishment that survives independently of confession, Holy Writing, even God? If so, has modernity not misrepresented 'religion' when it blames it for the injustices and insufficiencies of the social and public realm?

The entanglement between what has been happening during the European past, what is happening on the Western

56

political sense-making chessboard and the related issues of religion (or post-religion) is intimidating; moreover, the vocabulary and the methodological criteria accounting for this entangled relationship offer little guidance in their present state; in turn, this persuades a majority of observers to prefer the safe haven of silence to the danger of overstatement and the associated fears provoked by talk about the 'return of religion' or 'en-religioning.'[1] In our case, we find that this matter is far too bewildering to attribute it to 'repression' or 'hysteria'. Our thesis focuses on the way the 'relation' between law/politics, on the one hand, and religion on the other, is largely imagined as universal in two ways: either symmetrically, as a perduring coexistence (for which the secular sovereign provides and polices a watertight divide as opposed to the religious sovereign – e.g. the pre-Reformation Christian prince, the Iranian Supreme Leader, etc. – who, by contrast, removes the divide; or asymmetrically, as a continuous march of progress towards the final displacement or absorption of one of the poles by the other one. Rather than imagining this 'relation' in terms of a universal divide, a succession (religion as the past embodiment of public identity, law/politics as its present one), or a continuous journey of progress, starting from point A and continuously approaching point B, we shall recommend, again and again, the image of an unending oscillation, a see-saw movement, taking place within a bipolar structure of Western Christian origin, for which the distinction religion/non-religion (or 'post-religion', recently) provides the pivot. What we would like to save from the sense of anxious urgency that characterises the 'return of religion' debate on all sides today is that it is no longer easy to apply to the two poles: the 'winning' present – say the secular embodiments of public power – and its 'losing' ('obsolescent', 'overcome', etc.) past, made of religious bonds, the narratives to which they give rise, that of a dialectical 'relation', or that of an intelligible evolution. And it is a good thing, too!, for any such 'relation' would refer us again to the resulting need of being either sovereignly contained or administratively managed, giving rise, in turn, either to a renewed confrontation of state and religion, or to a state-controlled personnel of religion. One way or the other, we would embrace once again the idea that somewhere, hidden in the folds of the regrettably multiple past and the imperfectly homogenised present, there exists the secret recipe for a successful mediation: a viewpoint from which the journey towards a set of ever more consensual and Universalist conditions can take off.

The question that needs to be asked in this respect is not whether, but only how, it can be avoided. The 'symmetrical' view of the politics/law-religion 'relationship', held by those who think that it needs to be contained and managed, respectively, by an internal glorious sovereign – be it secular/multicultural or modern ethno-religious (say Iranian) – and the state's functionaries and administrators working with the personnel of religion, is dominant from Paris to Riyadh and from London to Tehran. The liberal position is that, if religious views are not, or not yet absent from communicative 'Public Reason' – as once advocated by (an earlier) Habermas – their public manifestation and presence must be restrained by the collaborative labour of the national sovereign and the courts (the exact reverse of which can be observed in Tehran). Despite its global spread, the false universalism of this view has been often exposed. The modern distinction between the secular state and 'religion' mirrors rather than dissolves the Catholic tradition that, in its own turn, transformed the ancient Christian idea of 'Two Swords' or two powers (sacred and temporal) into a 'political principle'. Scholars such as Saba Mahmood convincingly argue that the 'religious' and the 'secular' are not opposed ideologies, but rather concepts that are 'interdependent and necessarily linked in their mutual transformation and historical emergence', which gained a 'particular salience with the emergence of the modern state and attendant politics'.[2] Talal Asad contrasts the distinctly modern opposition between the sacred and the profane, according to the modes of classification particular to developments in anthropology and sociology in the nineteenth century that found its most famous exposition in Durkheim's *Elementary Forms of Religious Life*, with the opposition between divine/satanic transcendent powers and spiritual/temporal worldly institutions in mediaeval theology.[3] The reclassification occurred, claims Asad, in the aftermath of Europe's encounter with the non-European; it was through the designation of non-European practices, such as those linked to fetish and taboo, allocated exclusively to 'Nature Folk' or 'backward peoples', and the self-identification of enlightened Europe with 'profanation', namely the exclusive capacity to reorder society through 'forcible emancipation from error and despotism', that an essential separation was wrought between 'the sacred', now universally associated with mythic religion that Europe had left behind, and the profane, now associated with the history of European Reformation and Secularisation that others – including Islam – 'must' emulate. Asad further highlights the fact that, in structuring the 'right' relation between the state and religion, the secular sovereign as well as secular courts must first assume the paradoxical position of a secular body having to determine what counts as religious before deciding to what extent manifestations of religion can be legitimately limited in the name, once again, of preserving the 'separation' of church and state in order to show how contemporary secular liberal democracy retains structures and forms embedded in Christian dogma. These criticisms of the secular state extend to multicultural polities. Thus, the modern principle of state-guaranteed multiculturalism – as practised for example in the less-than-secular UK – can be linked genealogically, via Hobbes, Locke, etc., to the Christian prince's toleration of religious and other differences and, further back, to the mediaeval principle of 'unity in diversity', a maxim with a long history in the Catholic Church, subsequently also incorporated into the ideology of the Holy Roman Empire, assisting both in their parallel efforts to proclaim their appellate jurisdiction over the fragmented European feudal space.[4] The adaptation of the principles of the 'two powers' and of 'unity in diversity' respectively into the principles of state/church separation and toleration is explicable in the context of Bodin's reformulation of sovereignty as legislative (rather than appellate) and the rise of social contract theories among bourgeois Europeans in need to bring to a close their Catholic–Protestant wars and proceed with the business of commercial peace. These adaptations were first made possible thanks to the efforts of natural theologians who confiscated God's absolute yet self-limited power on behalf of man.[5] Moreover, B. Bhandar[6] eloquently argues that, notwithstanding their differences as political ideologies, secularism and multiculturalism (French-style) are 'deployed as techniques to govern difference',[7] suggesting that they share a 'common philosophical lineage' and a relationship to the collective and individual subject of Enlightenment and post-Enlightenment thought, namely a 'unitary if plural' sovereign political subjectivity:

> [W]hile secularism ostensibly decouples culture from religion to produce a common political culture, and multiculturalism purports to accommodate a diverse range of cultural and religious practices, both fail to accommodate difference that stretches the bounds of citizen-subject defined according to Anglo-European norms of culture, which implicitly include Christianity.[8]

Bhandar's insightful equivocation of secular and multicultural 'techniques to govern difference' in the light of their common presupposition of a 'unitary if plural' sovereign political subjectivity, can be related to the claim that our legal and political imagination may be over-determined by Christian postulates that simultaneously prep us for submitting to pastoralism, bio-politics, anomic administration and for doing so unbeknownst it as we are passionately glorifying any would-be God-like sovereign to replace the monarch we dispatched in the modern era.

We wish to challenge the reverse certainty, the blind trust that the law/politics/religion 'relation' is universally asymmetrical in the sense that it is a process of inevitable dissolution of one pole leading to the victory of the other; the presumption of such an encompassing dialectical historical process leading inevitably to resolution amounts to a hopeful programmatic claim/promise: 'where religion had been, the secular is to come'. If one can explain this certainty, indebted formally to Freud and content-wise to most of what might be called the church fathers of Western modernity, by referring to the success of Christianism past secular modernity – if, that is, we can say that Christianity offers the 'way out of religion', so that, paradoxically, '[T]he persistence of [Christian] political theology could be a prelude to its end'[9] – then the claim/promise of secularisation as religion's assured endpoint must be rephrased so as to render its actual illocutionary force uncannily explicit: 'join us Christian-cum-seculars in letting the world, previously occupied by so many different religions, be taken by the one, universal 'religion-after-religion': it's Progress!' This position is held, more or less explicitly, by an increasing number of Western philosophers as diverse such as Gauchet and Nancy, already mentioned above,[10] but also Simon Critchley,[11] Alain Badiou or Slavoj Žižek.[12] Radical critics like Critchley or Badiou insist that we need to reform our religious faith continuously so that its energies can be channelled towards re-politicisation. The devil with these positions lies in the fact that, despite honestly/unabashedly suggesting that the road to secularisation specifically passes through Europe, their understanding of 'religion' as primarily a matter of conceptual faith – which can thus be reformed hermeneutically – fails to critically reflect the specific historical transformations of European Christendom, above all other religious groups, culminating with Protestantism and the view of religion that is found in German Idealism, where love, ritual, art, imagery – the stuff of which affective meaning consists both in traditional religion (when they are sanctified in relation to the Holy) and civil religion (in which case they are sanctified by the absence of the Holy) – are relegated to the secondary status of inactive ruin, epiphenomena, 'folk culture', etc. As such, the positions of those who openly suggest to the world to follow the Western Christian path to secularisation and 'use' their faith to enhance the hermeneutics of progress come up with a problem: they coincide with, and performatively certify, the particular (and much criticised, as arbitrary and biased) handling of Christian and other religions' symbols, images and ritual practices by Western courts. Thus, for example, in Europe, suspicion grows that, despite claims to neutrality, state courts are prone to privileging Christian images and rituals, by arbitrarily downplaying them as a bit of innocuous national 'culture' in contrast with minority religions' symbols and rituals considered to be carrying 'really' religious messages. Thus the European Court of Human Rights (ECtHR) found that the crosses hanging in Italian schools are 'passive' symbols,[13] while on other occasions, it has found that the Muslim veil is an active symbol of the 'essentially' undemocratic 'religion of Islam'.[14] The message seems to be that while the cross symbolises the Christian/post-Christian prince's love of all humanity (or, to follow Rosenstock-Huessy, the cross as 'Cross of Reality' is the best reminder of what we all have in common[15]), the veil, or the circumcision, to take another classic example, are marks of tribal distinction; arguably, however, the fact of making children look up to the image of the impotent yet triumphal 'God on the Cross' at the place of their secular education is an efficient way to induce them to the love and trust of the cross' embedded message of political theology in a secular context: God/the sovereign is to be glorified, even if evidently weak and falling.

4.2

Occidental Christianism (i.e. the series Catholicism–Protestantism–Secularism) is, as we are being told, the religion that sets us on a path out of religion.[16] We are finally free to think about and doubt the creator God as much as any 'ontological' claim. How promising exactly is this in terms of its social sustainability? Questions of this type animate authors such as social anthropologist Roy Rappaport or legal historian (and 'dogmatic anthropologist') Pierre Legendre. For Legendre – whose international reception was pioneeringly launched by P. Goodrich[17] – the fate of metaphysical traditions is to bind their subjects primarily affectively, not conceptually. For Legendre (1997), the necessary emotional attachment to legal obedience and political love requires the affective identification of the human subject.[18] Even some constitutional lawyers acknowledge this.[19] Similarly, R. Rappaport (1999) has observed, in a different context, that traditions, be they explicitly or discreetly religious ('metaphysical'), bind their subjects primarily by way of loved images, rituals and formulaic ideas. In marked opposition to the secularised Protestant or Enlightenment view, and not unlike Agamben's observation that in the mediaeval and modern world deliberation is a misnomer for acclamatory rituals, Rappaport suggests that in any society, old or modern, and without any correlation to the superb growth of modern science, public consensus-based reason, far from only lending support to the inter-subjective trust destined to mitigate the problems necessarily generated by sense-based or language-based human order,[20] at the same time continuously presupposes trust that they are already solved. It is – explains the American anthropologist – by way of the performative validation of particular metaphysical canonical 'postulates' (which might be perfectly meaningless in themselves) that human cultures succeed in providing the 'blind' trust that sustains their social order. Yet the resulting particular social orders, 'sanctified' (and only thereby enabled) by such 'sacred postulates', are not static but subject to continuous processes of evolution. They are epigenetically adaptive: their unquestionable 'postulates' (say, 'chosen people', 'incarnation and resurrection' or moral 'progress') allow their subjects to conceive of change with a sense of order.

Thus, while today the modern political and legal thinking about what is called 'European Universalism' is predicated neither on simple preferences, nor on the European metaphysical tradition, but on universalisable conceptual meaning – on the structure-giving hope of reaching one day the level of integral enlightenment, in which all claims to validity are decided upon by the one competent tribunal of universally acknowledged Reason – political theology's re-emerging speaks another language. What it hints at is the claim that the occidental constitutional imagination is the outcome of the contingent, makeshift, multiply inflected rationalities that have accompanied, and preceded, the *ius publicum europaeum*. If we turn to modern law and politics and to constitutionalism, legal and political, we are confronted with the fact that all the key constitutional formulas, concepts and rituals (absolute-yet-limited sovereignty, Will exercised in-council, the separation of three powers, etc.) derive from mediaeval Christian postulates adapted to the circumstances of the different socio-economic situations of the various stages of European history. It cannot be stressed enough that these historically contingent and, often, idiosyncratic clusters of meaning have always been amplified by a decisive layer of affective structures inherited and constituting the capital, as well as the distinctive feature, of Western Christian/post-Christian societies. This is why it is so important not to forget that the rediscovery of political theology, with its turbulent impact on Western intellect, discourse and imaginary, extends far beyond the single issue of 'secularisation'. Secularisation is a phenomenon that remains within the limits of the conceptual level only. The death and disappearance of the God of the Western onto-theological tradition is doubtlessly an event incomparably more decisive and consequential than the political neutralisation and public downgrading of Christianity as a religious community[21] and its replacement by the separation of church and state. Even so, at a more immediate, e.g. affective, 'experiential' or 'icon-omic' levels of meaning, the Triune God of Christian metaphysics continues to offer His services to society, – even at the extreme opposite of everything that is normally identified with 'religion'. This fact is best epitomised in the consensual but also atavistic postulate that power is located somewhere in the relationship between order-giving law and sovereignty-supplementing politics, and in the falsely simple architecture that succeeds in transforming them into a plausible common entity.

In this light, the disputation about the primacy of conceptual over affective meaning does not present itself with the same urgency as the classics believed, most influentially among them some of the Greek philosophers who systematically belittled and disowned the affects. Writing in an entirely different world, most of the philosophical writers of the Enlightenment nonetheless convey the same message. The difference is that, while classical Greece was predicated on a political programme based upon purely conceptual – universalisable – meaning, her philosophers' treatises were never meant to be used as blueprints for a humanity-wide legal and political arrangement to be militantly pursued by a philosopher-king on an unlimited scale, as has been the case with all major political and legal philosophers of the second millennium CE. A first major inflection of this classical attitude occurred just after the end of the classical era, with Alexander the Great's universalism and his idea of an empire that would include 'all' (Athenians, Macedonians, Persians, etc.) on an equal standing, led by a conquering Basileus and his philosopher-advisor, thereby stunningly anticipating some of evolutionary achievements today attributed to Paul.[22] It was with this world in which all differences were announced as equidistant from the ruler, that Saul/Saint Paul had to align his Jewish followership when claiming that, before the One creator God, 'there is no difference between Jew and gentile'. Subsequently, once the Constitutio Antoniniana extended Roman citizenship to all freeborn inhabitants of the empire, primarily for fiscal reasons, the road was ready for the Christianised Roman emperors to extend further this universal formal equality to those born as slaves and women; unlike Caracalla, however, these Christian rulers justified this extension, by reference not to imperial *potestas* but to something new: their imperial impotence before the will of (Saint Paul's) God. But, of course, since the good God wants us free and since this is a 'fallen' world where differences and inequalities persist, *salus populi* required the management of the 'relation' between perfection and imperfection, ideal and real. As we shall show, for the Byzantines, who saw themselves as the last great empire before the Judgement and whose Trinitarianism does not envisage the Spirit investing the sovereign, the persistence of imperfection was a given that one had to be resigned to while trying to manage it as well as possible among fallible humans; hence, for example, their reluctance to join in the Crusades despite their military might which, had they wanted to join, would not have required the chaotic recruitment process seen in the Occident; hence, also, their setting up of the first welfare state and the ever more frequent use of dispensation from the austerity of the laws in the name of Christian charity.

Let us note, however, that this prowess absolutely did not entail any claim to impartiality; instead, they openly and unashamedly led them to privileging the *filoi* (Greek for 'friends') over others (non-Christian citizens, but also any Christians who, without access to a patron, fell outside the radar of ad hoc charity). As we shall elaborate in a later chapter, the first centralised state in which Saint Paul's lofty ideals were put to use was not the Holy Roman Empire or some Catholic occidental kingdom presided over by the anointed monarch; rather, the task of realising Saint Paul's ideals first fell to non-anointed Byzantine emperors who suffered from a deficient sovereignty and a legitimacy deficit; it is a vastly underestimated fact that for a thousand years, and long before the Catholic High Middle Ages that herald the rise of the righteous Occident, the Eastern Christian Basileus were mostly usurpers, and their end was often an excruciating one at the hands of the dissatisfied populace that had once acclaimed them as benefactors. For a long time, this was considered Europe's unfortunate and little studied prehistory. Our era, modernity, finds its roots in the achievements of the mediaeval Western Catholics, living in an entirely different setting (trying to institute unity and a centralised state that flourished via kingdoms and the empires, sometimes competing with them, while the problem of the Byzantines was to acculturate Christian ideals in a strong centralised empire), and developing a Christianism separate from that of the East, one in which this world could come to resemble heaven under the spirit-guided leadership of the vicar of Christ on Earth and those he anointed. For Byzantine Christians, their religion's acculturation led to an individualism without liberty, managed by a sovereign with no absolute legitimacy and needed to placate a sizeable group of *filoi*, 'or else', in an expiring, imperfect world, they themselves were directly in danger. For the Catholic Occident, this imperfection became a challenge to be overcome via the ever better-justified management of the 'relation' of ideal and reality, now articulated as the idea of unity as relational sovereignty entrusted in the hands of the anointed, righteous king or emperor. It is here, not in Byzantium, that we find the origins of the still active political and legal imagination that centres on the image of a perfectly tuned pendulum between, on the one hand, absolute/constituent power (first appellate then, after Bodin, legislative), irreducibly glorious, always-already justified, and on the other hand, modestly but decisively limited/constituted/responsible power.

Let us look for a yardstick to measure, first, how far we are from appraising at its value any non-occidental approach to law and politics, as long as our starting point is this pendulum of constituent and constituted power; and, second, how far we remain from taking the step from the underlying – and since the reformation long-suppressed – political theology ('hidden', as Krochmal had called it) to an awareness of its exceptional status in global terms. Such a yardstick is given by the logic and principle underlying egalitarian contemporary Universalist discourses such as – to give two very different examples – liberal John Rawls' 'veil of ignorance'[23] and leftist Etienne Balibar's 'equa-liberty'.[24] Is not the main source of Rawls' theorem, of its plausibility and legitimacy, the tradition that he never explicitly refers to, but that allows him, as well as his post-Christian Western reader, to still rely, be it discreetly or even unconsciously, on the affective power of the Cross as a symbol of martyrdom and resurrection for the sake of emancipation of humanity? Turning to 'equa-liberty', could it be that affectionate memories of such fables as that of the Pentecostal 'event' (i.e. the linguistic miracle of the Holy Spirit that allowed the apostles to preach their concepts equally effectively to the Jew and the gentile, each in its respective language) still preside over the performa-tive hiatus between being attributed or conceded equality and actively predicating it? If we do not dare to expose both levels of awareness at play here, the conceptual and the affec-tive, are we Westerners, who avail ourselves of both, not discreetly and in the all-overriding name of universalism, following the shortest path to our own advantage? Is it legiti-mate for those who were raised before such symbols as a cathartic cross, who know how to listen to such comforting fables of universal trust in concepts 'never lost in translation', as the Pentecost has been (it is still a national holiday even in super-secular France!), who know how to talk politics, constitutionalism, etc., without any mention of the fact that the religious environment of secular enlightenment has been Protestantism, namely the doctrine of a Christian confession that privileges conceptual faith. Should this implicit privilege not be challenged? Not only because, as argued above, there are alternative anthropological understandings, but also, and more importantly, because it operates as an undeserved trump card in the inter-civilisational context? Protestantism, and the secularism to which it has bestowed its place, disavow traditions explicitly centred on non-intellectual ('icon-omic' and experiential) meaning, while it secretly or unconsciously relies on one of these traditions; ridding the church and the public sphere of religious icons and rituals, the Protestant–secular framework is still but one of the mul-tiple ways for Christians to 'keep one's household together' (*oikonomia*), although it is perhaps just some sort of decorative minimalism coupled with hygienic symbolism. Transferring public-institutional bonds of love to 'secularised' constitu-tional rituals, images and formulaic propositions of Christian origins still leaves behind everything that is deemed to be

mere 'culture', silently considered to the present day as mere
leftovers of now deactivated pre-Christian cults. It does not
help, either, to include these pagan 'remainders' as so many
museum pieces or exotic details, adding a splash of colour
here, a fossil from earlier times there, placed where it helps to
orchestrate the overall Universalist–innocent effect of 'emptiness'. This being said, nothing precludes these objects, images
and rituals from getting massively reactivated, be it in those
new/old Christian/pre-Christian sects that most or all the
Catholic hierarchy and theologians currently have so many
problems with, be they, more worryingly, in the European
public space, which suddenly seems to be crowded by the
foreign objects brought along by immigrants. Today's Europe
is that of Switzerland banning minarets, of France banning
burqas and 'burkinis', and even of super-liberal Sweden
firing a well-integrated Muslim civil servant for refusing, on
conscientious religious grounds, to shake a woman's hand
while instead placing his right hand on his heart as a sign of
respect.[25]

4.3

If we are right to defend the thesis that conceptual secularisation presupposes an affective 'blind trust' that can only
be experienced inside particular civilisational families (even
as the concepts can be universally adopted as they are persuasive or simply because they are better at describing the
situation that comes about when one civilisational pattern
displaces another), it follows that any universal crisis of conceptual meaning (for example, of the crisis of legitimacy and
of the implosion of sovereignty) will also lead to particular
types of crisis of trust, indeed of trust disappearing without a
crisis. Thus a liberal European lawyer may be furious with the
way the ECtHR deals with current religious differences, but
that does not stop her from continuing to trust in the 'veil of
ignorance' – just as a Christian may be furious that Jesus was
crucified, but trusts in his resurrection. A leftist activist may
be furious with the way Greek Prime Minister Tsipras was
elected on the slogan of a radical alternative to neo-liberalism
only to embrace the excuse of TINA (for 'There is no alternative') in order to continue with catastrophic neo-liberal

policies, but this will not erode his trust in the potential, say, of the ill-fated Greek rebellion to engender a universal 'contagion of revolution'. If the modern constitutional imagination (based as it has been around the conjoined binaries of absolute and limited power, popular sovereignty and the rule of law, revolution and constitutional settlement, positive law and human rights, liberty and police, international and national law, globalisation and nationalism, trans-border liberalisation of movement of persons, services and goods and recidivist protectionism) is today in crisis, this may be so only conceptually, thus – for the Christian–secular subject – not fundamentally. While there is a plethora of new books that expose the paradoxical[26] nature of these binaries and a wealth of empirical facts bearing this out, this does not in itself destabilise the Christian/post-Christian subject, which still identifies affectively with the tradition that stages the imaginary notion of a sovereignty/decision/dogma as triumphal in defeat (cf. Jesus on the Cross) plus a 'peripheral' (therefore real) need for flexible *oikonomia*/management. While we can reason conceptually that this scheme no longer makes sense regarding what is happening now – under conditions in which *oikonomia*, in its systems-theoretical version, embraces it all – there is no one capable of robbing the Christian–secular subject of the certainty that he or she enjoys when in the act of performatively validating, as a social fact, a sense other than the communications and social systems-related kind: sense as identity. Hence the idea that sovereignty, plus the rule of law, 'rule ok' is validated by, say, voting in parliamentary elections or seeking judicial review (irrespectively of whether we believe or not in parliamentary democracy and the justice of the legal system), by participating in a demonstration led by a leader with a raised fist (irrespectively of whether we actually believe that this amounts to more than a mere rebellion), or in the necessity of leadership. When it comes to the Christian/ post-Christian subject, the much-talked-about crisis of trust is amended by the performative validation of particular Western metaphysical world-views of the universal. The idea of the world as a household or *oikos*, the housekeeping of which takes place under the watchful eye of a potent creator who however is also an increasingly impotent master (God as potent King, plus God as impotent human), is embedded in imagery, metaphors, rituals, including constitutional rituals and the architecture of public spaces that mimics, not the Roman Palatinus but rather the Christian Church, in leaders photographed looking out to a benign 'north-of-the-horizon' (a pose Constantine the Great pioneered), in formulas concerning the 'right' way of structuring society by exercising one of the two aspects of a single yet relational supreme power. In that sense, Berman was right to see the modern age as heir to an age of 'law and revolution'.

Even gifted with its characteristic ability of questioning and some incentives to seek to understand a complicated world, the current modern Western linguistic animal stands in need of a god or sovereign as source of preferential love and/or of a special 'role' for it to play, to invest it with the required meaning, and to guarantee the 'overall unity' of the social mediating the daily face to face and the anonymous, impersonal and disparate processes taking place in functionally differentiated societies. The principal contender for this job has been the Christian/post-Christian, Triune, relational yet sovereign-turned God, especially in the form in which he has been imagined for the past thousand years (that is, only in the form of a relation of God and Jesus or, by analogy, of sovereignty and government). By now, most of us logically comprehend such a notion as a 'counter-factual'. Yet while in science a hypothesis needs to be proved in order to be sustainable, the counter-factual of a sovereign-bound society survives, or so it seems, its deconstruction: it is fantasy in the sense given by Žižek at his very best.[27] Yet even then, the notion of an ontologically 'relational' sovereignty, for instance, must not only be seen as a counter-factual concept, but performatively validated as true social fact through our participation in constitutional rituals, such as elections and judicial review, but also as rallying around the revolutionary leader with a raised fist. In law, for a more particular example, it is not some logical benchmark or principle of deliberation that dictates whether we accept the justice of such interpretative judicial techniques as 'proportionality' and principles of the 'margin of appreciation', or whether we mistrust them as legitimating extensive government without restraint. In Western politics, all we have to rely on is metaphysically driven blind trust/mistrust that energise/

deflate 'revolutionary' politics and activism; we are otherwise increasingly unable to confront the neo-liberal TINA ('there is no alternative'), able only to 'avert our eyes' from the implosion of democracy.[28] There are also those who lament our era as repulsively meta-political in the sense that either 'law' or 'economy' emasculates 'the political' – respectively in favour of juridification or monetarisation – attributing this to a 'hatred of democracy'.[29] Some even enjoin us to reverse the situation through an extra effort of love of communism under a new, 'heretical', Christian European political theology delivering its universal message of equality without the need for Christian fables and without guilt about the history of this idea, under the leadership either of a party,[30] or, if the circumstances are not as favourable, at least a 'socialist Thatcher'.[31] Such 'secularised' neo-Paulian defence of communism has been aptly mocked by a critic as a desire for 'Christianity light', a 'Christianity without Christianity', 'not very different from the logic of the permissive capitalist society [Žižek] criticises', namely 'the same desire that goes into the logic of (Diet) Coke without caffeine – that is, to desire the property, the "proper" of the property, without the malignant substance that makes it up'.[32] Not very different, also, we might add, from those late mediaeval poverty-sworn Franciscan monks who, by wanting to enjoin property without legally owning anything have been so catalytic in the development of capitalist economic tools.[33]

We refer such 'radical' contemporary attempts to a wide gamut of similar attitudes, from seeking judicial review, to voting 'disagreeably', to raising a fist – rebellious, but not revolutionary – against neo-liberalism (think of Greek Prime Minister Tsipras and of all those far-right and radical left parties that have sprung up in austerity's Europe); however, most or all of these legal and political modes of acting now appear as 'empty rituals': they all validate in action, as true social facts, some 'sacred' postulate or maxim – the binary model of sovereignty as power constituent/constituted, or democracy/rule of law inherited from the binary model of God's *potentia absoluta/potentia ordinata/limitata* – but, paradoxically, they do so just at the moment when no one seems to really believe in them. If, as we argue, the fantasy of an absolute but self-limiting power of self-constitution was not jettisoned in Enlightenment-based constitutional theory but, rather, sequestrated from God and put inside the 'deficiently immanent' notion of a 'superpower of the Will', exercised through the so-claimed 'pure acts' of making/abandoning norms, the question to be asked is to what extent the same can be said of any presumption of epistemological supremacy over socio-political facticity. The latter, denied its radical exteriority, appears at the same time as the victim, either of the logos of sovereignty, be it according to the economic relation of norms and facts, or according to the 'eco-logical' principle of the 'appropriate' self-limitation of each of the different impersonal processes for the sake, say, of ever increasing functional differentiation. Last but not least, even theories of 'anarchistic politics' can be seen as derivatives of the Christian economic-political theology. Hence, for example, Agamben's repeated theologico-political references to the question of arche and especially of anarchy come with a fundamentally critical stance with respect to the latter: indeed, for Agamben, anarchy stands not for the object of some utopian desire of escaping the fate of being governed: it refers to the reality of administration without government. And yet the anomia and anarchy we all experience in the sense of what is happening now is also, at the level of sense as Western consciousness, inscribable as yet another chapter of modern history, the 'autobiography of Western man', just as Rosenstock-Huessy's title has it.[34]

Is it a mere coincidence if the current crisis of legitimacy, seen in its global and historical context – e.g. problems of social justice, regimes of exploitation – produces quite different results in different settings, depending on the interaction of occidental and other traditions of sense consciousness (i.e. of imagining, dimensioning and measuring legitimacy)? We are perfectly conscious that we shall provoke the contradiction of numerous internationalist advocates of the contagion of revolutionary imagination, from Tunis to Athens and from Wall Street to Tahrir Square, often the more passionate the further they are from the events. Indeed, we need to ask even further: is it a mere coincidence if political projects that are seeking, sometimes with the greatest honesty and seriousness, to address global problems without missing the particularities of the historical nitty-gritty and the intimately cultural configurations, and to avoid exceptionalising or reifying countries and peoples, so often end up doing just that? Gauchet argues that in a disenchanted world, critical politics, based on the constant questioning of legitimacy, cannot fail to replace religion.[35] We find here an example of a much-repeated constellation in current social theory – even a shared habit, though one always accompanied by an implicit agreement about its quasi-legitimacy – namely the present and certain assumption of a future transformation. The difficulty here consists in finding past experiences in which the future extrapolation can be anchored in ways that do not expose cultures to unnecessary trauma – that do not, in particular, deprive them of the 'bit of identity' without which they cannot go on. This is a game in the strictest sense, one that involves an irreducible gamble of chance. Now there exist various investment methodologies trying to link rationally justifiable decision making to unknowable possibilities yet to come. Yanis Varoufakis, who is an expert in game theory, tried his best to do this during his brief stint as official Greek negotiator during the Greek sovereign debt crisis. Yet the resulting calculus of risks, applied to responsibilities (collateral damage), finds itself fatally confronted, every time anew, to the incalculable. We shall not question that the real issue here, asking what is legitimate in dealing with the incalculable, remains wide open. The question becomes the more pressing as it is compounded with the further one of the role attributed to legitimacy by modern post-religious discussions, where legitimacy is expected to deliver the goods that can no longer be expected from religion? Or is it perhaps the case that the very notion of the legitimacy of the powers in place is a specifically modern concept and at the same time a late mediaeval Catholic postulate with no equivalent present in the enchanted worlds of, for instance, biblical Israel, Byzantium, or the classical Islamic civilisation?

4.4

What the thesis that Western Christianism is the religion that set us on a path leading out of religion[36] has in common with the claim brought up, seventy years earlier, by the German Catholic-converted theologian Erik Peterson in reply to his erstwhile friend Schmitt, that the notion of a Christian political theology is an oxymoron, worse: a contradiction,[37] is that both divert our attention from the philosophical examination of programmes, and direct it, instead, to their long-term resulting consequences over time. We are moving in landscapes made of tendencies and trends, cycles and loops, rather than of images, origins or imperatives.

In this view, what we need to ask ourselves is whether the hardest, but solely decisive question for us today is not rather how to find and implement a way of unhooking ourselves from the addictive happy-end-loop that epitomises the glory of progress according to the strategy described by Guy Debord studying the society of the spectacle. The loop seems to be generally construed as the superimposition of two images: that of a march, or path, and that of progress. On the march/path side the action of walking, marching, going,[38] is the master of the game, whence and whither matter little, and without thematising the use of time as an agent of dissymmetrisation, much as in the Chinese Dao and the Hebrew *halakha* – both of which are taking sides, one could say, with a performance-responsible ontology 'on the march' rather than with a doctrine of being as immobile and eternal, timeless and wordless, a self-possessed, self-obsessed and indifference-based doctrine. On the other side, progress connotes a justifying surplus value, transfiguring the movement into an inherent accumulation, a learning spiral, an unending improvement. From the viewpoint of progress, only the final destination is worth it. The reference to the march, barely a metaphor or even an image, is also neutral with respect to where it leads – relativising all destinations is the very point of front-staging the modest pedestrian movement; the surroundings of the walking person 'passes'. Progress, on the other hand, offers a legitimacy, a justification, a pedagogy. It can serve as a reference to a sequence of generations and, also unlike the march, it includes the possibility of an unending successful repetition of one identical operation. Progress, where the passing of time is matched by a material, objective, 'outbidding' process, can take diverse forms: 'growth', 'adaptation' add a supplementary difference. We are no longer dealing with an 'earlier' versus a 'later', but instead with an 'earlier-and-less/worse versus later-but-more/better'. Event-producing historical sequences in Western narratives that qualify as both path and progress, such as constitutionalism, with its late mediaeval roots, Reformation or Secularisation, include even more complex features: especially the transition from a binary to a ternary rhythm based upon the rejection of a middle term (or 'meantime') – the recent past – as shortcut to the imaginary return of the reference to an earlier time, a remote or immemorial past that has since been relinquished, and takes its value just from this fact. Arguably, all major European revolutions – as opposed to mere rebellions – had their chance courtesy of the claim of getting us back on to the right path from which we deviated by error or corruption.[39] This ternary rhythm confronts us with more complicated relations, involving two differences rather than only one, and as it were three dimensions rather than only two. It allowed the march of *homo economicus* to reach *an evolutionary speed* made possible only by the rejection of the reference to a recent past for the sake of investing into a timeless, deep-dead, distant past – the type of past that alone could prepare for the eventual emerging of the new, nameless and model-less future that would eventually replace it, giving rise to the general paradigm of 'progress'. And yet, for all these changes, the West identifies modernity with this image of 'progress'. Marching to pure futurity qualifies as a moral duty to pursue 'progress' for the post-Christian subject, so much so that it barely notices the costs or collateralities incurred, which stretch from the October Revolution to the neo-liberal reshaping of world society a century later. The stakes regarding the future of individualism, liberty, immortal (corporate) state sovereignty, limited government, even nationalism and, last but not certainly not least, capitalism, are thus raised at the point where an accelerated march towards pure futurity must qualify as progress: something that most likely will be easier for some than for others. How could human becoming be unhooked from Western Christianism's happy-end-loop qua humanity's march for progress?

For some, this is achievable by learning to march fearlessly forwards while 'disinheriting the past'[40] (especially as a decolonising tactic), not looking backwards – unlike the position with respect to the movement that Walter Benjamin famously chose, a century ago, as that of his own 'new angel'. The merits of this strategy, however, should be carefully

checked, in at least five respects. First, in so far as 'disinheriting' advocates an action without any mention of what
its end or accomplishment would look like, all it promises
is 'progress' – in other words, all it has to offer is a *march*
(and a march is uncertain as to where it leads or when it
will arrive); second, as long as it goes on, this action can
only be a self-imposed cure of *learning to stay indifferent to the
past* (the proof that the past is effectively indifferent is that
nothing changes had it been otherwise). Third, it accords with the
desire of *homo economicus* to speed-walk ahead without being
burdened by thoughts about the past; fearless and unrepent-
ant Tony Blair would approve. Fourth, it features an affinity
with what is top of the agenda in times of exceptionalism
and crisis, of individualism coupled with (less meaningful)
liberty, of sovereignty coupled with (less meaningful) constitutional restraint. Finally, learning to disinherit the past
suggests mastery gained by single-handed conceptual labour
but, as psychoanalysts know all too well, the ghosts of the
past, which do not primarily dwell in one's intellect or experience, tell us that ridding ourselves of their taxing influence
requires paying a price to someone else. For these reasons
we propose that unhooking from Western Christianism's
happy-end-loop may be a task much harder and worthier
than simply marching without looking backwards.

The endurance of western post-secularisation political
theology is courtesy of the energy produced by the tension
and tides of two *functionally related but antinomical* paradigms:
'political theology which founds the transcendence of sovereign power on the single God, and economic theology
[NB: strictly speaking not a theology but the displacement of
Greek conception of a household onto the theological field],
which effectively replaces this transcendence with the idea
of an *oikonomia,* conceived as an immanent ordering of both
divine and human life'.[41] The paradigm whereby modern
secular government coexists with the power to declare a state
of exception (a power Schmitt rightly described as analogous to the premodern miracle) is one in which these two
theologies – political and economic – are co-articulated in 'the
idea of *oikonomia,* an administrative praxis that governs the
course of things, adapting at each turn, on its salvific intent,
to the nature of the concrete situation against which it has to

measure itself'.[42] Thus, the ceaseless activity of coping with upcoming challenges, conceived in terms of a domestic and not a political activity amounts to an 'immanent praxis of government'[43] that we think is only deficiently immanent in so far as its mundanity 'coincides' with the 'supermundane mystery'[44] of salvation.

5

Political Theology beyond Schmitt

5.1

Political Theology: Four Chapters on the Concept of Sovereignty, Schmitt's most sulphurous opusculum, written in a half-scholarly, half-propagandistic vein, throws its ideological *weltanschaulich* roots right in the post-First World War defeat of the German left, evincing its contribution to the German revolution. Only two years before it was written, in January 1919, Berlin had experienced the murder of revolutionaries Rosa Luxemburg and Karl Liebknecht.[1] Even considering the questionable humus that had been favouring the growth of the seeds it had planted, Schmitt's brochure did have the indisputable merit of having fired the first broadside against the fortress of secularist and scientistic convictions, against those for whom the theological paradigm needed to be viewed as obsolescent or simply 'overcome'. Schmitt must be credited for his early understanding of the fact that the pivotal 'difference' of modernity, in the name of which the so-called Dark Ages are lost in oblivion, is conspicuously fragile, and sits uncomfortably with the double rejoicing about the innovations that had been achieved and the further innovations and achievements that, from this base, could now be hoped in the future.

Carl Schmitt's unmasking of the concepts of the modern theory of the state as depending closely on 'theology' was immediately supplemented with a second reading according to which 'political theology' also offers the means to escape the 'small-p' politics of parliamentary, liberal and social-democrat modernity, and return to 'capital-P' politics. Yet a third reading of the Schmittian argument is possible, focusing on Schmitt's failure to even start to fine-tune what exactly 'theology' refers to. Such a third reading requires rejecting the common assumption implicit in the first two: that we find in 'theology' and 'secularisation' two mutually exclusive elements. Rather, they produce together and as complements the half-carelessly and half-wilfully ambiguous unity of the reinvented political theology that Schmitt seeks to offer. We are dealing here with two distinct flawed ideas: that 'theology' epitomises something like an immemorially mediaeval discipline, linked irremediably to a non-modern mindset; and that 'secularising' consists of dismissing and replacing religion in each and all of its occurrences, vocations and employments, by something 'non-religious'. The two mistaken views – one of the theological past, the other of the secular future – need to be interpreted as partners and accomplices: twin expressions of one single and identical rationality, claiming that both are placed within the same series and on the same side of Christianity's genealogical bifurcation. We need to keep in mind that 'theological concepts' do not refer to anything like an anthropologically early, undeveloped state of things in which religion was 'everywhere' in society, intimately intertwined with politics and law; theology – especially of the scholastic type, which Schmitt refers to as it alone makes sense in connection to what he tries to promote under the term of 'political theology' – is a late original invention of the second millennium CE, and it is suffused by social arts of distinction and habits of choice. The theology of Schmitt's 'theological concepts' is a reference to a certain moment in the history of occidental Christianism, a moment that we might schematically describe, with reference to the great title that age has to institutional originality, as the inaugural age of the university.[2]

'Secularisation', on the other hand, refers only marginally to the rejection of the religious from the sphere of institutional matters and decisions, and only at one specific historical moment within a *longue durée*. It does not refer essentially to anything like a replacement, whether sudden or gradual, of the Church by the State (except, of course, in the specific episode of German church expropriations after the Napoleonian wars when the word 'secularisation' [German: *Säkularisierung*] was coined). Both the rejection of the religious from the public mind or discourse and the unfriendly takeover of the Catholic

Church's social agenda by the state administration need to be redefined as an early yet inessential aspect of a wider process of 'secularisation', which needs to be understood as among the top-ranking distinctive forces or potencies of Western Christianism. This force or potency was already at work in the process by which the revolutionary Western church, pushed by the Gregorian reform programme, took up the task of supplying European society with a strategy of social differentiation that would lead to the creation of the unprecedented entity called the university; this was followed by a sequence of centuries (including those of the Protestant reform and European religious war) marking the Church's slow retreat towards a merely 'spiritual' role. The decisive point, if there is one, resides in the fact that the notion of 'secularisation' deserves to be restituted the sweeping dialectical energy of which it was shorn, despite attempts to the contrary (Hegel!), by a certain slant towards the micro-logical. Western secularisation started ages before anyone could talk of the self-assertion of the state 'public sphere' against 'the Church'; even the increasingly competitive relationship, throughout Western Christendom, between a Church that claimed ultimate appellate jurisdiction throughout Europe and pre-state European principalities (and later, states) was sufficiently successful not only at motivating an ongoing chain reaction of escalating polarisations but, even more importantly, at channelling internal social evolution towards differentiation processes, which were ultimately capable of giving rise to a difference between (secularising) Church and the (secularised) public sphere that has ever since functioned as the sole relevant one (the 'difference that makes a difference', in Bateson's classical definition). In sum, far from acting as an eventual correction addressing theological concepts from a non-religious perspective, secularisation goes all the way back to the inaugural centuries of Western natural theology, understood as a field dedicated to the praxis of presenting and defending claims to validity in relation to God, a specifically instituted process of continuous inquiry – we would speak of an 'academic discipline'. All or most of this happened around the dawn of the twelfth century, a time that coincided with the new understanding conferred to 'theology' – the term, the discipline – by Abelard.[3]

In the following we choose an interpretation that does not

necessarily correspond to what Schmitt wanted to say, even less to what Schmitt wanted to be seen as doing in making the programmatic suggestions he made in his in 1922 manifesto. It is exclusively based upon our own experience as Schmitt's readers: we find that his argument leads to perplexing and/ or misleading results, and that this is a consequence of paradoxes and contradictions, but also sloppiness and inconsistency, only some of which is either harmless or necessary given historic conditions. However, their basic inspiration can be corrected without too much ado, at the price of discarding what we consider as a specifically Western fixation alternatively or cumulatively with religion and the need of getting rid of religion – a fixation that results from the torsion structure at the core of Western religion, and that extends to Western religion's external or exceptional role with respect to society and its 'public idols' (*idola fori* according to Francis Bacon), its mediatised ideology at large. Instead of polarising secular modernity and religious mediaeval times against each other, we propose to cast the parameters of our own predicament as a largely immobile and ultimately undecidable no-man's-land, which is at once 'modern' – insofar it relies upon an intellectual discipline that proceeds through constructive distinctions – and 'mediaeval' insofar as its unique or overwhelming topic remains 'theological' (or more exactly religious) throughout, and is indeed, in our view, fated to remain so indefinitely. This is why we suggest the revocation of any periodisation that ultimately boils down to a species of the 'religion/science'[4] distinction.

Here, setting aside both Schmitt's decisionism and his 'Catholic-gone-stale'[5] way of exploiting the fragility of Protestant Hegelian philosophy professors arguing the West's historic/post-historic insuperability – Hegel's *Geschichtsmächtigkeit*[6] of 'world spirit' and Weltgeist, today represented by an academic-cum-mediatic consensus acting as the Weltgeist's legitimate lieutenant – we shall highlight a bigger problem with Schmitt, which is his 'modesty' in matters of scholarly ambition. Schmitt – who was a keen reader and had a particular predilection for two groups of authors: first, his 'enemies', present or recent, including obviously their reactionary nineteenth-century 'enemies' (thus his 'friends'); second, Patristics, especially of the

Greek/Byzantine brand – went out of his way to avoid any possible close encounter with any of the theologians to whom he erected his shrine in honour of political theology, which is still well-attended today.[7]

5.2

Effectively, Schmitt never ventured to circumscribe the precise nature of the political role and intellectual import of the theology of the so-called 'schoolmen' whom he saw at work unfolding the modern political systems.[8] The most decisive questions thus remain wide open. There is especially one point, one short-circuit, it is tempting to say, that still awaits thorough elucidation. As research in recent decades has abundantly shown (albeit rarely under the name 'political theology'[9]). As research in recent decades has abundantly shown (albeit rarely under the name 'political theology') the role of the mediaeval political theologians to whom Schmitt refers, mostly without naming them, falls far short of doing justice to the role that Schmitt wishes them to play – in short, that of so many authoritarian pillars of timeless, modernity-incompatible power structures, so many fossils of the undifferentiated land mass that includes both law/politics and religion; they now appear as proto-modern pioneers of the most analytical brands of modern legal, political and economic rationality. This is what couples Schmitt's great merit, his opening of the file of 'political theology', with what needs to be understood as its core incoherence. It is precisely those teachers, often friars, who, in the decisive decades of the late thirteenth and early fourteenth centuries, presented the most radical versions of God's power that Christian political theology has ever come up with, and who at the same time, often, and as it were inadvertently, sowed the seed of modernity, giving rise to the most unexpected contributions to the evolution of the society in which they were active.

In their teaching, the maximalism of their attribution of absolute (but at the same time ordered) power to God goes together with a radical reduction of the social and political attributions qualifying the human being, both individual and collective. Without, in the main, goals other than justifying their form of life – one that excluded them from the networks of rights, status, institution, etc. – the followers of Saint Francis developed new and well-functioning conceptions and conceptualisations, dealing with various matters legal, economic and political, some of which (notably subjective rights) have been crowned, centuries after the fact, by the most amazing historical success in the evolution of modern society. Subjective rights,[10] the structure of trust,[11] credit and banking rationality,[12] the societal trajectory leading through 'juridification',[13] all of those have their roots in the works of some follower of Saint Francis, most largely some ambitious and repressed exponent of his teaching. The Franciscan spirituals strive to set themselves apart from the state of fallen nature that follows from God's revocation of natural law as instituted in paradise, arguing that an exceptional and exclusive return to this abolished condition is awarded to those only who have made theirs the stainless poverty chosen and practised by Christ and the apostles. Thus, rather than fitting into the tragic image of champions of a well-ordered, hierocratic world condemned to be defeated by the modern introduction of mutual indifference between law/politics and religion, the evidence we stumble upon shows these austere brethren not only as an important constituency, but also as a crew pioneering precisely those technologies, including political technologies, that we rightly or wrongly identify as modernity. They have thereby, and – if one tries to reconstrue their situation – clearly without wishing to do so, assured for themselves the fame (though in their eyes this would rather amount to infamy) of having played the triggering role in some of the evolutionary episodes that have led Western society to transform into the world that the twentieth and twenty-first centuries identify as theirs.

Thus, if contract law and subjective right point as to their origin to late thirteenth and early fourteenth-century Franciscan theologians,[14] then the question to be asked is how these two capital modern-scientific contributions to mutual indifference and the decoupling of law/politics and religion can have thirteenth-century roots.[15] If so, this would have meant that, in the process of opposing law (or: law-plus-politics) and religion, the unsolved riddles of their division versus indivision, of identity versus non-identity, extend their genealogy much further back than even Schmitt's own chronology of the beginning of modernity would allow. Be this as it may, we must resist the temptation to see in those radicalised Franciscan friars the heroes or harbingers of early modernity; rather, the contributions they epitomise were unintentional side-products of their efforts to approach their unique speculative object: God represented as a power-holding being. By imputing such eminently exploitable inventions to mendicant monks whose sole ambition was the absolute poverty they wanted to share with Christ and his apostles (but no one else), one runs into the difficulty of having to imagine a very special group of inventors: collateral inventors, inventors by accident, who never wished to invent what they had invented.

Do we need to admit that historical effectiveness gains, very generally, from being understood, not as a matter of important deeds, but as a matter of the post-history or epigenesis of impulses that, on their own, are of little importance? If it somehow feels morally wrong or sinful to give in to this epistemic temptation, the reasons are not hard to see: it undermines the basic wager underlying the Western conception of public life up to the threshold of modernity, within political discourse even far beyond this threshold, as it is captured in the glorious, politico-centric image of society in which Will, divine or human, is the author of history (one might also call it the mythological, or the politico-centric view of society).

In modernity, Giambattista Vico's celebrated phrase *verum factum* remains a faithful expression of this view. While the onslaught of empirical dissonance and unresolvable multiplicity had led to spirited measures of simplification, unification, uncluttering, already present in pre-Christian antiquity and ever since – for instance by interpreting the *universitas rerum*, the compassing order of all things, created by the 'demiurg', to individual human action – Vico's early eighteenth-century version only retains one element of the myth: the quality of each thing as 'made' (*factum*). In modernity it is 'us', at least some of us – the makers, the doers, the go-getters, the settlers, the decision-makers – who play the demiurgic role and who steer society on its way. The world presents itself truthfully to secular humanity in the form imposed upon it by those who 'make it', namely 'us' and – as Bush junior would certainly concede – those who are 'with us'.

The notion we strive to express is that the ancient-modern Western doctrine that 'the truth is in the deed/the making', and the equation 'truthful = made' seems to become more fragile with every step into the thicket of our world and, in all probability, any world to come, and the happenings and evolutions that constitute it. Our basic notion is that the world, the cloud of happening that constitutes it, does not need a myth of sovereign Will in order to become readable – even if we readily admit that (1) some of us, more than others, continue to find shelter in the mythical sense of a maker or making agency, while (2) others continue to validate it performatively even if no longer convinced of its truth. What needs to be reopened (though ultimately to be left open) is the entire issue of 'alternative paths', the complex of the genealogy of modernity, including the notion of 'revolution'. An overly simple grand concept like that of revolution might be an obstacle in the way of construing appropriate historical reconstructions or narratives. The birth of, say, the concept of a subjective right needs to be re-explained in terms of an effect that is not only unintended and unforeseen, but also merely collateral or epigenetic, rather than as the gift bestowed upon itself by a courageous humankind on the triumphal march of its self-realisation.[16]

5.3

To the extent to which it offers itself to be *understood*, at least subliminally, as a long-term anti-modern rehabilitation of Old European hierarchic structures, Schmitt's assertion of what would need to be classified as and called a 'geo-Western' political continuity in the sign of a decisionism-based secularised (as opposed to a pastoral-power-based, i.e. non-decisionistic administration-based) political theology also offers a spectacular example of a pious but philosophically misleading politico-centrism. By sinking his teeth deeply into the self-referential theme of the 'power-holder's' 'decision-power', Schmitt conjured, a hundred years ago, a romantic idealisation, an acro-political icon or idyll, that still today combines only too well with our own confident politico-centric idealisations. It is apt to say that, in comparison to the earlier nineteenth-century German champions of an 'unending conversation' (*unendliches Gespräch*), highly praised in their own times, but severely criticised by Schmitt in the early twentieth century for their 'political romanticism',[17] his own romantically politico-centric view of decisionist power and mastery has been even more successful – namely at generating those misleadingly reassuring projected futures in which a large share of the political-intellectual consensus of early twenty-first century times recognises itself. The Schmittian early twentieth-century obsession with power-wielding mastery, with the master's sovereign decision, etc., offers barely the best conditions for an accurate understanding of the great dispute between theological and philosophical political doctrines in the mediaeval West. Despite what Schmitt wishes to make his reader believe, the history of power, politics and sovereignty in the West has been a long, winding and often turbulent history, especially an unpredictable one (cf. the sudden availability in Latin translations, from Greek and Arabic, of most of Aristotle's hitherto unknown, now game-changing, work throughout the twelfth and thirteenth centuries). There is no doubt about the 'winner' between the philosophical/Aristotelian and the theological/Augustinian school in the main intellectual conflict of the later Middle Ages: starting with the 'successful' condemnation of 219 philosophical propositions by the Paris bishop Etienne Tempier, the definitive and lasting victory went to the theological side – not unlike how theo-political issues had been resolved, or were being resolved, in the Islamic political world.[18] The error is in the notion that the occidental game has been one of mastery and of submission to a master,[19] according to a doctrine of the overlordship of the theo-political, as imagined by Schmitt.

The most innovatively and radically theo-centric positions of the late mediaeval dispute between philosophy and theology was the one held by Franciscan followers of Augustine, at a decisive moment even the dissident Spiritual branch of that same community. The West, during the hundred years straddling the thirteenth and fourteenth centuries, saw both political controversialists (in liberal amounts) and theologians properly speaking being caught largely in a Moebius loop-type tension between Aristotle and Aristotle; that is between, on the one hand, an interpretation of Aristotle as an intellectual enabling device, without the recent discovery of whose essential work scholastic thinking would never have even started to achieve its power or subtlety, and an opposite interpretation of Aristotle as a seductive teacher, whose doctrine could be, and was, read at the Arts Faculties – as a manifesto for an autonomously philosophical life and knowledge that does away with the very need of a revealed truth. What was not around, by contrast, are political theologians as imagined by Schmitt – with the possible sole exception of the last period in the life and work of William of Ockham, who, as an exiled intellectual at the court of proscribed Roman-German Emperor Louis of Bavaria in Munich, found himself however in a very particular situation, not incomparable to that of Edward Snowden today. Yet even if in William's case one is tempted to conclude that, during the last two decades of his life, which he documented in his political writings, he no longer worked as a theologian or a philosopher, he transformed not into a 'political theologian' – the term did not make sense in his time – but rather a political controversialist. Even if one is perfectly aware that the term 'political theology' has a long and well-documented history, Schmitt's specific conception of political theology is an unwarranted retrospective fantasy; a close reading of the authors one might have in mind leads to answers different from those expected by Schmitt (which were essentially inspired by early twentieth-century right-wing German ideas). As to the great philosophical and theological period around 1300, its main entries are the thematic series contingency, modalities, will/voluntarism (followed, later on, by the fourteenth-century explosion of nominalism). Most of all, the Scotist doctrine of the univocity of being, in its application to the power wielded by both God and man, could not be more opposed to the basic Schmittian mythology of the power-holder, the Machthaber.

Although situated on different sides, as creator and creature, God and man are according to Scotus' theo-theory not distinct in the way in which, say, master and subject are: according to one of the most significant chapters of John Duns Scotus' Reportatio Parisiensis, God and man are equal in the sense that both are 'beings', in one single, perfectly identical sense of the word 'being.' Obedience to positive law is emphasised; indeed, in this scheme, God, holder of *potentia absoluta*, is at once construed, by dint of his *potentia ordinata*, as the most law-obedient legal subject; our understanding of the English-Franciscan idea of God even gains from imagining Him, be it for a second, in the guise of a well-educated English or Scottish upper-class individual, perfectly well-disciplined, uncorrupted by even the remotest temptation to have recourse to limitless *potentia absoluta*, capable of keeping his place in the queue without frowning. Half a millennium after the politico-theological supernova that started with the Franciscans' steep career within the Church during the last quarter of the thirteenth century, and was followed by their equally breath-taking institutional defeat and persecution in the earlier fourteenth century, the French Enlightenment philosophers would sing the praise of the 'political sense' of the English. In retrospect, one wonders whether both moments, separated by centuries, are not part of a single story featuring as its canonical 'message' the notion of a protagonist maker-being endowed with both absolute and limited power. In the course of centuries, this message, which was first announced in theological guise – notably through the legal 'turn' that John Duns Scotus imparted upon the common Western theological doctrine of God's 'twofold power' – has been sent through a succession of so-called 'secular' metamorphoses, at the end of which it came to function as the ultimate blueprint of Western public power construed as the coupling of sovereignty and rule of law. Hence, sovereign 'power' remains capable of its own absoluteness when self-controlled, capable of limiting itself, of conducting itself by its own means;[20] this is the point Duns Scotus refers to, by univocally subjecting any actor, God as well as man, to the rule required by the moral insistence on *ratio recta*. To be sure, if anyone had the idea of suggesting to Montesquieu and Voltaire, the chief members of the French eighteenth-century fan club of English political sense, that Jean Duns Scot, the overly 'subtle doctor', proponent of a thought that they classified as a scholastic and theocentric chimera typical of the dark ages, was responsible for what they admired in English political history and tried to import and imitate, they would have been surprised.

Looking at the contemporary scene, the question here, of how to think of this classically modern, classically

Enlightenment way of rejecting into nothingness the medi-aeval past, distant by some ten or twelve generations only, treating it like some intruder from a different galaxy, 'inter-pellates' us. The problem was not merely one of overdoing the distance but of considering the mediaeval as being part of a stage of history now overcome, almost as if belonging to an extinct species, as remote as the Neanderthals. Clearly, the eighteenth-century French Enlightenment elite vantage point, concerned with establishing a viable secular and non-despotic political system, relates to European preoccupations other than those of the years around 1300 (or for that matter, those of our times). For instance, the philosophers were right about the fact that England alone was, at the time, in posses-sion of a modicum of relevant success stories on procedural-political matters. Moreover, as inmates of the world of the Old European state- and church-based structures of domina-tion that resulted from the fusion of inherited clerical and feudal networks, they were driven by the need to find ways and examples of successful resistance that were based on identifiable ideological and politicised polarities. Voltaire's anti-clerical rallying cry, 'écrasez l'infâme!' (French for 'crush the loathsome thing!'), was one of them.

There is a question of method involved here. We are searching for the lost keys of the locks sealing our captivity. Forgetting the past looks like an official pedagogy destined to discipline the inmates. Any step we would like to make is predicated on clues capable of shedding some light on the genealogy, the enshrined commitments, the hidden bifurca-tion points, etc., of the highly path-dependent evolutions and factors responsible for the situation that is now ours. Inmates of a different world, in which 'storming the Bastille' does not cut it, we grapple with a depoliticised but moralised/legal-ised world, torn between the responsible quadrature of the irresponsible circle, i.e. anonymous and narcissistic and yet consensual and remotely controlled by the spectre and the vital worry inspired by the possible failure of what is consen-sually, normatively, transferentially understood as 'too big to fail'. If we, too, stand in need of enlightenment, it is about this world, not that of the eighteenth century. Relying on the minimal degree of cognitive confidence, our assumption is that understanding the emergence of a new fragmentary global society might enable us to understand its constraints, even if we cannot hope to twist ourselves free of them. In addition, the coexistence of ordered and absolutist power in God (human actors possess only ordered power) – in its many more or less sophisticated late mediaeval interpretations – is present in the search for a potent and robust conception of power, any conception capable of guiding 'constitutionalist bricolage'.

The success of the Scotist theory of God as self-disciplined and all-powerful, omnipotent yet patiently waiting in line, epitomising the transition from late mediaeval natural theology to early modern natural philosophy, simultaneously (1) taints the argument that modernity reversed the loss of philosophy's 'right' to assert the standing of revealed religion and the successful mid-term solutions that proposed some un-prejudged combination of revealed truth and philosophical truth under a *primus inter pares* position of the former; (2) shows that the most radical and successful conception of mediaeval theology did not go in the direction extolled by Schmitt, who carelessly gave the assurance to his 1922 readership that what is argued in the politico-theological tradition of Western Christianism is basically a doctrine in favour of strong, dictatorially personalised exceptional powers.[21] Even neo-Thomism, the doctrine construed by Pope Leo XIII in the last years of the nineteenth century as a base for the new social doctrine of the Catholic Church that would allow it to compete with the 'godless doctrines' of the socialist labour movement,[22] and that leads in a direction that is perfectly and diametrically opposed to the Schmittian fixation on decisionist politics, defined itself, not disingenuously with respect to its thirteenth-century source, as a social movement. In this sense, it needs to be admitted that the moneying of 'political theology' as an 'alternative' for Weimarian, etc., parliamentarianism, is hard to distinguish from what is now known as a Ponzi scheme, except that it is based not only upon the intractable unknowability of the future, but also upon the ignorance of the past (which, in principle, could be rectified). While Schmitt rightly confronted the sheer phobia of the Middle Ages, the anti-theological allergies and preconceptions which obsessed the establishment that he encountered in the twentieth-century institutional world, he showed insufficient interest in the proto-modern quality of just those political theologians that he tried to draw attention to. It remains difficult to decide whether he should be congratulated for his capacity in matters of cunningly targeted forgetfulness, or whether, on the contrary, one needs to accept that he simply could not bring himself to consider late mediaeval political theology as a potential source of relevant twentieth-century information.

And yet Schmitt, as a thinker of 'post-Lapsarian' politics under modern conditions, did share part of the Franciscan legacy. Was he unable, or was he understandably unwilling, to admit that the classical champions of mediaeval political theology also held positions that, on closer examination, shared important affinities with the militant branch of their 'atheist' descendants, and even with the contrary liberal, positivist type of modernism? All we can say is that exposure of this proto-modernity would barely have served his argumentative/propagandistic needs. What is worse than any tactical sloppiness is that the Prussian state councillor was a helpless subject of that paradigmatic tendency of professionalised politics which consists of overloading the future with hyperbolic promises, as if it were an Eldorado of inexhaustible riches. No wonder, then, that he had no access to issues such as whether a group of partly dissident Franciscan friars of the half-century straddling the year 1300 needed to be considered as the unwilling inventors of the absolutely fundamental feature of modern society's legal order that we identify as subjective right. The point to be retained, to which Schmitt did succeed in alerting us, is that, even if unobserved, the ruins and remains of mediaeval theology discharge a vital function in the current political horizon – the function of offering the modern imagination a counterpoise to the weight of the classical antiquities from democratic Athens and Republican Rome, which officially rule gloriously over the modern legal and political constitutional imagination. The more warmly embraced stony ruins from two millennia or so ago have succeeded at surviving modernity and still today constitute the main frame of reference for the constitutionalist debate. Schmitt's rescheduling of political theology beyond the academic disciplines of theology and history – even passing through sceptical receptions, such as that of

Agamben's archaeological investigations – had the merit of challenging a whole class of smooth, 'classical' readings of politics.[23] The constitutionalist discussion is far from offering the sole example here. Other examples, evolving before and after Schmitt's politico-theological broadside, include the reign of the differentialist paradigm, be it clad in structuralism and/or cyberneticism, in psychoanalysis and/or a doctrine of the linguistic turn (or one of its many followers). Even Hegel's famous meta-claim about Reason – that Reason itself is cunning, never to be captured in any claim, realising itself in history at once despite and by means of no matter what argument, actor, or campaign, always turning the tables on its self-appointed partisans, has been subject to an almost industrial over-use as a comforting drug by communities of disorientated twenty-first century intellectuals.

It is therefore not a coincidence that, meantime, Schmitt has been invested with the role of the main outside ('rogue'?) reference in current geo-politics, in the age of geo-economics and the world agon of counter-terrorism and terrorism. Recycling an old joke, one can say that, if Schmitt and certain arguments of his had never existed, the global situation today is such that one would have had to invent them. Taking up the politico-theological remainders of the Catholic era, complete with their inherent claim to universal mastery, such as the regime in charge of exceptions and justifications, is an indispensable counterweight to the imperceptible but unstoppable triumphal march of differentialist routines in charge of the continuation of societal conditions. One of the structural changes in how society lives out its own existence and temporality throughout the past hundred and again, increasingly, the past fifty years has been the double process of emptying the promise of law/politics of its glorious meaning and reasserting it under the condition of its own newly achieved emptiness. If, during the last third of the twentieth century, Western Christian religion resisted the proceedings without giving rise to sudden structural breakdowns, instituted as it is as a dialectic of the death of God and faith in God, it is not surprising that today it has become the central site of the debate on the waning of sovereignty and the rise of 'administration without government',[24] pursued alongside the rise of popular and populist-led protest movements.

5.4

The intricate and very special relationship between, on the one hand, the multidimensional object that we call 'Christianism' and, on the other hand, the concept of 'religion' – a concept integrally rooted in a Christian genealogy[25] – tell us that it is best to avoid haste in staging anything like a comparison between the mutual virtues of different 'religions'. Only once this has been appropriately taken into account, we can ask the question of what 'religion' actually means and what it does not. Admitting the double-faced status of the one religion we single out as 'religion-after-religion', recognising that it is perfectly classifiable both as religion and as non-religion, we shall retain only one fundamental notion: that the personnel of most other religions do not count universality among the attributes with which they exalt the ultimate object of their cult. Why is this so? Singular Gods, singular pantheons as well, usually come with an inbuilt claim to universality, either for having created the world with all its ingredients, out of nothing, of chaos, or of any other primary resource, or just in the name of their sheer overwhelming glory. Restricting ourselves to the first two 'abrahamic' religions,[26] we see that sometimes, this inbuilt claim to universality gives rise to cults of a glorious but by now distant creator God who in some Jewish traditions even figures as generously dispensing with his own presence in his own creation, and gradually delegating all mastery to his creature;[27] hence the resulting heroic, but at once deeply inglorious, spectacle of subjects religious enough to relentlessly offer themselves to remedy His creation *à leur propre corps perdant*. The motive is illustrated perfectly in the parodistic image of ten men earning their lives by upholding, with the force of their arms and working in eight-hour shifts, the roof of a five-storey bourgeois townhouse in Moscow that is threatening to collapse.[28] Sometimes, on the other hand, it produces an inglorious but process-entangled and indispensable superhero-type agent of 24/7 salvation, redemption and remedy,[29] cast in the equally inglorious image of Christ's intervention in the fate of man. The fact is that all mono-theologies find themselves confronted with this encompassing condition of a singular God/pantheon who does make claim to it all, either discreetly or less so; this common un-commonality is at the bottom of their – shared – success, which is acquired, for each, at the expense of its competitors.

Religious history offers vast evidence for the claim that different mono-Gods can be attributed too many similar powers and omnipotences to see them fuse. Religions – including their theologies as religion-dependent intellectual 'production sites' – are eminently comparable among themselves, on condition that their one-gods are remote 'totallers', each total(is)ing the entire potential of their domain. Religions are neighbours, competitors, shareholders, stake-holders, and as such are vitally rooted in continuous processes of mutual distinction. Feverishly defining themselves in view of gaining an identity of their own, religions in today's world have become less definable than ever; they are compositions or clusters of elements selected from traditional or neo-traditional beliefs, claims and practices, who gain their identity by the actively pursued effort of distinguishing themselves from each other. There is of course no need to insist that this mode of being of religion, voluntarist or choice-based, is, historically, a recent acquisition. Non-choice, or, for the individual, the fact of simply being born into a religious framework and existing within a given religious integrity – in other words the existence of religion in the form of an extended form of kinship – has long provided the general framework of the existence of religions. Whence, then, the particularities of Christianism? If, according to Serge Margel's insight, the Christian religion, describing itself as the true religion, can be described as a comparative religion,[30] that which distinguishes Christianism from other cults against which it has profiled itself right from its beginnings and from which it keeps distinguishing itself, is the very fact of its self-profiling, or self-distinguishing, through a choice-based mode of relating to the Christian 'message'. On this basis we believe that, starting from the seventeenth, and continuing in an accelerated manner through to the twenty-first century, is a process, not of a de-Christianisation (as certain historians of mentalities would have it), but of the 'Christianisation' or 'meta-Christianisation' of world society, which proceeds by successfully subjecting the subject's relationship to no matter which particular religion, to a conversion process towards religiosity that is offer- and choice-based (a value that is distinctive of Christianity).

What we are witnessing is not a conversion to one religion, away from another religion; it is a conversion of all religions to the mode of social existence of religion that has long been represented and was originally invented by Christianism. In this sense Christianism has historically taken possession of the religious potential of Westernised humankind not only and not primarily through actual conversions, but through ever more individuals and groups 'embracing'[31] choice-based religiosity; by today, all individuals/groups who 'embrace' ethno-religious identities, even and indeed particularly non-European-Christian ones, are in this sense Christianised. In this sense, furthermore, the problem of weak Church attendance is not a big issue: indeed, in this regard, there is no longer a difference between Jew and gentile. That said, of course there are still different religions distinguishing themselves from each other in relation to other aspects. For one, Christianism is a religion that did not want its omnipotent and glorious God of love to be tainted by the all-too-obvious failures of His creation; hence, the theological split between His being and His praxis that angered the Gnostics and that, as Agamben notes,[32] gives early theology its particularly flexible economic character. This last general point could help provide a starting point for being (or not being/no longer being) 'religious', and is much more easily accessible for a Christian than, say, for a Jew or a Muslim; when however, we consider the empirical impact those intermingling fractions or halves of constantly varying practices and beliefs that we call 'religions', and that compare and compete with each other, have upon the life- and meaning-horizons of the individuals that 'embrace' them, we must bear in mind that their multiplicity is based, not upon any mutually exclusive claim to an original identity, but upon the continuous, mutual, distancing and unrelenting production of distinctive features. Different from nations, whose distinctive features often refer to some immemorial absolute beginning (at least this is the typical state of all those entities the roots of which fail to go back further than modern or early modern times), religions, throughout their evolution, gain their identity and self-description from constant processes of exchange, comparison, and rewriting of their role-distribution, in the tension of orthodoxy and heresy.

While in the Western *longue durée*, the binary relation law/ politics–religion has produced a widely admired and imitated model that boasts a harmonious fit to society's industrial evolution, it must be recognised, looking at the political reality and its capacity to digest the achievements obtained through the process of functional differentiation, that all ventures of meaningfully coordinating them, of establishing a positive institutional relationship, have failed, except for a small belt of Northern/Western, Protestant, work-ethic based cultures, where a discipline of mind enables the subject to see the lack of positively achieved success sufficiently compensated for by ongoing further effort and work-in-progress. Otherwise, the 'need' to manage the tension generated between law/ politics and religion (hence, also, the capacity to be capable of managing) is constantly touted. In other words, the polarisation between law/politics and religion that made the differentiation of society possible must also, at a more fundamental level, be seen as a necessarily inconclusive half-way solution. Thus, *pace* the argument that Christianity, like all monotheisms, yet a step further from the others, is destined to lead us the 'way out of religion',[33] the paradigm of economic-political theology to which we can attribute this success of Western power, is more like a bitter relationship between divorcees – especially where religion is being routinely pilloried as an institutionalised remainder, an internal brake diminishing the tempo of social evolution, if not as the culprit for the sloth with which the specific modern achievements gained by means of a de-religionised practice of law/politics have been obtained. The disentanglement between religion and politics/law has given rise to modern secularism (a social-historical category all too often represented by a trinity of 'thinkers': Machiavelli, Bodin, Hobbes[34]); the main event of this episode is the defeat of religion as a public matter (known as such in the 'winner's' historical account, written in its own triumph at the instigation of social modernity).

Conversely, the strong renewal of scholarly interest in the politics and political theology of the Middle Ages – this 'denigrated intermediate past', as it has been called by a perspicacious observer[35] – is understandable as a reaction against the amnesia of the Middle Ages, which has dominated Western understanding of the eighteenth and extensive fractions of the nineteenth and twentieth centuries, dominated by the notion that there was little or nothing interesting to be found. It is with this invitation to oblivion in mind that the study of mediaeval political theology needs to be assessed: as a double-edged remedy or *pharmakon* (Greek for medicine or poison) for amnesia. The study of mediaeval-cum-late mediaeval political theology is of course an anti-modern dispositive, a remedy against Western modernity, to the extent that it relativises the modern-enlightened innovations of the two most recent centuries by claiming their uninterrupted dependence on the preceding half-millennium or millennium; yet at the same time, it is also an anti-anti-modern remedy, a remedy against the anti-modernists, offering proof that the most in/famous theo-political doctrines, especially epitomised by Carl Schmitt, are themselves not new, but date back to the years and decades of what might be called the primary secularisation of divine power, the 'digestion' of Aristotle's, non-religious, philosophical approach to power, by Catholic natural theology. Aristotle's brief enthronement in Western Liberal Arts faculties of the third quarter of the thirteenth century, stopped by the official condemnation of a digest of 219 philosophical claims in 1277 by an anti-philosophical Paris bishop, was followed by centuries of philosophico-theological coexistence, conditional acceptance, mutual stimulation and emulation, between the two poles of what one might call the dual (philosophical and theological) constitution of Western Christianism. This evolution that tellingly contrasts with the full-blown and lasting rejection and banishment of philosophy and philosophers from late mediaeval Muslim cultures, which are the site of a less compromising, less 'flexible' way to rid theology of its philosophical 'parasites'.[36]

Schmitt's claim of a mediaeval–modern continuity with respect to politico-theological doctrine points to a mediaeval Christian God as a holder of power at once legitimate (*potentia ordinata*) and limitless (*potentia absoluta*) – a harbinger of the modern so-called 'constitutional paradox' obtaining between the notions of 'constituent' (law-making) and 'constituted' (law-limiting) power.[37] It confronts a certain bourgeois consensus that their sovereign was post-mediaeval because located after the decline/overcoming of absolute power. The pattern underlies the progressive ingredients of the Weimar Republic and resembles the pattern present two centuries earlier in Weimar classicism when it coalesced with the idea that a resurrection of classical Athenian fifth-century BC democracy was desirable and even possible.[38] Setting aside Schmitt's unsavoury allusions (deadly illusions, more likely) to a Führer who overcomes the constitutional paradox and fuses the distinction of limitless and legitimate power, attention should also be paid to his admiration for the Catholic Church and its capacity of flexibly combining dogmatism with pragmatism.[39] Any Schmittian eager to find more on this theme – of how the Western paradigm is one of sovereignty plus flexible administrative logic rather than sovereignty alone – must be referred to Foucault's and Agamben's work.[40] Christian economic-political theology, in its occidental mediaeval acculturation, has indisputably been at the root of modern individualist ideas and related images of subjectivity since it first expressed and 'sanctified' the scissile, mutually reinforcing, simultaneous desire for authority and revolution, order and transformation, in equal measure.

The legal and political see-saw played by late modern revolutionaries and constitutionalists is intimately connected to a Janus-faced subjectivity, a prototype of which is the 'earliest modernity' – the one emerging in the midst of the Catholic Middle Ages. This 'rightfully rebellious' proto-individualist, even proto-nationalist[41] individual and its subjectivity is effectively best exemplified by the popes who, as Rosenstock-Huessy insightfully claimed, offered the model for a new type of subjectivity by means of their self-appointment as sole and legitimate Vicars of Christ.[42] The Roman pontiffs – starting in the eleventh century with the 'revolutionary'[43] party of Pope Gregory VII – first embodied the justifiably rebelling individual who takes up his/her stance, unlike Antigone, not against all human authority but on the contrary those invested with authority. The popes held the spiritualised, extra-legal 'right' to reject tradition and law – 'perversions introduced by the princes of the world', to use the formulation of Gregorian reform party apparatchik Anselm of Lucca – and to point out and declare war on the Antichrist (as proven by a long series of mediaeval tests, a label that attaches with admirable adhesive power to whatever adversary it is thrown at). Further, this new subject, unlike Athenians and Romans, does not rebel

at the risk of unity (of rocking the proverbial ship of unity-
providing government) but acts on the chance of imposing,
henceforth, a new type of unity in diversity. A wide range of
institutions including, eventually, the papacy itself, individuals, peoples, classes, etc., have been singled out in this way as
embodying the 'power' that prevents those of good will from
being successful at bringing salvation/emancipation to universal man. Thus, the new aspiration to power and liberty of
late mediaeval individuals and their corporations was, from
the start, guaranteed by the Catholic Church 'establishing
itself a feudal court for the world at large',[44] and 'lending
its spiritual justification to . . . social change', with the Pope
acting as 'trustee of all Christendom against the imperialism
of the Germanic Roman Empire'.[45] To say it in words not yet
available in the days of Rosenstock-Huessy: the revolutionary potential of the new liberty was structurally contained
in the other distinctly occidental and Catholic invention (one
that Rosenstock-Huessy does mention): the idea of 'mere
government', considered as relatively independent from the
ruler's dignity. By granting the free right to appeal to every
Christian soul, the popes did nothing less than invent the
modern idea of omnipresent but centralised government:[46]

> The Pope, who for a thousand years had anxiously
> avoided calling himself universal . . . because he feared
> that the expression would be derogatory to the other
> churches, was now settled, as the vicar of Christ, the
> earthly representative of God, the breathing law and
> official living interpreter of the Christian canon, on the
> universal apostolic throne of the world . . . Gregory [Pope
> Gregory VII, 1073–85] is the man who discovered the
> fusion of omnipresence and centralisation, the anti-classi-
> cal and anti-pagan core of the Middle Ages.[47]

True as it is that modernity defined and defines itself in
contradistinction to 'theology-stricken' mediaeval Western
consciousness (to the point of having given rise to the very
term Middle Ages in order to identify and isolate, distance,
disqualify, and ultimately proscribe an establishment that
early modern and modern elites wished to leave behind),
the historically most momentous group to benefit from a

theology that was understood and used as a doctrine of power and self-enforcement, the elite party behind the Gregorian reform/revolution of the eleventh century, fits perfectly the (modern) image of power politics. This is paradoxical; it is neither particularly surprising nor unique; it suffices to think of long-time NASA director Wernher von Braun, the father of the V2 rockets and director of a German weapons industry known for its heavy reliance on slave labour, flown out of freshly defeated Nazi Germany as a matter of urgency to ensure the success of the US space programme. From the earliest moments of the history of modern self-assertion, militants, Protestant as well as Catholic (admittedly or otherwise) have borrowed essential elements from ancestor-militants, unfazed and unimpaired by the notable differences in the 'ultimate goals' inspiring their actions. In this sense, the credentials of earlier stints of institutionalised revolutionary militancy have always been the core trophy conquered and recycled by revolutionary Western movements. This explains in part those revolutions which, like the French and American ones, anticipate their settlement with a new constitution – even if this new constitution ostensibly harkens back to the opposite side of the Gregorian hierocrats, namely Greek democracy (which was yet at least equally as important as the Roman republic). This trophy, this surviving militant core in mediaeval and early modern history, consisted in effectively prioritising the overriding concern of the unity of an *ekklesia* as against its intrinsic and natural tendency that, since Athens, has always tempted and threatened to lead the political community towards *schisma* and *stasis*: disunion and civil strife. This is why, when we read that sovereignty is at odds with democracy, the latter term referring to 'a modestly egalitarian sharing of power',[48] we must also make clear that sovereignty is also at odds with the less egalitarian aspects of Greek democracy insofar as sovereignty prizes stability above all. Neither civil warfare nor immobility (which nourish each other), but stability; it prizes, to be exact, the institutional flexibility that Schmitt admired in the Catholic Church and wanted to be reflected by the latter's institutional successor, the state, on the basis of the wisdom that one that can always justify the economic negotiation of problems through a combination of hierarchy and anarchy.

5.5

The political universe of the older world was one of causality – of all happening being the effect of one identifiable and identified constitutive cause, with the power-holder figuring as ultimate cause of it all – a vertex powerfully governing the pyramid carrying it, alias its 'subject matter'. *Arche*, power, verticality, causality: all formed aspects of an infinitely and gloriously meaningful identity. Even so, it is by no means the case that the awareness that 'stuff happens', that contingency is out of control, came as late as is usually thought. Throughout history, power-holders had to develop routines of neutralising rival claims to causality, covering them with their own claims in an endless competition for origins. In this process the vertex had to compensate, or to receive compensation, for its irremediable incapacity to sign for its responsibilities. In Western history the second millennium of occidental might is marked by the initial split vertex of Western Christianity separating itself from Eastern Christianity in the eleventh century, denying its origins in Constantinople and even suggesting by fraudulent means that Constantine had 'transferred' power back to Rome (the Donatio Constantini); this division never stopped giving rise to further forms of split vertex leading to a twentieth century of civil wars, world wars, cold wars; even today, when globalisation/Westernisation has reached such a degree that we see any conflict only as an instance of a global civil war[49] (in which the global reach of interior politics provokes the rise of unglobalisable, or 'meta-global', resistance) – the most general attitude is to speak of 'us' versus 'them'. When the realisation hits that the repercussions of fighting 'them' go further than anticipated, we say: 'stuff happens'; this expression appears on the face of the 'whole extended universe' (Spinoza's *facies totius universi*) at the moment when managing a contingency-out-of-control, which smashes its way into the self-interpretation of governmental politics, is included within the business-as-usual of governmental routines. It is the moment when, within the sphere that Michel Foucault called the 'art of governing', collaterality replaces causality.

What is revealing here is the light that a glance at the classical concept of the author and its vicissitudes, fortunes, misfortunes and 'progress', throughout the course of Western centuries and millennia, can cast on the matter of collaterality, of 'stuff happens'. To start with, *auctor*, a word that forms part of what might be seen as the 'sovereign dynasty of words' within European history and is bonded to the meaning 'increasing', designates someone who has received the glorious right of being attributed, of being awarded the right of passing themselves off and of being irrefutably and publicly being recognised as the origin of some fact, deed or product – of being the cause and carrying its insignia. In Rome, being an *auctor* was the exclusive right of high-ranking (and generally, well-born) individuals and provided the structure of protector/client relationships. The words *auctor fio* (Latin for 'I approve'/'I guarantee') are of paramount relevance in Roman private law. Someone who held in his hands the reins of an overflowing causality as a matter of name or title, and whose guarantee made, for instance, a difference to the buyer when he had doubts about the seller's right in the thing he was buying, took it upon himself to allow his name to stand in so that a causal chain could be counted on and ward off any doubts. In short, Roman authorship was the result of complicated procedures of authorisation in the sense of a guarantee of present transactions; causality was upheld and any idea of uncontrolled happening was rejected as a matter of principle; currently, we see our own regime, based upon the directly opposed principle that everyone has legitimate authorship (legal capacity), on how to converge with it: because 'stuff happens', nearly any valid transaction requires 'authorisation', which in turn depends on the presence of an 'author'. Yet it needs to be understood as the great achievement and distinctive feature of modern society to be able to cope with ever increasing contingency and complexity: public standing is increasingly conceded to contingent happening. At the same moment – and we leave it to the reader to judge whether this is a coincidence – 'stuff happens' becomes part of official governmental discourse. Looking backwards from here, what offers itself is a differentialist view. Old societies were based upon the notion, the fiction no doubt, that whatever happened was not 'stuff', but was either the will of the power-holder, or at least possessed a 'standing', was taken into account by it. This fiction was shared by all: the community, which was a community of subjects to causal power, was predicated, in its very life and integrity, upon the fiction of including mastery, rather than excluding it. Mere 'stuff' was not allowed to happen, at least not admittedly so. Subjects were not asked to pay allegiance to contingent ways of dealing with contingent fact.

No other thermometer than the notions of 'stuff happens' and 'collateral damage' measures better the glaciation period that followed the warmth of the age following the Second World War (or, alternatively, of a much more extensive period), and the civilisational aspiration of a society based on ongoing mutual dialogical exposure. The high-hearted (though admittedly also condescending) Habermasian utopian conception of a paradise of dialogically exchanged and consensually weighed claims to validity has been substituted by the dystopian conception of the hell constituted by the constant exchange of merely defensive disclaimers: 'stuff happens' providing its most concise formulation! This journey has its own Western church history, too. It is summarised by nineteenth-century Pope Pius IX (the Pope of the First Vatican Synod and of pontifical infallibility), author of the famous phrase: 'La tradizione sono io!' ('The tradition is I!'). And it leads from the personal usurpation of the hierarchical tradition (which anticipates – in a mock-humorous way – what would later become known as the Hitlerian *Führerprinzip*) directly to its apparent opposite, the 'stuff happens' disclaimer of the consequences of governmental action. Once again, it would be a naïve error to interpret the substitution of the later disclaimer for the earlier claim as revealing some radical difference or opposite direction taken, let alone a 'paradigm change', rather than simply the opposite phase of the swing of a pendulum or a see-saw. The West lives through the disintegration of hierarchy and indeed refers to it as to its programme, explicitly campaigning for it, pushing it worldwide including in places where the circumstances on which it is unleashed are, and mostly have ever been, deprived of any resemblance with those that gave rise to it in the first place.[50] (Identify this 'first place' as sixteenth-century Western Europe staging the secularisation of the thirteenth- and fourteenth-century theological claim to divine all-powerfulness, by taking it back from God and putting it in the service of the absolute ruler.) Placed back into its genealogical context, the new word 'collateral' sounds like a half-playful, half-managemental way of pronouncing a judgement of 'beyond care', or irrelevance, on whatever it is applied to.

Nor is this all. The managemental switch from claiming all power to disclaiming all responsibility, from absolutism to collateralism, needs to be understood not only as an accident or even a problem, but as a success, indeed as a solution – even if it is a solution of the 'emptying-the-baby-with-the-bathwater'-type – to a widely felt problem. The problem relates to the withdrawal symptom or phantom pain type; it concerns the destitution and post-history of hierarchy. As to its solution, two steps need to be distinguished. The first step leads from hierarchy properly speaking – i.e. from holy/legitimate power as a mainly religious phenomenon – to secularised hierarchy, that is, to the usurped and self-contradictory hierarchy-without-holiness that corresponds to the modern meaning of the term, which it reduces/trivialises to that of a form of mastery. The example here are absolutist monarchies of early modernity, and again the *Führerprinzip* as a more recent fascist or 'totalitarian' substitution of personal power for institutional legitimacy. The second step portrays our own current situation today. Now it is not only that hierarchy has been understood as a religious illusion and is therefore in need of being replaced by secular master, but mastery itself has been revealed/exposed as being unable to deliver on its promises. Of course institutional and traditional orders have been replaced and hierarchies emptied, multiple times in history, by other competing such orders, especially through warfare and defeat, be it between the Persian and Macedonian Empires, or between the Napoleonian Empire and the Holy Alliance.

But this is not what is now at stake: for now there is no new order challenging an older order (that it was inaccurate to take this as an 'end of history' is another story). The suggestion that we are confronted with an epic civilisational battle for sovereignty between the secular and the religious, a battle that is bound to end with the triumph of one of the two sides over the other, is as misleading as is the suggestion that we are confronted with yet another stage in class struggle that will predictably move the wheels of universal history to its next stage by means of revolution. What is happening has little to do with hierarchy, or even legitimate power. It is rather the game that imposes its own stakes, which 'losers' of globalisation can be seen as accumulating, producing immense masses of what sociologist Zygmunt Bauman calls 'wasted lives'[51] – like the pieces that backgammon players build up around the board as they play. We are no longer dealing with wagers, finalities, commitments, goals, targets, strategies, or with any other of the game-describing and game-transcending references that in the past both motivated and justified every move in the game. The traditional institutional terminology that so cunningly joined game-immanent and game-transcendent meanings has reached its limit: there are no game-transcending references available now. It is down to the game itself to motivate and to justify every move in the game. The more we are confident in assuming that the game-transcending puppeteer emperor is not only illegitimate (naked) but absent to start with, the greater becomes also the desire to establish legal rules that allow us to locate the line between moves that are 'in' and moves that are 'out' upon purely procedural, game-internal, criteria.

Hence also the need for the notion of 'collateral'. Participants in the game cannot do without knowing how to refer to what is located both inside the range of its effects and outside the remit of its responsibilities. In a historical and economico-theological perspective, the collateralisation of consequences is only the managemental account of a far more compassing process. There is also the abandonment and obsolescence of political 'measures', of compassing (collective) beings, decisions and operations, at large. Vico's equation *verum factum* might have been formulated, and eventually welcomed, as an anti-Cartesian *pronunciamento*, claiming that what is true is a matter of making, of creation, not a matter of observation by a cogitating mind. Yet it also portrays perfectly the conditions of availability of a certain sense of making, of deciding about and of imposing the 'true'. In the language of Vico, 'true' corresponds well enough to a certain colloquial use of the word 'real' today and, like 'real', it caters at once for beings, decisions and operations. The formula summarises the state of the world at it is, or as it has developed, throughout a particular episode of history, which might actually be in the process of reaching its end, with a new one unfolding to take its place. For an immediate illustration consider once again the situation in crisis-hit Greece; 'in power' is a radical left party some of whose MPs believe, or want their public to believe that they believe, that whatever can be said to be 'true' is not like a particular state of the world, which is 'made' by some agent, and therefore knowable by everyone, but rather something like the tactics required to 'radically transform the situation we are in'. A pity, then, that SYRIZA's 'tactics' include more austerity, more privatisation, more expulsion of refugees (who are transported with tied hands on marine vessels to Turkey and to Greek-based closed camps in breach of the Geneva Convention and in breach of SYRIZA's electoral pledge to shut these down), all of which those same MPs voted for.

It is undeniable that all of this contrasts maximally with the instructive Giambattista Vico, for whom only something that has been made can be the object of a truthful statement. First, when the enlightened Neapolitan, writing in the earlier eighteenth century, speaks of a 'truthful statement', he does not refer to the relationship between a statement and a state of fact. Instead, he refers to something like 'true being' or 'intrinsic' truthfulness or 'reliable' orientation. Truthfulness emanates, according to the position that Vico wishes to see accredited, from that which has been 'made' (by humans; God 'creates' rather than 'makes'). That which is made by humans, exclusively, provides truthful instruction. All that really counts/is relevant (or in another philosophical lingo: all that is), has been made. There is equally some common ground here between Vico on *factum* and Marx on production; the 'making' for Marx includes the ongoing class struggle, which will last until the *factum* of the revolutionary socialisation of the means of production has relativised every other, earlier *factum*. Now it has been often remarked that Marx has only the vaguest, and indeed a bit childish, ideas about what the post-revolutionary time will look like (according to Kolakowski, Marx imagined that the whole world, after the revolution, is to become some kind of an Athenian agora), almost as if he did not really believe that it would ever happen (not unlike, closer to us, the Brexiteers in the UK referendum

on EU membership). Let us, however, set aside the speculation and concentrate on the 'trivial fact' – supported by flaw-
less universal consensus – that the revolutionary socialisation
of the means of production has not happened so far (nor,
perhaps, will Brexit ever deliver on the Brexiteers' nationalist
longing for 'talking back control'). The question of whether
proletarian or national socialist revolution – as opposed to
mere rebellion – happened or not, however, might fit much
better one than one first thinks. Again, Vico has the great
merit of inviting us to have a closer look at this apparent
triviality. It is effectively difficult to gauge how the status
of the *factum verum* equation would be modified after the
'revolution' that puts an end to capitalism, whether it would
be proven wrong or inapplicable, or replaced by some other
relationship. However, while capitalism, far from flourishing, exacerbates and trivialises its grasp every day under the
paradoxical dictatorship of its endemic crises, it could be an
instructive point to find out whether the *verum factum* equation is still sustainable today. The question can be posed in
this way: is our making, is its being made, what singles out an
item as being 'true', in Vico's sense of this term, that is, does
it indicate what really is? Is the fact of being made still that
which shows, epitomises, qualifies, describes a being or thing
as *verum*, as that (or: as participating in that) which it truly
is? We suggest a negative reply (with some noteworthy but
'conservative' exceptions: sentences, artefacts, books, poems,
etc.).

Over recent years, decades, even centuries, causality exercised and power wielded, both accepted since time immemorial as providing the basic and indispensable conceptual
cornerstones of any access to social-happening-in-time, have
all but imploded. Power, wielded by a ruler, has lost its
visibility – allowing us to see that the sovereign throne that
Hobbes thought indispensable and Habermas treats as a necessary part of our 'counter-factual' constitutional imagination, is no more real than the Throne of God which, according
to the inter-testamentary and subsequent Christian tradition,
God created before, and independently of, the world.[52] The
dissymmetrical relationship of causality is a question for us
here exclusively in view of its socio-political/religion dimension, as a representation of mastery, or as embodying the

vitally necessary key to a commonly shared, because integrally mastered world. Today, of course it has been all but
eliminated, replaced by a host of newer, less cluttering and
more 'immanentist' concepts, 'structural coupling' among
them.[53] The subject side continues to be characterised by
exposure dependence; at the same time; the question *whose*
subject, or in other words the question which master, remains
conspicuously without answer.[54] Yet it is the presence of such
a master that was the decisive point: the omnipotent divinity
embodied this role and had been for long the indispensable
supplement of subject-ness. The difference that this makes
comes to mind as soon as one remembers at what point the
world-creating God was causal first of all, far more promi-
nently so than 'religious'. According to the account favoured
by these far more disciplined or immanentist concepts, it
makes little sense to relate social-happening-in-time to a
simple origin that, be it by way of emanation, dissemination,
creation or no matter what other model of efficiency, proves
God's power or omnipotence (in which Aquinas sees only a
special case of His 'power of being'). There is no denying that
universal, *en bloc* attributions of power/efficiency prove able
to galvanise attention and provoke deep dramatic impres-
sions and operatic identifications. They still serve the needs
of politics today, with recent right-wing populism taking
pride of place. Nigel Farage left the leadership of Brexiteers
once the people had voted to leave the EU, satisfied that the
seeds of his nationalist utopia were sown; likewise, when
Greek Prime Minister Tsipras was challenged in an interview
about how he had betrayed the anti-austerity hopes he had
nourished, he replied by quoting Saint Paul, 1 Corinthians
15:36. Here is what the passage says, in a contemporary translation: 'What a foolish question! When you put a seed into the
ground, it doesn't grow into a plant unless it dies first.' The
fact that the Apostle's argument is barely sustainable – if one
is looking for a description of what happens to a seed when
it gives rise to a plant, 'death' is frankly a rather egregious
choice – has not stopped it from providing the basis for powerful political discourse, peddling social hope and managing
to cope with the unending news of its disappointment, certainly in Greece in 2016, but also ever since Christian times.

Yet just how instructive for understanding society is causation, scientific or otherwise?[55] The new horizontal and immanentist conceptualisations that are on offer to replace those traditional top-down or centre–periphery-based concepts with point-to-point or item-to-item connections are built upon multiple horizontal networks that allow far more accuracy, even if they are much less spectacular, much less 'satisfying' than their monolithic vertical predecessor – even much less 'interpellating', to say it in Althusser's clumsy terminology. Looking at society from this new, flatter, but also less flattering vantage point, the causal actions that give rise to a fact, and that preside over Vico's notion of *factum* – and its underlying *facere* ('making') – appear as glamorously, proudly, even cockily hierarchic and 'verticalist', far too much so to offer a cognitively promising rendering of how contemporary society reproduces on an everyday level. Whatever is at stake in the seething need to identify the power-bearer or 'master of it all' is given far too much attention; the idea of a universal master or puppeteer, though decisive to the success of certain successful television series, is too spectacular, too insufficiently analytic as well, to allow an understanding of the problem landscape in which current society evolves; all it allows us is to stick to sovereignty beyond the implosion of sovereignty. If, on the other hand, we change the over-all parameters of the problem, and accept that the social world is built out of multiply connected immanent networks or systems, related not through an overarching causality but by a multiplicity of structural couplings, if we effectively dismiss any transcending power-holder or puppeteer and any last-instance ordering capacity, then there are indeed ways of understanding opening up in front of us. The question, then, is: Why is it that we still hesitate to make, and especially to *claim*, such a disillusioned approach to matters social? Why won't we, just yet? What retains us and condemns us to continue seeking refuge in totalising phantasies, religious or political – no matter how aware we seem to be that no one holds causal mastery? In the name of which social Majesty or Glory? These are good questions and, once again, there are no more dependable answers to them around than those delivered by genealogical study.

But first, how did it dry up? The history of the downfall of the over-powerful attractors 'causality' and 'power' in favour of immanent networks is based upon a small number of not-too-apparent but still contagious modifications. When, back in the seventeenth century, naturalists discussed processes related to ageing and coming-of-age, the discussants were split into two groups, the preformationists, who held that every feature observed later in an animal had already been present right from the start, and the epigeneticists, who claimed on the contrary that a new living being achieves its form and visible qualities courtesy of factors exercising their influence during the course, roughly, of its own growth. Whereas for the first group of researchers, the human being is already there at the beginning, as a homunculus (a small or microscopic yet already perfectly shaped human being, that springs into existence at the union of egg and spermatozoid), the second group located the factors determining each and every state of a being, including what is commonly referred to as its grown-up (earlier often called its 'perfect') state, as being the outcome of changes and modifications happening within its ontogenesis, its individual biography – i.e. in the very process of its becoming. For them, there is, in the existence of a living being, no longer such a thing as a perfect stage preceded and/or followed by stages of lesser perfection. Being-in-time is understood as a series of successive emergences: features come into existence as soon as the conditions for their appearance are assembled.

We would like to suggest an affinity in what is at stake in such post-causal approaches and their nexus to the later demise of Vico's *verum factum* thinking. The biological theory of evolution has already passed by: once the conditions are provided by earlier coincidences, a new layer, perhaps a new stage of further coincidences, can be expected to take place. To suggest, by contrast, that each later outcome is, as a rule, made – *factum* – by the will of man or the cunning of reason, albeit on the base of earlier outcomes, comes close to a preformationist narrative – if of course one of a secularised, human-centred type. Hence, the 'danger' is that it can, and often does, result in an overly optimistic account of action, of its capacity and of its efficiency. To believe that history is a matter of our making leaves us with an insufficiently complex account that is all too close to the creation-centred theological tradition, even in Vico's resolutely human-centred view;

to repeal it does not equal buying into the 'huge learning experiment' version of history. It does not force one to agree with the habitual 'can't make omelette without breaking eggs', which can apply either to the retrospective, half-critical whitewashing of, say, Iraq's destruction through an ad hoc British 'public inquiry' (designed to generate 'lessons'),[56] or the murders instigated by Stalin, Pol Pot, etc.

There is more to be said in this connection about history in relation to learning – precisely about the doctrinal crossroads between them, starting with the doctrine that plugs genesis directly into experience by claiming the transmission of acquired characteristics. This, as is well known, was the doctrine of count Lamarck, working a century and more after the preformationist–epigeneticist debate, a doctrine that famously prompted Charles Darwin's very different conceptions, at a different time (that of Marx, for example). The one point here that retains our attention in the context of modern society's re-actualisation of Old European *oikonomia* and its evolution towards encompassing management is the notion of environment. The intersection of the Lamarckian notion of learning and the Vichian account of 'worldmaking' (as Nelson Goodman would call it) appears in the light thrown back on both of them by Darwin's front-staging of the environment as a supplementary articulation added to the exposure to which the evolutionary candidate, the 'survival candidate', is subjected. The point that distinguishes Darwin's understanding of evolution, which generates a large following, including in the social sciences, is that environments are at least as 'specific' as the beings or species themselves. In fact, environments have a rather surprising number of features in common with the beings/species whose fitness or survival depend on them. The decisive difference between environments and biologically or socially evolving species or living beings is that environments are themselves located in the field of adaptation and learning, i.e. they themselves 'have' environments. In other words, environments, phenomenologically speaking, are or can be multiple, protean (amorphous and/or anamorphic), subject to change (thus even 'fragile'). Most decisively however, as this refers to what might be called their basic contradiction, environments, while being utterly powerful and decisive with respect to that which they environ, are unconscious, fickle and irresponsible. We would therefore tend to suggest, as far at least as social evolution is concerned, the neologism 'environjects'. Darwin endows what he calls environments with a peculiar double status. On the one hand, as sites of selection, environments are masters over life and death of whatever species they environ; and yet an environment is not a 'master', as it cannot exercise any power or make any decisions; there is no intelligence, no responsibility, no will – therefore no power, strictly speaking (this is why we suggest 'environject', in order to stress its commonality with an inanimate mere 'object'). As the environed life is subject to limitless, life-long, vital exposure, undistinguishable from any other subject of 'absolute power', the absence of a corresponding holder of mastery is frustrating. The simplest and most accurate way to describe this situation is not to gloss over this frustration. Instead, it is to stress the tautological aspect: the environment is what it is (the relevant suggestion of social systems theory).

This para-theological view of the environment provides at once an opening to our topic, as it allows us to recognise the concept of environment in comparison with, and in counter-distinction to, the theological concepts of divine power and all-powerfulness. It would thus be tempting to conclude that the environment, according to Darwin, belongs to the paradoxical family of absent, spectral or otherwise deficient power-holders (including perhaps parents – together, say, with William Blake's 'nobodaddy'), along with no less obvious yet analytically instructive examples. The markets of capitalism, which Adam Smith and his followers have introduced as the only 'real' object of economy, belong here. Another connection is, however, more relevant and also more troublesome. It touches the delicate topic of the correlation of the paradigm of infinite ('life-long'?) learning with political preferences, more exactly the undeniable attraction that the architecture of Lamarckian theory, staging an ongoing process of perfecting the species via the transmission of acquired characteristics, exercises in those inspired by an enlightened and/ or 'progressive', and most especially a socialist worldview.[57] The discovery of environments and the step it announces from conceiving adaptive processes as related to a general, nameless, indifferent 'nature', towards processes related to specific, potentially unique, even temporary and evanescent environments (in the plural!), is of the essence here. Suppose we would like to distinguish what might be called 'absolute', i.e. Lamarckian, as opposed to 'relative' Darwinian evolutionary arrangements, and compare the situation each prepares for the 'candidates' for evolution, identifying the conditions in each for flourishing or, more modestly, self-continuation. Such a 'candidate' is exposed, in the first case, with a compassing totality (referred to as 'reality', 'nature', 'the world', etc.), while in the second case, it will encounter the supplementary unknown that is constituted by the specific fragment of the world referred to by Darwin and his followers as the 'environment'. Looking (unlike both authors) at social evolution alone, it is likely that we would come up with a list of optimistic strategies for the perfection or self-perfection inspiring most political action in the modern sense of the term; those appear as connected to the Lamarckian scenario, for the simple reason that, here, learning and adaptation make sense not only in an individualist but in a Universalist outlook, as the possibility of transmitting acquired characteristics allows the hope of learning for the sake of others and not only for oneself – clearly favouring a progressive type of world making. In the Darwinian, environment-centred model, all that can be 'learnt', being perfectly portrayed in the notions of 'fit' and 'fitting', will result in an agenda for learning, for pedagogy, for social action, that is socially much less ambitious – for in the Darwinian setting any item learnt, any character acquired, will provide information only and exclusively in relation to the individual environment within which it has been learnt or acquired.

From the angle of our attempt to demystify/reassess the vocation, the ambition, the self-appraisal, that distinguish the Western political tradition, it is difficult to overstate what is at stake in the divide between a conception that limits itself to an encompassing, immobile nature, and one based upon the multiplication of environments. The paradise of religious traditions is a garden whose inhabitants' lives are located in a vast if enclosed space, in which they dwell, roam, sojourn, but also act, learn, even 'adapt'. Their full roaming and general access rights to the garden remain inalienable. They cannot become hostages, victims, prisoners, debtors, etc., of their own deeds and their post-history. Straight, learning-based, making-based accounts (Lamarck, Vico) apply perfectly to the conditions of life in paradise. They do not apply to the conditions of the social world in which we are now accommodated – a world related to individual environments. We can as well adopt the terminology of the naturalist controversy mentioned above, stipulating only that we endow the terminology of epigenesis with a slightly different meaning – defining as 'epigenetic' mainly the unintended or the collateral: side-products or consequences, which are triggered – rather than 'achieved', 'created', or 'made' – by the actions that give rise to them. The world that results from the long history of modernisation is based upon an unrelenting displacement of intentionally produced action-events (deeds) by epigenetic fact-events (consequences), with unintended or unseen consequences always attached to them in excess of the intended ones. It is these consequences and outcomes that require to be dealt with, coped with, managed, *après coup*, in order to allow, in fact, nothing more ambitious than the continuation of all that continues. On the one hand, the displacement works always to the emerging advantage of management; yet on the other hand – and at this point we can take up again the file of political theology – by doing so, it destabilises and calls into question the basis of politics understood as an exclusive sphere of highest-intensity matters, i.e. politics, understood as action,[58] just in the way Schmitt understood it. This is what is crucial here: even if the inglorious *oikonomia* of actual world management humiliates sovereignty, the latter – at least in the Western imagination – triumphs in defeat, not unlike Jesus on the cross.

Part II
Historicised Political Theology

6

From Jerusalem to Rome via Constantinople

6.1

An interlude is appropriate. We have seen how modernity, including constitutionalism, has been the collateral, epigenetic product of a particular religion, Christianity, which, like all other religions requires not only conceptual faith but, primarily, affective identification with cosmological postulates and views of the universal, which survives their conceptual deconstruction since it is anchored in imaginations that are effective even as ruins. The continuing impact of Western political theology, centred on the notion of an absolute power that is deployed oikonomically, is precisely explained by such love of ruins. We have argued that, as a result, the current crisis of the legitimacy of government is experienced differently across civilisations with only the Western Christian/post-Christian subject availing of a blind, affective trust in sovereignty. Thus, if an example is needed, we risk having to predict that the prolonged negotiations that will eventually follow Brexit, once Article 50 of the Treaty of the European Union is finally invoked, will lead to a situation that will make the popular 'sovereign' decision to leave the EU sound hollow, and yet there will be no upheaval, no violence in British streets. It is now apposite to offer an example of Westernised political and juridical cultures, fully modern, where, however, subjective identification is also directed at the ruins of different, non-Western premodern religions and where, as a result, the affective trust in the sense of sovereignty with *oikonomia* is weaker, leading to potentially much more explosive reactions at the level of human consciousness. To put it differently, while the whole world has bought into Western Christianity's loop of progress narrative, which rests on the image of a see-saw between sovereign will and management, causality and contingency, when the chips are down, only some of us can remain perfectly stoical, as if we believed that, at the end of the day, whatever happens must be part of a mysterious *oikonomia* that has always played out as a see-saw between willing and managing.

Israel, the 'only democracy in the Middle East' – which survives in said part of the world so-called by the colonial British India Office by virtue of vast amounts of US military 'aid' spent on nerve-wracking wars and the infamous occupation/annexation of post-1967 Palestinian lands, is frequently seen as a re-emerging 'theocracy;' yet for us, it offers a good example of how traditional political theologies are in fact the irrelevant, collateral waste that emerges as the modern ethno-religious identities of certain non-Western but Western-styled nation states absorb Western modernity; in order to do so, they must acquire blind trust in the Western Christian/post-Christian political and legal imagination, as it were artificially and ex post facto – unlike their Western counterparts, which already possess these as pre-adaptive advances, having successfully passed the relevant tests already 'at the first sitting'. Like all other modern states Israel's sovereign decisions/actions are nothing if not transient instances within a self-referential economic-securitarian crisis management and its administrative apparatus; but if in core Western nations this co-articulation of 'glorious' national self-determination and inglorious, anomic management of populations and resources is as old as the Christian notion of a universal *oikos* of 'humanity' in which there is no Jew or gentile and which is 'presided' over by a Triune God-cum-scissile (constituent-constituted) sovereignty, the story of modern Israel is one where, for less than a century, one theo-political imagination has displaced another. The identity of Zionism assumed by most of the populations of Jews that were not literally wasted by Hitler but 'deposited' in what is now Israel as if no one lived there – thus generating further human waste, this time of Arab populations – is fully integrated in Western modernity's loops: between glorious, liberating sovereign decisions/actions and crisis management of 'Jew versus Arab' and 'secular versus religious' relations at the hands of the bloated administrative apparatuses

118

of Israeli and Palestinian Authority civil servants, army or police and beyond; there also rabbis issuing, say, kosher certifications (for a fee), settlers and even gay activists whose successes in carving a niche for themselves in an otherwise conservative and religious country is very useful for the purposes of *hasbara* (the propaganda that highlights Israel as the 'only democracy in the Middle East'); there is also the sizeable Palestinian bureaucracy living symbiotically with the bureaucracies of its foreign funders, as well as various ethno-religious agents from mullahs issuing pastoral advice to Hamas operatives.

In fact, no one is excluded from this see-saw of sovereignty and *oikonomia*, although some are assigned the role of mere human waste, useful if at all as dead weight for those pulling, now on the side of sovereignty, now of management: notably, but not only, the Palestinians of the occupied territories – especially any who do not want to replace one sovereign for another, including assertive homosexuals and other moral offenders who irritate not so much for breaking a 'traditional' moral code but for prioritising their way of life over the nationalist super-cause. Though their suffering is not to be compared to the occupation's victims, there is also something wasted about the lives of roughly half a million Israelis of Russian descent who cannot marry in Israel; their Jewishness was accepted by the state – hence they became citizens under the 'Law of Return'– but not in the view of the rabbis who control the institution of marriage. Their situation, of course, invites even more decision/management. Among the human waste within the recognised borders of Israel, we wish to note those – be they 'religious' or 'secular' from the point of view of this distinction – whose institution as subjects still occurs with reference to the ruins of a Judaism that has nothing to contribute to the game of sovereignty-plus-management except as pieces early set aside in the 'backgammon' called Israeli public life. It has been the pleasure for one of us to interview pre-Israel Palestine-born individuals who really live at the very margins of the power of the Israeli state and of its justice system and who are derided as utterly irrelevant by both the ethno-'religious' and 'secular' Zionist majority. One of these is a leading rabbi among those faithful Jews of the anti-Zionist Neturei Karta movement who live in abject poverty since they refuse any involvement with the state; they even decline electricity and ambulance services unless they come from the Palestinian Authority (PA) or some other Arab country; the other is Uzzi Ornan, an atheist and a pioneer professor of linguistics, who calls himself a 'Hebrew' and refuses to identify either as a Jew under the 'law of return' ('I was here before your state' he likes to tell officials), or as a member of the other recognised ethno-religious groups that the Israeli state manages, and who leads a small non-governmental organisation (NGO) that keeps launching failing judicial review procedures against the requirement that citizens be identifiable under said ethno-religious categories. Both kinds of individuals, in different ways, live marginalised lives in a sort of civic limbo; but, equally, they both deeply embarrass the establishment, for they embody the critique of modern Judaism as a Western invention (another 'religion'), as well as the critique of all sovereign modern nation states, no matter what their official 'religion', as Westernised in the sense that they are the products of Christianity's 'secularisation.'

The ruinous, irrelevant state of the Neturei Karta becomes more telling if we bear in mind that, when it first emerged as a political programme for the Jews at the end of the nineteenth century, Zionism was a movement that eluded categorisation in both religious terminology and the religious images and rituals of the past, insofar as it promised a political solution that was neither redemption nor exile. The notion of a sovereign Jewish state established by means of human action was radically different from the tradition of the messianic gathering of the exiles that would be marked by a transformation of the Jewish condition and the human condition as a whole.[1] As such, Zionism attracted the ire of many Orthodox Jews (Hebrew: *haredim*: 'the ones who tremble') who saw it as:

[a] satanic rebellion against God and as a vehicle of secularisation, attempting to shape Jewish identity by means of such worldly instruments as a shared language, a group loyalty, a land, and a common memory, which would together usurp the foundations of the traditional identity of Jews, the old identity based on commitment to Torah and Jewish law.[2]

How did this strict position become diluted or economised? It was first done through the production of a new ideology that allowed the *haredim* to be at once ostensibly 'anti-Zionist' and fully immersed in the political economy of the Zionist state.

It is worth taking the time to follow closely A. Ravitzky's analysis of this process in his *Messianism, Zionism and Jewish Religious Radicalism*, for it illustrates perfectly the overwhelming dominance in modernity of the model that comprises the economic 'relation' of religion to law/politics under sovereignty; as M. Halbertal emphasises in his review of Ravitzky's book, Rabbi Yitzhak Reines, the founder of the first religious Zionist party Mizrachi in 1902, dismissed the *haredi* criticism that Zionism is an attempt to force redemption. Zionism, this Rabbi maintained, was not a substitute identity for Jews because it had 'nothing to do with messianism'; it was 'merely' a practical way to ensure the improvement of the political condition of the Jews and, as such, it should be accepted by everyone, believer or unbeliever, who cares about the fate of the Jews. By neutralising the messianic element, Reines legitimised cooperation between the religious and the secular in pursuing the narrowly defined, merely 'practical' goals of Zionism. This, of course, is not what has actually happened in the course of the twentieth century and beyond. The Holocaust, the birth of Israel, victories in the face of annihilation, the glorious Six Day War, all exacerbated a powerful temptation for apocalyptic interpretations of Zionism and of a new sense of ethno-religious identity similar to any modern nation state: glorious martyrdom. The ideology of religious Zionism, articulated mainly by Rabbi Abraham Kook in the 1920s and 1930s, and concretised by his son R. Zvi Yehudah Kook in the 1960s and 1970s, has since overwhelmed the youth of the Zionist world; rather than emptying Zionism of religious significance, as Reines had done, the Kooks openly endowed it with redemptive importance. If the anti-Zionist *haredim* insist that only in messianic times will the gathering of the exiled be allowed, their more 'flexible' antithesis, the religious Zionists, countered that the messianic era has already began; deeply influenced by Hegel's philosophy of history, rabbi Zvi Yehudah Kook was a firm believer in 'progress', which he understood as the 'dialectical process of historical redemption, whereby a higher synthesis of sacred and profane is being created. In other words his Messianism was a Messianism without a messiah, as the culmination of the teleological movement of history as progress.'³ Now, if we are right in our claim, along with Rappaport, that conceptual meaning always presupposes affective trust, then anyone, keen to insert their community into the modern humanity of nations, must do so with some reference to premodern tradition. Abraham Kook's attempt to explain Jewish history and to reinterpret Messianism drew upon the cosmological and mystical symbolism of sixteenth-century-rooted Lurianic kabbalah according to which the *cosmos* [in ancient Greek: order, jewel, decorum; in mediaeval Greek: a world ordered by God, universe; in modern Greek: world, people] is the result of a set of internal movements in the divine:

> God contracted himself so as to provide space for the cosmos, and Divine rays of light were sent to that space, but the vessels failed to contain them. The breaking of the vessels and the falling of the rays constituted a cosmic catastrophe. And so the cosmos awaits emendation. This emendation is a long eschatological mission, and it culminates in redemption.⁴

All this dialectical and cosmological machinery was applied by Kook to the understanding of secular Zionism. Secular Zionism is, on its surface, a *contradictio in adiecto*, a self-contradiction or self-negation, quite obviously heretical in appearance; yet the ideological pathos of the Zionist pioneers, and their search for social justice and for a renewal of the nation's life, are imagined as part of this unfalsifiable dialectical movement towards redemption. The Zionists were breaking with the law in order to expand its horizons; and the overcoming of the narrow spiritual Jewish existence in the diaspora necessitated a shattering of boundaries. Abraham Kook described the pioneers whom he met when he immigrated to Palestine in 1904 in the following terms:

> These fiery spirits assert themselves, refusing to be bound by any limitation. The weak who inhabit the world of order, the moderate and well-mannered are intimidated by them. [...] But the strong know that this show of

force comes to rectify the world, to invigorate the nation, humanity, and the world [. . .].[5]

In sum, economic cooperation between the religious and the secular was legitimated by a notion of secular Zionism as an unwitting but admirable instrument in the mysterious engine of redemption as continuous progress. 'There are people who do not have the slightest idea what an important role they play in the scheme of Divine Providence', Kook wrote.[6] 'They are called but do not know who is calling them. [. . .] But this terrible concealment will end with a great disclosure of lasting import.'[7] Abraham Kook, who died in 1935, did not embody his messianism in a particular political programme; the channelling of the messianic energies into a concrete political agenda took place years later, through the work of his son and his disciples, the leaders of Gush Emunim, who looked upon the State of Israel as a divine instrument, its travails – and any collateral damage – now interpreted as steps in this irreversible, messianic movement. The Six Day War and the conquest of Jerusalem – in which, previously, native Jews or Hebrews had enjoyed a relatively peaceful coexistence with Muslims and Christians as both our above-mentioned interviewees were keen to tell us – were thus seen as a main step in the redemptive process (and so any territorial compromise with the Arabs came to be perceived by the messianic right as a retreat in the scheme of salvation). Here again we find the twofold image of a path that is not merely a path but a glorified march to progress. By means of the settler movement in the West Bank and Gaza, young recruits to the cult of religious Zionism, who were previously marginal to the Zionist effort, began to feel that they were nothing less than the vanguard of Zionism, facilitated by the secular Zionists for reasons of expediency (and not without a certain indifference towards the cost not only to the Palestinians but also to the religious settlers themselves). Again, moreover, we find that such political 'steering' generates unforeseen, undesirable consequences. The secular Labor Zionist establishment, which had a soft spot for the idealism of the religious Zionist youth, and later the conservative Likud government, which used them to define the future borders of Israel, quickly found themselves to be prisoners of this hardcore ideological grouping. While the religious Zionist group is numerically marginal – even among the right – its members have been at the centre of the Israeli–Palestinian conflict, exploiting their strategic position in the occupied territories but also, not infrequently, putting themselves and their children in harm's way. In their determination to use force, and to die as martyrs, and constantly testing the boundaries of the Israeli legal system, the settler movement became a political force that no Israeli politician can ignore.

Religious Zionism constitutes a shift towards messianism, increasingly defining its terms of cooperation with secular Israelis. The impact of this change on Israeli politics is one of the cruel ironies in the history of Zionism. Etatist secular David Ben-Gurion's intention was at once to keep all potential sources of power within the confines of the new sovereign state – perfectly in line with modern Western political universalism – as well as to use religious symbols, etc., as a source of identity and unity (perfectly in line with modern Western views of particularity). His stated objective was to 'put religion in his "palm"',[8] and this required, he calculated, two steps; discrediting the Neturei Karta as 'religious zealots' who opposed the new 'revolutionary approach to Jewish salvation';[9] and tempting the *haredim* into religious Zionism by making concessions in what he thought were matters of low politics (control over dietary laws, marriage, Sabbath observance and the possibility of choosing a purely 'religious' education system for their children). While some *haredim* were appalled (Yeshayahu Leibowitz called this 'prostitution of religion for the sake of power, political, factional and personal interests'[10]) many more gave in to the temptation. As Patricia J. Woods summarises, the calculations of secular Ben-Gurion proved to be miscalculations as, precisely in their interactions with the life-cycle events of ordinary people, the new, Zionist-friendly, hierarchical, state-funded religious 'authorities' and institutions (Israel has two 'Chief Rabbis' overseeing a huge religious bureaucracy), 'became increasingly salient in the everyday life of Israelis and in all manner of political debates in years to come'.[11] In other words putting the Jewish religion in the state's 'palm', making it march on the path to redemption alongside the secular Zionists that had come from Europe, had the unintended consequence of tying the electoral chances of most Israeli politicians to the desires and dictates of the ever more numerous converts to the new religion, namely 'religious Zionists' who are thus able to ensure that they continue to enjoy major, both long-standing and more recent, exemption from civic duties while receiving state benefits, and increasingly to shape state policy. Secular Zionism, which was a movement that attempted to break away from the messianic script, thus became, to a large degree, dependent on the actions of the messianic latecomers, its interns, in its midst.

As Halbertal reminds us, Gershom Scholem, a Zionist who was exercised by the price of Messianism, 'posed the following question: "Can Jewish history manage to re-enter concrete reality without being destroyed by the messianic claim [that re-entry is bound to] bring up from its depths?"'[12] It still remains to be seen whether religious Zionism itself can be awakened from the messianic nightmare, and whether secular Zionism can reclaim the possibility of a Jewish politics that is based neither on the ruins of exilic Judaism nor on the ruins of Christian eschatological political theology. As Ravitzky argues, a central reason for the *haredi* integration into Israel's political life is the growing dependency of its members on economic support from the state. Ben-Gurion and his successors sought to neutralise religious Jewish anti-Zionism and to instrumentalise religion for nation state building purposes by means of offering the *haredim* a package that few would resist, including exemption from military service. The ultra-Orthodox *haredim* who accepted this offer, as represented by the Agudat Israel party, initially developed the ideology of 'exile in the holy land': the transformation of Jewish political conditions, the settling of the land of Israel, did not bring the Jews out of exile; it just moved them to another address but maintained their sense of homelessness even in their 'historical home'. As Rabbi Menachem Shach, the leader of the Lithuanian wing of *haredim*, declared: 'The Jewish people is still in exile, until the arrival of the redeemer, even when it is in Eretz Israel. This is neither redemption nor the beginning of redemption.'[13] As things turned out, however, this 'neither nor' entailed not exile but the status of privileged citizenship. Most ultra-Orthodox, who once despised Zionism, learnt to love it, for they were thence able to enjoy its fruits as a form of patronage while being exempt from taxation, military conscription and the state's educational curriculum; their institutions are subsidised by the state and their leadership controls the lucrative business that comes with handling all family law cases or issuing *kashrut* certificates, etc. In the past, the economic life of the *haredim* was based upon a division of labour between scholars and other members of the community – mainly fathers-in-law, the merchants and the businessmen who supported the scholar's life of study. With the unprecedented expansion and near-universalisation of state-funded *yeshiva* learning among *haredi* males, however, the generation of munificent fathers-in-law has disappeared. The state has become the father-in-law, the *mechutan*; and the *haredi* community is dramatically in need of state support. At the same time, this community, initially participating in political life only with the aim of preserving the *haredi* way of life, gave rise to *haredi* politicians increasingly attempting (and succeeding) to influence Israel's public life and seek an ever greater share in the nation-building process (e.g. by opposing the state's inclusion of reformed Jews in the ambit of the Law of Return and already making marriage in Israel impossible for nearly half a million Israelis whose 'Jewishness' they doubt).

Thus, the price of the establishment of the greatest *yeshiva* community ever to exist in Jewish history – a Church would be a better term – has been the 'mechutanisation' of the Jewish state. As Halbertal comments, this speaks to the failure of the *haredi* leadership to maintain the consciousness of exile within a Jewish state:

> Philosophically, it rejected the use of state power until the advent of the messianic era. Practically, it succumbed to the temptation of power. The haredi newcomers to the power game not only accepted and internalised the fact of Jewish sovereignty, they also threw their support behind the more militant trends of Zionism. The man who consolidated the alliance between the haredim and Benjamin Netanyahu was Ariel Sharon, a symbol of military power and not a man known for his devotion to the traditions of his ancestors.[14]

The 'economic' frame of mind of religious Zionists is also evident in their response to the accusations of religious anti-Zionists; for example, in response to the accusation that Zionism is a breach of the so-called the 'Three Oaths' – a Midrash found in the Talmud,[15] which relates that God adjured three oaths upon the world, two of which pertain to the Jewish people, sworn not to migrate from Exile to the Land of Israel en masse and not to rebel against the other nations, while the other nations in their turn were sworn not to subjugate the Jews excessively – religious Zionists respond that today's Jews are free from their oaths to God because the *goyim* had, first, broken their oaths (by trying to annihilate all Jews); their support for settlements and their unwillingness to contribute to Israel's state economy and security, other than by praying, has become a major factor in sustaining the permanent state of crisis in that region and, therefore, the need for conflict management by the local but also international political, military, security, economic and ethno-religious lobbies. Even Tony Blair managed to get a generously compensated slice of the action as 'Peace Envoy' of the so-called 'Middle East Quartet'.

6.2

The case of modern Israel is just one of the many Westernised modern nation states where the ruins of non-Western political theologies are included, much like pieces in a museum, in the modern Western paradigm of governance which, in turn, rests on the ruins of occidental Christian mediaeval political theology. In view of this it is instructive to attempt an archaeological survey of said non-occidental ruins in order to speculate what these may have meant outside their current museological placement. We shall restrict ourselves to such theo-political ruins from Jerusalem and Constantinople.

Throughout Second Temple Hebrew history, royal legitimacy was constantly challenged: there is conspicuously little symmetry to be observed between what was the Hebrew royal power and that of the rulers of the era of European absolutism (which provides the antithesis to limited government in Western political and legal imagination). Moreover, what started as a personal divine power endowment made to Moses personally eventually gave place to the Davidic element of authority that was destined to coexist precariously and ambiguously (rather than to gloriously master it out of a safe transcendence) with the power of Levitic priests. Relationships within the equally split summit of meso-Byzantine and classical Islamic times were comparable, with the only difference that here the process was reversed. Whereas in Old Israel, the rulership personnel of the later stages of history struggled to keep the integrity of its unique inaugural endowment, under Byzantine and Islamic conditions it was on the contrary the imperial and clerical powers embodying the antagonist position that had to be – but eventually failed to be – synthesised in order for a coherent conception of political authority to arise. It was in the Catholic/Protestant/secular West that the appropriate political theology arose along with the image of a glorious if impotent sovereign 'reigning but not governing' – the image that overdetermines social contract theories. In contrast to the latter's transcendent–immanent mutual bond (king, people, 'social' contract) the biblical myth of Israel's political self-constitution refers to self-submission to a covenant (Hebrew: ברית – *berith*) that was not founded on any legitimacy or any form of Reason; unlike a contract, the covenant was understood as being only indirectly an alliance of humans, its etymology suggesting a leap of faith involving the consumption of a particular pre-revelation tradition and the cutting-out of a new particular entity with which to ally.[16] As a result, a dimension of communal 'origin' was structurally inscribed only by reference to an unbridgeable gap between the Hebraic community and its possible 'causes' – be they immanent, material and final (nature and tradition), or transcendent, efficient and formal (a withdrawn creator and a mysterious messiah). This is the exact opposite of what constitutions today are expected to do when seen as repositories of original intent or as 'living constitutions'.[17] The Old Testament is not a universal treatise on politics as the West has read it since the Middle Ages and through modernity, e.g. in Hobbes (the Byzantines did not fall for this error). It is, rather, the story of a nation. Arguably, however, the Hebrew covenant does testify to a universal truth, proving that what is at the heart of every human association is neither an inexplicable power that 'naturally found' individuals, nasty yet prudent, discover in themselves in order to redeem themselves by jointly making peace, nor is it the horde's 'spontaneous' decision to cast out or prevent the approach of dissimilar others. Rather, we have to understand that, at the core of the totality, there is an unsurpassable gap: not any founding reason, but its marked absence. Action, happening, history, take place without waiting, at their impatient pace – while the stork that brings the child of legitimacy or justification only flies out early in the morning of the next day.

The lesson from such a reading of Hebrew 'political theology' is that retrospectively justifying community by anchoring its genealogical causality in a mythical origin is not the only way to constitute a community. An alternative route leading to the same destination is, or can be offered by, an unjustified, gratuitous 'leap of faith.' An act of pure self-dedication to some unquestionable postulate can equally be enough to overcome both fear of the future and the mythical appeasement of those who are defined as 'losers' by past conflicts and grievance. Moreover, nothing prohibits the assumption that a compact unit 'aporetic-faith-cum-political-aporia' can, at least indirectly, support praxis and, therefore, perfectly sustain and embody the distinction of the political (*le politique*) from mere politics (*la politique*) and be on the side of conflict and change. One can make equivalent readings of other 'political theologies'. Thus, in Eastern Christianity and Islam, lacking the Catholic Church's hierarchical structure, the constant bickering among rabbis, bishops, juris-consults, etc., can correlate to a secularised political imagination that is open to the idea that praxis is not oriented to overall unity of differences. Praxis can lead to disunity – can 'rock' the proverbial collective boat, as in the case of the Greek polis, and as we know from history, nothing guaranteed Athens the privileged status of *fluctuat nec mergitur* (it rocks, but it doesn't sink) that is emblematically predicated of a Western second-millennium European metropolis – and still can remain praxis for all of this. To engage in praxis is not, then, to aim at a singular and 'constructive' principle of truth or to one consistent conception of production/reproduction. It can also mean to 'speak and elucidate the void all the while acknowledging that there is no foundation of the political',[18] without any reassurance granted in advance. One might object that in ancient Israel such acting-out of the political, such praxis, remained unthe-orised, relying mostly on 'mad faith' and prophetic activism.

We note, however, that reflexivity alone does not ensure praxis, for reflexivity suggests thinking only the present, while disregarding, at its own peril, the fact that sense also, and alas primarily, operates in the form of consciousness-seeking identity and genealogy (indeed a glorious one), to boot. In fact, in the democratic Greek polis – where the very idea of praxis first came up, in opposition in certain contexts from *theoria*, in others from *poiesis* – it figured ordinarily as an object of fear and repression – and was consciously undertaken only retrospectively and conditionally, in times, precisely, of stasis and 'crisis'.[19] At the very least we should acknowledge, on the one hand, that the idealism of Socrates was never meant to give the state a reason to consider him as someone who undermines the state religion; and also, on the other hand, that the intellectual curiosity of non-citizen Aristotle was enough to prevent him from flattering the constitution of his adopted state as the 'best' possible. Yet modern secular legal constitutionalists have sought to 'emulate' the Hebrew Covenant – now read as a bourgeois contract – minus what they considered as its inherent ten-dency to theocracy, a tendency that they suggested to dis-mantle by emulating the Athenian constitution (also read as a bourgeois contract) – minus what they perceived as its inherent tendency to factionalism and stasis (civil strife, civil war). In turn, modern secular political (including 'agonistic') constitutionalists purport to emulate the critical spirit of Socrates, Aristotle's logic and Saint Paul's universalising of the Hebrew Covenant – minus the lack of rebelliousness of all those mentioned, and minus Saint Paul's 'metaphysi-cal' beliefs. We hold that such imperative abstractions and self-serving discounts in our heritage are not an option, and that it is urgent to identify an alternative. We suggest that instead of retroactively attributing to the biblical elites a theo-political absolute power that in fact emerged only much later in Western Europe (through the prism of Aristotelian classifications in politics, which itself reflected the unsati-ated, obsessive Greek desire for a permanent constitution and the successful avoidance of stasis), we can re-imagine the Hebraic kingdoms as fragile states, made possible by the same perpetual aporia that always threatened and often destroyed their unity.

Likewise, we shall now argue, instead of retroactively attributing to Byzantium the caesaro-papist outlook of the Russian Czars we can re-imagine the Eastern Roman Empire as a sort of populist 'Byzantine republic',[20] where the holder of the imperial office is always suspected as potentially illegitimate – a false messiah – and is tolerated only insofar as the administration is conducive to the *salus populi*, not of everyone in the people to be precise, but of enough supporters and friends to keep him in office – the *filoi*.[21] The key unanswerable questions confronting rabbis throughout are well known: would the Messiah come – or had he, perhaps, already come – from the tribe of Judah as an heir to Davidic kingship or from the tribe of Levi as a descendant of the priesthood of Aaron? Or perhaps from a 'mixture' of the two tribes; i.e. as a sovereign reunifying the power that Moses had divided after having exercised it in full as one? Jewish traditions contain a myriad of answers based on the many Old Testament texts, which evoked God's promise to David that his house and his kingship would last for ever or . . . at least until the coming of the Messiah,[22] but perhaps even after His coming, another division may prevail . . . or, perhaps, a union between kingship and priesthood would occur as prefigured in the mythical figure of Melchizedek (a name – if it was a name, and not only, as it was sometimes surmised, a description, or a title – which meant 'my King is just').[23] In the writings of the period referred to as inter-testamentary – later than the Old Testament and already heralding the New – we find yet more hesitant speculations.[24] A similar unanswerable yet also un-unanswerable (insistent) question baffled Byzantine bishops when confronted with their emperors' claims to be the Melchizedek; in fact, the issue was even more taxing for them, insofar as, for them, Jesus had assigned the Old Testament to the level of dead history.

6.3

The same problematic fits other 'leap'-related communities, as is revealed by a careful look at the – all too often neglected – historical documentation from Byzantium, i.e.

from an entity, a political space, in which the model pre-
miered by a long-gone Jewish sect was first elevated from
a tribal model to that of imperial Christian religion. Once
again, it is important to stress, against the customary Western
mythological assumptions about Eastern history, based as
they are on the hopelessly inappropriate term of 'caesaro-
papism', that the Byzantine Christian empire, while trying by
all means to impress the populace and foreign powers,[25] was
characterised by a weak – doubtlessly to the Western reader a
dangerously, uncannily weak – quasi-sovereignty, with each
Basileus enjoying full recognition as dominus while facing
a perennial legitimacy deficit insofar as he was now placed
between the two comfortably powerful earlier chairs, being
no longer the Pontifex Maximus of the Roman religion nor
truly a Christian priest free of any compromise. Rather than
trying to understand the Christian legitimacy of Eastern
emperors by retroactively generalising the later occidental
perspective of the separation of 'two powers', temporal and
spiritual, and claiming that Byzantium was some totalitarian regime where the two powers were 'merged', it would
be methodologically sound to ask the not-so-naïve question
whether, originally, the Christianisation of the Roman Empire
boosted the supreme power held by the ruler – as it is largely
and almost automatically assumed – or, on the contrary,
weakened it. In the view of Dagron,[26] Christianity meant that
each Eastern emperor's claim to legitimacy made sense only
in the context of the claimed continuity between the Old and
New Testaments (or a projection of one onto the other), with
the emperor's role being identified with that of Melchizedek,
invested by God alone, a superposition of the New Testament
and the Old Testament that was theologically problematic
insofar as it was increasingly asserted that, by His incarnation, God has 'cut history in two halves', subjecting history
(and thus genealogy) to a hitherto irreparable basic rupture.
Taking into account its Trinitarian theology – whereby the
Spirit emanates only from God (and not from the Church)
– we understand that the Byzantine Church would provisionally recognise each emperor's claim to be the Melchizedek
by the grace of unction, in contrast to the occidental model
of anointment, which was in and of itself a valid conferral of
legitimacy. It is characteristic that the ecclesiastic part of the

Byzantine crowning ceremony was followed by a public theatrical representation, staged in the huge hippodrome, of the
exact circumstances that brought the new dominus to power,
circumstances more often than not involving violence or
deceit. Second, again contrary to widely upheld convictions
among (Western) specialised scholars, we acknowledge that
Byzantium was not a lawless monarchy, but rather some sort
of a populist republic in which assemblies played a major
role, especially in times of danger.[27] While this new reading
of Byzantium is often meant to buttress claims of the irreduc-
ibility of 'democracy' we endorse it in order to claim, with
Agamben and others, that once we step outside the classic
Greek polis, especially in the context of the Christianised
empire, said 'assemblies' were less about deliberation and
more about (staged or manipulated) acclamation.

While Byzantium understood itself as an *ennomos politeia*, a
'law-contained state' (and indeed, it is quite possible that no
second historical example society featuring a similar wealth
of laws, that were regulating in detail just about everything,
has ever existed[28]), its public space, imagined as part of the
house of God was nothing like the Greek agora; moreover
it was a polity where the law, its rigour and its austerity,
had to give way to philanthropy – a philanthropy owed by
the emperor qua humble servant of God to His people, and
exercised by way of welfare policy and *oikonomia*, yet here
in the sense not of a legality of the household, but in the
different, even opposed sense, of an ad hoc dispensation
from the law. In practice, this was an exercise of the Basileus'
parental love of his 'friends', his filoi. Equally revealing as
to the importance of being well connected are letters sent
by the Fathers of the Church to emperors requesting, now
that this official caught stealing should be pardoned, now
that this struggling peasant be excused from his contractual
obligations to a (richer) landlord – the latter example shows
at once an excellent strategy to reduce the dangerous possibility of magnates emerging here or there in the empire
who could, then, threaten imperial power. It is in order to
conceive of Byzantium as of a politico-social entity availed of
an explicitly economic-political theology that lies beyond the
grasp of the modern distinction between political economy
and political theology – in this modern form a distinction

which downgrades, if not obfuscates, the economic character of Christian theology at large. The obfuscation has itself its genealogy. An overwhelmingly Western phenomenon, it is due, first, to Catholic legalism and, subsequently, in modern times, to the Protestant and secular over-emphasis either on the homo oeconomicus – whereby 'economy', as it is commonly understood even today, synecdochically takes over from the wider parent concept of *oikonomia* – or on the homo politicus – whereby 'politics' is on the contrary put in direct opposition to economy. In uttermost contrast to this decisionistic dissociation, the overarching doctrine of Byzantine economic-political theology is the concept of symphonia[29] between state and church, namely: 'the principle of . . . deal-making as an integral part of good order . . . elevated as essential safeguard . . . to the principle of the rule of law.'[30] In its classical form, a concept that epitomised a sensuous apprehension of the politico-theological field by reference to the musical model of symphonia, did exist for some centuries of the history of the earlier mediaeval West;[31] even so, this model, originally developed under sixth-century emperor and law-giver Justinian, was actively continued within the Eastern churches and, arguably, captures the political imaginary in certain nation states of modern Eastern/South-Eastern Europe. It was however first formulated and enacted in Emperor Justinian's lasting contribution – including and, eventually, most particularly within the West – which is his new imperial legislation from the thirties of the sixth century onward. The purpose of this promulgation was eminently not that of defining the proper spheres of the imperial power (imperium) and the ecclesiastical authority (sacerdotium); what the law-emperor Justinian (who was also a theologian) wanted to ensure was a conditional blessing of the exercise of political power for the common welfare of the Christian society (church and state), to the extent to which the ruler remains faithful to the Scriptures and the Christian dogma.[32] Effectively, the Byzantine Church shaped and managed its relation to those emperors who knew how to conduct themselves to its taste, with its typical 'economy'. In short, the basic move was not one of problem solving or decision making: it was one of knowing how to dispense with the problem posed and how to avoid the irreversible intervention into the multiply inter-connected fabric of social coexistence. In other words, the task was not one of questioning imperial legitimacy – after all, it was God who had willed each emperor to be emperor, to come to power, in the light of the circumstances at hand, and in favour of the 'general' good. Now, at the same time, the Eastern Church readily and frequently withdrew its support from emperors that did not rule up to its expecta-tions. In such circumstances, there existed a generic formula that offered the general denominator of the shortcoming of the Basileus. This was coined in the accusation of having lent himself to the flaw of 'judaising', as it is documented, for instance, in the case of the iconoclast or iconomach (image-persecuting) emperors. At times, also, the Basileus was straightforwardly accused of 'being the Antichrist.' As Dagron suggests: '[W]hatever they did, the emperors were permanently suspect, caught in the mesh of a rhetoric of the 'almost-priest' and of a Melchizedekian model associated with the beginnings and with the historical development of of their power since Constantine the Great, but which back-fired on them at the slightest moral or religious 'sin.'"[33] The 'legitimacy deficit' of the (otherwise feared and respected) dominus led, inter alia, to the abandonment of legislation as an expression of sovereignty and to a greater reliance on dispensation from the austerity of the law, which was in turn necessitated by an increasingly complex administration of the newly found 'social question', often displaced to, at least disguised as, an 'imitation of Christ.' Each time an emperor failed to be successful at keeping those that could mobilise popular rebellions in good spirits he would have proved himself to be a bad imitation of Christ, a false messiah, a Roman tyrant, a Judaising priest, and usually would suffer a rather miserable and not particularly Christian end.

Theologically, too, we are dealing with key differ-ences between the earlier Eastern and the later occidental models (we have already hinted at this in the chapter on Trinitarianism). First, the Eastern Church understands its role not as a necessary conduit of salvation and Vicar of Christ, but rather as an assistant and mediator in the individ-ual's supplication for divine grace after the model of Christ's mother, Mary. Incidentally, in this Mario-centric (rather than

Christocentric) perspective, we find that all-too-frequent confessions and especially Holy Communions are discouraged – which, along with such features as the fact that the lower-rank clerics marry, further underlines that the institutions of the Byzantine Church are, in one sense, closer to Judaism than those of the Carolingian-protected and later Gregorian papacy, and the Western tradition at large, which is far more individualist- and Christocentric-minded. The relevant Eastern self-description refers repeatedly, and indeed paradigmatically, to a corporate role, for which the imitation of the virgin mother Mary offers the appropriate model (as opposed to Christ, who as a model is rather limited only to individuals). Second, we are dealing with Eastern Trinitarianism in a strictly literal, unaccommodated and uncompromised sense: the Holy Spirit, the third person of the Trinity, never talks through Man or Church, but only through God, without the possibility of any further 'tracing'. In the corresponding political theology, the Byzantine Roman Empire, like its church, did not need to be 'created' or 'instituted' as a righteous, God-serving entity (unlike the 'Holy Roman Empire'). It was taken for granted that it was simply plausible that the institutional survival of the Roman Empire after its Christianisation was God's will. Yet unlike the occidental selected Pope or anointed monarch, there was no assumption that this or that potentate was indeed God's choice. God being *anarchos*, without limiting beginning or fettering 'principle', the economy employed in dealing with each imperial legitimacy crisis was not understood as a necessary 'exception' to a rule but both as the sign of a mysterious divine providence and as the first step in the next emperor's rise to power. Let us not forget that a further difference with respect to Western rulership consisted in the fact that the ruler was usually not dynastically preselected.

The obfuscation of anomic *oikonomia* behind the fiction of a divinely and, later, mass-imposed 'exception' to rules and principles happened only later, and only in the West, in the context of the Latin modification of the Creed. Only then was the original Byzantine model of Christian politics understood as politics restrained and based upon a generalised suspicion of power and also upon the precarious and only ever provisional acceptance of the legitimacy of the sole *dominus*, superseded by the model, so well known in the West today, of dual legitimacy. In the West, the top end of the power pyramid, sovereignty, was instituted and 'legalised' as coherent but bipolar – absolute, and yet at the same time, also limited, albeit by means of its division. This occidental formulation of sovereignty as containing all possible political tension later became the indispensable condition of the modern state as a proceduralisation of conflict, and was maintained as such by all doctrines of the separation of powers. It is important to understand that these institutional–governmental–theological innovations have their roots in the Western modification of the Trinitarian doctrine, according to which the Spirit proceeded from the Son as well as from the Father, which meant that the Spirit was now subservient to Christ and His Vicars on Earth – not a coincidence, as this vicar typically presided over social bodies striving collectively for salvation; This adaptation was retroactively sanctioned as canonical by reference to the Gelasian idea, or theory, of 'Two Powers' – or 'Two Swords'. This had the double merit of presenting the East as 'heretical' and allowing the Catholic Church to enter into permanent and principled legal arrangements with the Teutonic prince who coveted the authority of the second Rome and whom the Church declared 'Holy Roman Emperor'. The latter was the reverse image of the Byzantine Basileus: a weak lord whose calling it was to oversee a myriad of largely autonomy-endowed kingdoms or principalities; however, at the same time, he also disposed of much more, including an almost limitless legitimacy the type of which Byzantine emperors never enjoyed: what early thirteenth-century Pope Innocent III and the main proponents of the classical thirteenth-century canon law would routinely dub *plenitudo potestatis* (fullness of power).[34]

In the context of this mediaeval-occidental natural theology and its corresponding dualist political theology, the meaning of Christian 'economy' in relation to the question of political legitimacy was reversed: while, according to the Eastern Christian view, any legitimacy of command assured in advance inside the Christian *oikos* was excluded as an impossibility, if not a blaspheme, according to occidental Christian theology, by contrast, always-already legitimate power was possible, thanks to the employment of the legally or politically appropriate architectonics of state and society relations combined with the belief in the occasional necessity for temporary exceptions in which either the state or the people could justifiably suspend the rule of law. Ever since the occidental Church was thought to share authority with the temporal sovereign, rather than compete for it or settle on temporary arrangements as in the East, state violence was no longer justified either just mythically or with reference to secular legal or political need, as in Byzantium; rather, the ultimate location of power was itself embodied, not in any identity or substance, but in one ultimate, unquestionable 'relation' – which was, paradigmatically, the one between pope and emperor. An abstract, always-already justified, absolute and immortal power, attributed to a sovereign king/people, generated and stored in church-cum-state institutions, etc., was put in perpetual 'relation' with the 'limited sovereignty' of day-to-day policy, legal implementation and administration.[35] Unlike in the East with the immense role it bestows upon the compassionate Holy Virgin (because one can never know for sure if one's mouth is used by the Holy Spirit or the devil) the Christocentric West's transcendent and immanent claims to authority constitute a cybernetic mechanism in which there is only one thing that is out of the question: that either transcendence or immanence may ever obtain a definitive victory over the other or, in other words, that one of them may prevail over the other. Whereas the Western mechanism results in a competition between transcendence and immanence that is perfectly calibrated to generate a permanent surplus of legitimacy of sovereign violence, the opposite is the case in the East.

Seen in this light, the great European revolutions of the second millennium CE that supplied their contribution to bringing about modernity, as well as the constitutional settlements that followed them, can be considered as not only immanent actions but indeed without exception as re-enactments of Gregory VII's papal revolution: an immanent, 'political' act of rebellion against an unjust regime and, at once, a declaration of transcendent, 'lawful' authority to restore what has been corrupted and to use legislation to make the world as close to the heavens as possible. Insofar as the modern secular division between legal and political brands of constitutionalism derives from and depends on this metaphysical scheme it is a moot point whether natural law should prevail over positive law or vice versa, and whether one sides with a reformedly Kantian or un-reformedly Kantian, an utilitarian or a Hegelian humanist, etc., view on the issues of responsibility, agency and freedom. Revived as a symbol of the subject that stands up to non-universal man-made law in the name of the gods/the Right, the magnetically attractive figure of Antigone mainly obscures the indebtedness of our imagination to the Christian model of *oikonomia* in which the Church/state reserves for itself, respectively in the East and the West, the role of an imitator of Mary (suggesting humble compassion for the weak and dispensation from the austerity of the law) and of Christ (suggesting salvation through martyrdom). Today, the relevance of this theologically inflected imagination is gauged in the extent to which governments are still expected to rule legitimately in either sense as we see their function being reduced to no more than police and tax collectors, even without welfarism. Beckett's 1956 characters Estragon and Vladimir, waiting for the elusive Godot, offer a better analogy than Sophocles' Antigone for the late modern 'subject' of law and politics, which finds itself lost in a world of impersonal processes but still imagines the social to be steered or, at least, 'presided' over, by a missing sovereign, be it one whom, though he is absent, it is always-already necessary and legitimate to presuppose as present – even as a mere counter-factual or popular usurper who marches to occupy the empty throne from where he will dispense with too much austerity and injustice.

6.4

None of this is mere philology: understanding power in the Hebrew states as constitutionally split, remaining without resolution over very long periods, and in Byzantium, which lacked a proper notion of corporate sovereignty, as only precariously 'banded' and easily unstitched each time a new usurper made the exact same claim that he, rather than his predecessor, was the Melchizedek, can help us understand later legacies. In grounding his claim that the Triadic God's providential will not to 'ban' or abandon the world slips at the scene of law into the possibility of exception or abandonment of the law, Agamben, in *The Kingdom and the Glory*, briefly references canon law in the seventh-century Byzantine Church and specifically Leon VI's tenth-century imperial legislation. Agamben's Byzantine excursus is welcome as a historiographical intervention – in the sense that it depicts the one thousand years of Eastern Roman Empire (i.e. of uninterrupted Roman imperial rule), the use of Roman law and coin as well as para-political practices for manipulating public opinion (the use of claqueurs in acclamatory rituals, etc.) as the 'prehistory' of the subsequent millennial history of the European age of revolution and public law, constituent and constituted power. Yet Agamben's Byzantine excursus is much too brief, if not superficial, and, as a result, partly misleading. His theory of eternal sovereign glory is based on connecting two archaeological findings: on the one hand, as we saw, he begins with theological developments in the third to fifth centuries CE, performing the split between God's being and His praxis (and the new discourse of *oikonomia* that holds them together) as well as the use of the ancient symbol of the empty throne found in early Christian art to signify the glory of government. These insights, however, are brought to bear, without further ado, on the history of the Occident, bypassing a thousand years of Eastern Roman history. The leap occurs in Chapter 4, 'The Kingdom and the Government', whose theme is a figure from the Holy Grail, *le roi méhaigné* – the mutilated and impotent king who reigns over a *terre gaste*, the devastated land as Western Europe, during and in the immediate aftermath of the Migration Period (400–700 CE) (previously known as the period of the 'Barbarian Invasions'), was represented, when the only available literature were the Bible and legends of the Holy Grail variety, which were read interchangeably. A look at the Byzantine 'princes of mirrors' literature, by contrast, reveals that it anticipates and even exceeds Machiavelli in secularism as it consists of manuals based on classical Greek sources that the literati of the time knew to read in parallel with Christian sources. The *roi méhaigné*, the useless Fisher-King – a myth the Byzantines never had – symbolises the occidental notion of a divided sovereignty that retains its unity thanks to the dual economic-relational arrangement starting with the Two

Swords theory that theologians had come up with hundreds of years earlier, which turned God into 'this circle in which two orders', the transcendent and the immanent, 'continuously penetrate each other' as Agamben notes. As a result, Agamben's chronology of the evolution of the dualist model of 'Glory' and 'Kingdom', as if it had already begun in the third or fourth century, appears retrospectively as tainted. While it is right to point out that in the first millennium CE the paradigm of *oikonomia* locked law and politics together in a fictive 'relation' of *oikonomia* in which some forms of life are anarchically privileged over others, it was nonetheless only during the age of 'law and revolution' in the second millennium, that this *oikonomia* was associated with the 'rightful' government that features in Agamben's title: *The Kingdom and the Glory*. In Byzantium, *oikonomia* was not yet obscured by claims to Right: emperors suffered from a permanent 'legitimacy deficit'; un-Christian official behaviour was not excused but portrayed as necessary in a fallen world.

Premodern rabbis, Eastern bishops and Muslim *ulamā* (Arabic for 'the learned ones') and *fuqahā'* (Arabic for 'jurisconsults') differed from the late mediaeval Catholic scholars who re-engaged Roman law and Aristotle's thought so as to create a political theology suited to their times, as well as from the Protestant-cum-secular modern thinkers who sought to firmly replace (or develop) Catholic political theology with (as) a civic religion; they differed in that their message was to obey the law, but to do so neither for the reason that it is authoritatively dictated by a state official (legal positivism), nor because it passed the test of some philosopher's or other universal truth-claim wielding specialist, but because it originated from your local wise man whose authority depended on his popularity and oscillated according to local political dynamics. The fact that expectations of a neutral and general authority were kept low outside occidental Christianism(s) is clear when we take into consideration, for example, how the ideas of *filia* (Greek for friendship) and patronage were an explicit criterion for decision in Byzantine politics. The same fact is apparent in mediaeval Jewish communities which, throughout history (but before the emergence of occidental Jewish philosophy that made Zionism possible), had nothing else to go by when looking for 'authoritative' guidance but the aporetic and – in comparison to the Byzantine patronage model – liberating double maxim: make a rabbi for yourself (Hebrew: *Aseh lecha rav*)[36] and acquire for yourself a friend (Hebrew: *Kneh lecha chaver*) which, as Maimonides explained, involves the freedom to choose unqualified, unprofessional masters lacking authority and pedigree, and treat them as your 'friend', meaning with fierce loyalty, commitment and love as one does with one's spouse.[37]

Today we find traces of curiosity in the political implications of such aporetic treatment of authority in a post-parochial, post-neutral politics, inter alia in a number of works revisiting selected notions from Jewish ethical traditions. Walter Benjamin's critique of authorised, state, and legal violence, and the contrasting concept of 'divine violence' are to be named here, as are Emmanuel Levinas' and Jacques Derrida's radicalisation of ethical responsibility as primary, gratuitous and infinite and as a proclamation of the structural incompatibility of justice and law. In the field of jurisprudence, the primacy and excess of responsibility over rights and of ethics over law can and has been used to evoke a contrast between responsibility-centred Jewish and a rights-based Western model of law.[38] There is little to add here except that this retraces a distinction that has, by now, been contained in the globalised occidental paradigm. What is postulated here is an economic relation between all 'positive' and all 'natural' laws. The tension in which is structured by some imaginary, sovereign or counter-sovereign, sense-as-consciousness (the image of Antigone versus Creon comes to mind) also casts its shadow on those within so-called 'critical jurisprudence' who invoke absolute ethical responsibility both to denote the deficiency of law without justice and call on us to assume the all-compassing, extra-legal responsibility before 'the Other';[39] working as counter-weights against the notion that 'we' are absolutely free to legislate as befits the circumstances, they take up, in diverse ways, the notion of a gratuitously infinite individuated responsibility for the positing of new law, and even for the abandoning of old law. Do any of these authors, one of us included, provide as much as a first inkling of an exit from the legalistic and discreetly violent totality of the 'social contract' paradigm? Or do they succeed only in offering a symptom of its deficiency? Much depends on whether and to what degree one gives in to the strong temptation, for its modern interpreter, to interpret the Decalogue as being the first paradigmatic product of some well-oiled legislative machinery. This is a temptation that needs to be resisted: the Ten Commandments must be read sequentially and with utter emphasis on the initial prohibition of idolatry, first of all, as it is to this prohibition that the Decalogue, and biblical normativity at large, remain indebted.[40]

In this regard we must point out that despite their good intentions, all militants, past, present and probably future, who imagine a kind of responsible praxis that will finally fuse ethics and law, responsibility and decision, are only the obverse of those positivists who, on the contrary, sought to separate them once and for all. Critical or positivist jurists, in other words, enjoy a ride on the see-saw, the ultimate message of which is not resolution, decision, settlement, but, simply, more of the same game – more management/*oikonomia*. This feature inserts crits into the tradition that, we have argued, is that of one particular community, one among many, but which claims the position of *primus inter pares*. Insofar as 'absolute ethical responsibility' is owed not to a particular collective or its members but, exclusively, to a transcendent–immanent Other, who is 'presiding' over the common household of 'humanity' embodied either in God or his immanent lieutenant (which includes the popular sovereign, cf. Erdogan's Turkey in 2016), this only bears a minimal difference with respect to the divine model of a perfectly disciplined God found in the Catholic concept *of potentia ordinata dei*, a model that, as we have seen and as everyone knows, can give rise to maximal divergences. Finally, there are also some who make a reference to the idea of absolute ethical responsibility, only to suggest that it lies in ruins and most often than not in the ruins of sovereignty that 'structures' the relation between natural and positive law.[41] Also, today's liberal lawyers, as well as materialist militants, would be well advised to take notice of the fact that Jewish rabbis, Eastern bishops and Muslim *ulamā* and *fuqahā'* developed, over the centuries, highly rational jurisprudences without turning into Hartian 'officials', that is without colonising, indeed without even hoping to contain, the political domain with all its intrigue and conflict. Avoiding the role of vicars of the divinity, they turned instead into ad hoc political advisors or, in secular times, into embodiments of the people's Will (or indeed into public intellectuals supremely gifted with the art of interpreting the movements of history as progress). For example, many of the letters sent by the most prominent Greek Fathers to the emperor offering him political advice refer mainly, not to the Bible but to classical Greek and Roman sources – in other words to just the two pre-Christian cultures that, as priests providing moral guidance, these Fathers helped to vilify. In sum, the improbable group just referred to, consisting of premodern rabbis, Eastern bishops and Muslim *ulamā* (a tiny number of which still exist if only as an endangered species) can be seen as catering, on the one hand, for (what positivist jurisprudence and psychoanalytic theory presuppose to be) the human subject's need to obey a law 'because it is the law' (and not due to its 'merits'), while on the other hand they consistently refrain from partaking in the institutionalisation/*étatisation* of the function of law/politics. This meant that they were, and chose to remain, in a position that is particularly enviable: on the one hand, they did exercise practical freedom (interpreting holy texts; devising solutions for moral dilemmas and legal disputes, etc.); yet on the other hand, they were 'trembling' while doing so, being painfully conscious of the fact that their everyday exercise was deprived of any guarantee or external recognition that they were correct, justified, 'good' or 'right', principled, or expedient, in what they did, in deciding what they decided, admitting what they admitted, rejecting what they rejected. This, in other words, was an important but not a glamorous job. The difference that the uncomfortable and unglamorous nature of their employment actually made is not easy to establish, or even understand, within Western human scientific or social scientific discourse. The reason corresponds to the best kept secret of the Western institutional consciousness and mindset; the French public lawyer and psychoanalyst Pierre Legendre has dedicated a life's work to applying the notion 'sensuous apprehension of thought' – a term coined by T. S. Eliot for the English metaphysical poets of the seventeenth century – to the subjective take on institutions, arguing that understanding what is at stake in this is not a particular forte of the occidental mindset.

If, 'everybody needs a master' – we had been told by colleagues at law school, when we asked them why they attended every Žižek lecture – we need to be conscious that said master is not, cannot, discharge the unglamorous function of trembling Jewish rabbis, Eastern bishops and Muslim *ulamā*. Those who do offer themselves as masters today cannot *not* have glory and universal love – at least in their own minds – and are dutifully ready to do whatever it takes to get there. In politics as, also not infrequently, in academia, sociopaths thrive. Genealogy matters here, too. In *Power and Persuasion in Late Antiquity*, Peter Brown reopens the question of how the Empire's transformation from 'paganism' to Christianity affected its civic culture while it remained a system of laws, at a time when crises and the social question were as important as today. He argues convincingly that imperial government depended on the cooperation of local elites, composed initially of officials and administrators who were responsible for the collection of taxes, with the emperor and his representatives. Throughout the empire's huge territory, said multi-ethnic elites were distinguished by their shared upper-class culture, inculcated by the system of education known by the Greek term *paideia*. *Paideia* bound the ruling classes in codes of courtesy and assigned philosophers a special role, that of persuaders and admonishers of the powerful. A long and intellectually demanding training in Greek literature and rhetoric provided social distance from the lower classes, an ethic of friendship (Greek: *filia*) that created widespread networks of contacts, and ideals of deportment that helped limit violence by prizing self-restraint. Since the emperor himself was expected to stand at the apex of this pyramid of cultivated social values, even the monarch's behaviour was bound by educated opinion. When educated opinion proved insufficient against the power of the emperor, however, tradition assigned to the philosopher the duty and right of parrhesia or freedom of speech (literally the duty of saying it all), to act as privileged moral advisor to the court (a tradition continuing today through the work of secret government advisors as well as 'rebellious' public intellectuals). In this way, the elites, in their own eyes, were connected to the ultimate source of political power and were convinced that they could exercise persuasive control over it. Contrary to what some leftist public intellectuals today may think, however, they are not the direct descendants of those elite philosophers of the fourth-century empire.

During the last decades of the fourth century, Christian

monks and bishops began to replace the philosophers as the moral bridges between the rulers and the ruled: it is they who were the forefathers of both the mediaeval Franciscans as well as of today's public intellectuals advocating social justice. These Christian notables emerged from the old upper classes and shared many of the ideals of *paideia*. However, instead of basing their claims to eminence strictly on membership of a cultivated social group, the Christian leaders presented themselves as 'lovers of the poor'. A worsening economic situation and an apparently rising population throughout the Eastern Empire made the poor, those without a defined place in society, an increasingly visible and political presence. Overflowing the countryside and crowding into the cities, the poor were readily mobilised and integrated into the retinues of the bishops. In Christian literature of the fifth century, the juxtaposition of autocratic secular authority and the mass of impoverished humanity provided with a new language of power. Power was recast in a Christian image; and so was philia, i.e. the network of those worthy of the emperor's particular attention. Appeals to the emperor moved away from references to the shared classical culture of an elite minority and began to emphasise that just as God had condescended to become man through Christ, so the ruler should condescend to recognise his common humanity with the broader masses he ruled. Arguably, some of today's public intellectuals do continue this tradition of elitist parrhesia,[42] yet with one crucial difference: gone is the trembling of rabbis, Orthodox clerics and monks and Muslim jurisconsults, which has been replaced by programmatic certainty coupled with the after-the-event logic of 'stuff happens'. Take for an instance the overwhelming certainty with which Žižek embraced the tough negotiating anti-austerity tactics of SYRIZA as bound to succeed because backed by the will of the millions of Indignados. Once these tactics led to the imposition of capital controls and eventually the capitulation that have rendered the social crisis much worse, Žižek now shrugs off the 'power' of direct democracy as the 'last myth of the Left' ('stuff happened') and, with renewed confidence, now offers us a new blueprint for universal emancipation in the form of an 'invisible state, whose mechanisms work in the background' – a sort of 'bureaucratic socialism, but not in the

Stalinist sense'.[43] What can we say: welcome to the *oikonomia* you wanted to overcome, Mr Žižek!

The offshoot of our historicised comparative analysis of political theologies is not only to invoke the particularity of Christianism vis-à-vis the other 'great religions' – let alone the less great ones – as well as the particularity of dualist occidental political theology vis-à-vis Byzantine political theology. More importantly, what we suggest, *pace* Gauchet and Nancy, is that the occidental phase of Western political theology might represent a 'stalling' of the historical process of disenchantment with the great religions or else of the 'auto-deconstruction' of monotheism. This would help explain the endless fascination with the relation of religion to law/politics at a time when a large part of those fascinated declare themselves atheists. Anxiety over the so-called 'revival of religion' is a symptom of such fascination with the Western God, very alive in his quality as the harbinger of metaphysically rooted world hegemony, even as the Western God of onto-theology is dead. While this is especially noted in relation to Westernised fundamentalists who fetishise 'sovereignty' in the name of what is recognisably only a putatively different God – a God supposedly other than the Christian one who passed his throne to the 'People'. The Turkish president's religious nationalism, successfully sold to a majority of Turks and successfully provoking the West, does not pit one God against another. The universalistic imperialism of, say, Alexander's Macedonians, the Mongols, or the Western Christian Crusaders, can indeed be explained as repetitions of one archetypal form of sovereignty, which, from the point of view suggested by Gauchet, remains below the level of historical legitimacy. Who is the judge of historical legitimacy, one might be tempted to ask. Gauchet is not difficult: according to his teaching, empire, or whatever power wielded by whoever is on the top of the pyramid, is in principle justifiable, if not as God-ordained, then nonetheless as benefiting humankind; it all depends on how well whoever 'looks after' things as God's human proxy manages. We note that in Christianism, where the main postulate is the incarnation of God's Son – encompassing the divine and the human animal – the first emperor to act as Christ's proxy in managing the fallen world while awaiting the Second Coming, Constantine, undertook this role by his own tactical choice, prompted, of course, as his propagandist Eusebius tells us, by the miraculous appearance of the sign of the cross above the battlefield of the Melva bridge with the Greek words 'En toutō níka', usually translated into Latin as *in hoc signo vinces*. The message that triumph will come under the sign of Christ's glorious defeat was by all means helpful as an innovation in comparison to earlier or non-Christian empires such as the Macedonian, Mongols, etc. It is undeniable that the incarnation assured Western power against the psychological repercussions of ordinary defeats and failures in the course of governing.[44]

But, contrary to widespread opinion, it is not the case that the Christianisation of the Roman Empire acted overall and immediately as a fail-proof bonus of legitimacy for the Byzantine Basileus. Being merely blessed by the Church – not anointed, as his Western counterpart was – the latter could not rely on the authority given him by God to play down actual losses of control or challenges of power. Sovereignty thus remained personal rather than invested in an immortal, naturally or irreducibly glorious office, advantageously articulated with a smoothly functioning managemental–decisionist administration. The Byzantine Basileus merely presides over administration. As argued elsewhere,[45] (based on the assessment of Gilbert Dagron's brilliant inquiry into the notion that the first Christian emperor was at once 'Emperor' and 'Priest') and contrary to the occidental misreading of the situation, the Christianisation of the empire was, from the vantage point of the imperial office, not a power-increasing move but on the contrary a negative development; it was the origin of an evolution that was mired in a legitimacy deficit. The Christianised emperor stopped playing the role of the sacred pagan Pontifex Maximus; instead, his authority was suddenly only that of an 'as if' Christian priest. In addition, there was no tradition of dynastic succession by primogeniture, and coronation rituals represented the violent or conspiratorial events that brought the emperor to power. In the Byzantine 'game of thrones' each emperor started as a wannabe Jewish Melchizedek, blessed but not anointed by the Church; he typically ended his days dethroned and often humiliatingly savaged. This made ruling via law increasingly untenable and brought about a transformation: emperors henceforth would rely on a combination of Christian self-humiliation – depicted in churches as bowing and wearing poor clothes, appearing in the hippodrome no longer holding the *mappa*, the silk cloth used by the Roman consuls to start the races. Instead, what the Byzantine emperor held in his hand during ceremonies was the *akakia* [literally 'guilelessness'] – a cylindrical purple silk roll containing dust, and symbolising the mortal nature of all men. The precise legal meaning of this expression of humbleness was the underscoring and, tangentially, the augmenting of the dispensational character of legislation, while politically it meant increased reliance and dependence on patronage.

Contrary to what most of us learnt at school, the Byzantine Basileus was not a super-autonomous sovereign, unbound by law and wielding a double-hatted imperial and sacerdotal power. In legal-historical scholarship much is made of Justinian's *Digest* stating that the emperor was the source of all law,[46] and therefore not bound by laws,[47] even if he did choose to abide by them on a voluntary basis.[48] This is perfectly correct as far as the Justinian-based law of the Western Middle Ages, early modernity and modernity, are concerned. To Byzantium it barely applies. Justinian's restating of the classical Roman jurist Ulpian's *Princeps legibus solutus* must be taken with a taste-altering big pinch of Christian salt. In reality, Justinian had many opportunities to learn that the new world was not made more governable by the passing of laws. In addition to his compilation of selected fragments from the works of the classical Roman jurists, Justinian issued an impressive 600 laws over thirty years (which is, however, not as many as earlier emperors issued). Imperial legislative production aimed for codification slowed down exponentially after the fifth century when the second and longest phase in Byzantine legal history began. It was during these long years of established and triumphant Byzantine cultural, military and economic supremacy, as has frequently been observed by Western legal historians, that Byzantine law-giving, in the form of imperial statutes called Novels, took on its characteristic dispensatory nature. A closer look at the legal and political history of Byzantium reveals that the Christianisation of

imperial power – specifically the merging of God's anarchic praxis with the Roman legal concepts of *aequitas* and
epieikeia, which gave the Byzantine Republic, from the fifth
century, its characteristic law-dispensing character, and
Byzantine politics its characteristic obsession with the social
question – occurred, not, as Catholic Agamben implies it
did, in the name of universal salvation, but in that of the
emperor qua patron, sometimes also in that of the particular individuals, or classes of individuals, officials, clerics
and lay persons whose interests and intervention had each
occasioned the issuing of a dispensatory law, even where
the language and rhetoric used constantly referred to the
emperor's love of the poor. The ethos of the Byzantine sovereign never quite extended to the self-righteousness we
find in, say, Shakespeare's kings. Here is an extract from the
resignation speech of Justin II (r. 565–74):

'You behold the ensigns of supreme power. You are about
to receive them, not from my hand, but from the hand of
God. Honour them, and from them you will derive honour.
Respect the empress your mother: you are now her son;
before, you were her servant. Delight not in blood; abstain
from revenge; avoid those actions by which I have incurred
the public hatred; and consult the experience, rather than
the example, of your predecessor. As a man, I have sinned;
as a sinner, even in this life, I have been severely punished:
but these servants (and we pointed to his ministers) who
have abused my confidence, and inflamed my passions,
will appear with me before the tribunal of Christ. I have
been dazzled by the splendour of the diadem: be thou wise
and modest; remember what you have been, remember
what you are. You see around us your slaves, and your
children: with the authority, assume the tenderness, of a
parent. Love your people like yourself; cultivate the affec-
tions, maintain the discipline, of the army; protect the fortunes of the rich, relieve the necessities of the poor.'[49]

Such were the problems that plagued the first Christian
emperors. There were others: how, for instance, was it possible to justify wars led by the emperor as an official follower
of the 'turn-the-other-cheek' religion?

The politico-theological paradigm that emerged later in the West neutralised all of them. Specifically, the pope claimed to be Christ's vicar, alone at first and later together with the Council-cum-layman who was anointed potentate, a German anointed as the 'Holy Roman' emperor presiding over numerous kings and princes, who would eventually be anointed in turn. Here, rather than in Byzantium, lies the birth of the idea of a permanent, irreproachable, abstract, always-already legitimate power that was used to justify absolute monarchy at first and then both the revolution and the law – the 'see-saw' movement by which we imagine the structure of occidental political theology. Recently, Chris Thornhill showed us precisely how the modern state inherited from the Catholic church the notion of continuous, abstract 'political power', always-already legitimate, and capable of being stored in ecclesiastical-cum-state institutions.[50] It is arguably just such an abstract, always-already legitimate 'power' that is enlisted by the institutional sovereign – who, as Schmitt, unlike Bodin, understood as having no absolute power to legislate, but rather a prerogative – not a delegated power – to proclaim enemies and introduce exceptions so as to bridge the inevitable gaps between norms and facts at times of crisis. Further, we can interpret the attempts of liberal lawyers[51] to counter Schmitt's emphasis on unity and constituent power,[52] as well as leftist attempts to enlist his ideas to promote an agonistic democratic politics that advances pluralist rather than fascist agendas,[53] asking whether, taken together, what they do is not simply to iterate and certify performatively, in the first case, a distinction between constituent/constituted power inherited from the Catholic Middle Ages (derived from their distinction between God's *potentia absoluta* and His *potentia limitata*),[54] and, in the second case, the need to economically manage the tension between them, officially in line with ideas of legal or political right but, in effect, factually, in as arbitrary a fashion as the circumstances require, in line with the secularised Christian postulate of *oikonomia*.

If pure, explicitly anarchic, *oikonomia* marked the Byzantine political and legal system, if power as-dispensation-from-the-law gradually replaced legislation as the main expression of sovereignty, and if Byzantine rulers found it equally expedient to appear as merciful Christians by annulling onerous contracts binding the meek and pardoning their corrupt officials, the liberal-constitutional states in which the luckier among us individualists live do not avail themselves of the Eastern Christian apophatic theology, which essentially endorses anomia as mystery (in ways that both sustain and bring down power). Our constitutional states rather follow a path marked by the innovations introduced by Catholicism's late mediaeval natural theology, whereby, in sum, *oikonomia /* exception is not the law being mysteriously silent as in the East,[55] but a justifiable suspension of the law. Take again the issue of the justification of state violence. Whereas the young Jesus, losing his temper with the representatives of the commercialised temple, has recourse to some degree of violence, the Jesus in Gethsemane, some years later, rebuked Peter for attacking a boy named Malchus and even miraculously reattached the latter's sword-severed ear. The preference for violence manifested in the first event could only have embarrassed the first imperial Christian state, the Eastern Roman Empire, which survived the implosion of the Western part, to so-called 'Byzantium'), which, lacking a doctrine of 'just war', went to great lengths to avoid war (by means, inter alia, of bribing the enemy and paying shameful subsidies), and to describe its wars as purely defensive.[56] Not so the West, which even rebuked Byzantium for not joining (or at least co-sponsoring) the Crusades – imperialist warfare that was presented in the more auspicious image of a pilgrimage. While there is no reason not to assume that, historically, Christians have killed, maimed and enslaved at least as many as other religionists, there is little doubt that, starting with the Catholic doctrine of 'just war', the West has excelled in the provision of economic justifications for its contingent decision making on violence or preferential non-violence, hence, the perennial Eastern topos of Western hypocrisy. In order to correctly appraise the degree to which this entire form of political rationality is intimately connected with the bipolar design of secular forms of theological *oikonomia*, consider, by contrast, the fact that (though admittedly much would need to be said about this) no one accuses contemporary Chinese foreign policy of hypocrisy.

7

The Transition from Secularism to Post-secularism

7.1

Philosophy does not deserve its name unless it aims for truth: a sense of what is happening independently of the needs of the human psyche; in this respect Greek 'sophists', 'cynics', Epicureans and others deserve more respect than allowed by Platonists or Stoics. By contrast, all religions cater to these needs of human consciousness, offering, above all, metaphysical postulates and cosmological axioms embedded in cult images and rituals as an affective basis for blind inter-subjective trust, thus alleviating the problems of the lie and the alternative faced by the linguistic animal; certain strands of philosophy, notably the heirs of Platonic idealism, and all successful religions, such as Christianity, offer seductive amounts of consolation through a mixture of truth and blind trust. Occidental Christianism, with its mixture of religious postulates, neo-Platonism and neo-Aristotelianism, still conserves the notion of a truth that makes the difference; although this is equally, if not more true, of all other religions – each with its own special blend of truth, blind trust and consolation – the fact is that most non-Christian religions have by now, and for very real reasons, lost almost all connection between their affective or cult side (the 'iconomic' as well as the liturgical sense) on the one hand, and any conceptual, 'philosophical' sense on the other. Thus, for one example, in Islam, there is no premodern historical precedent for seeking and receiving fatwas mass-produced by, say, Egypt's now state-run al-Azhar University or by dedicated internet sites. In fact today, all religions that cause anxiety do so because of attempts, especially in the post-colony, to harness their affective power (their symbols and emblematic images, etc.) in order to fight Christianism within the latter's conceptual game; fundamentalist Islamists, for example, use sophisticated social networks to seduce disaffected youth with such old Islamic slogans as 'there is no sovereignty except in God', in order to recruit the youth in crusades aimed at bolstering the sovereignty of an 'Islamic state' in which the 'correct' interpretation of Islamic law takes place in a pyramidal hierarchy, as it is in the Catholic Church, and applied on a territorial, rather than personal basis (thus, quite unlike the situation in the classic mediaeval Islamic era to which fundamentalists rhetorically hark back). Thus the world now indeed makes sense in most consciousnesses as a global *oikos* that needs a master, just as it was postulated in the Christian mediaeval imagination; what Giorgio Agamben has reminded us, however, is that the real innovation at the core of this imagination – still not quite grasped by the Christian/ post-Christian subject, let alone others – is that mastery is irrelevant; thus, in order to understand events taking place in the emerging global *oikos* – from Raqqa, Syria to London, UK – we all need to look not at theories of sovereign design and social engineering but at techniques of social administration and management of unintended (collateral) consequences of decisions and actions. Overall, the Christian/post-Christian theo-political model – comprising the fiction of sovereignty with the reality of *oikonomia* – is bolstered, not threatened, by the contemporary so-called 'return' of traditional religions. Whether we look at fundamentalist Islamism, religious Zionism or Hindu ethno-religiosity, what we find is that all these 'movements' are thoroughly modern, perfectly adapted to undergo Darwin-type conditions of competition within economic, political, or mediatic parameters; rather than representing the antediluvian survival of a phenomenon otherwise extinct, they are inconceivable outside of the context of a Westernised world in which 'religion' is pitted against 'secular' law/politics with the effect of obfuscating *oikonomia*, and saving it by rendering it 'subject to sovereignty'.

In view of this we need to rethink the current double crisis of the modern occidental constitutional imagination, consisting, first, of the realisation that sovereignty is nowhere to be found and, second, of the collapse of trust in the legitimacy of government. Most of us have learnt – and now need to unlearn – to expect a sovereign master to provide order; but only some of us (occidentals) blindly trust that the question of a legitimate sovereign trumps the question of his inefficacy or even non-existence. This, as we showed through our references to Byzantium and Eastern Christian political theology, constitutes a schism even within the Western world. While the first ecclesiastical coronation of the Christianised Roman Emperor took place as early as 457 CE, this act was not felt to be constitutive of legitimacy. Whereas the anointing of kings in the West can be traced back to the sixth or seventh century, in Byzantium the purely ecclesiastical rite of anointing was introduced into the inauguration ritual only in the twelfth century at just the moment when papist-occidental power threatened not only the Church but also the Empire of Byzantium; for by then it had become necessary to show that the Eastern Empire, too, was 'Holy', having been anointed by the Church under Christ the Anointed One (again: for most of Byzantine history, the Basileus, who seldom established successful dynasties, did not dispose of the full ecclesiastical endorsement of his claim that he was indeed God's choice in the good old Roman fashion).

Let us recall Marcel Gauchet's thesis that, paradoxically, religion is the way out of religion.[1] It rests on the argument that 'divine otherness, whatever its shape, has been transported into the social space', rendering 'the instituting force . . . visible and accessible', often incarnated by 'humans completely different from their fellow beings in so far as they participate directly or indirectly in the invisible sacred centre fuelling collective existence'.[2] This:

> [gave] rise to a critical corollary, namely that the same gods are brought back within reach and, in practice, become socially questionable . . . Here we see the gods increasingly dependent on what is supposed to depend on them, that is on the actions of an ever changing system they are supposed to keep intact. This political severance introduces a dynamic, a principle of change, into the heart of collective practices on the physical, spiritual and symbolic levels.[3]

Clearly, the dialectics ensuing from the simultaneous and mutually dependent thriving of Hebrew kingship and prophecy are an example here. Even on this level, however, the decisive news come from the Christian millennia and especially the modern centuries. It is, we argue – not unlike Gauchet – the peculiar contribution of the Christian/post-Christian theo-political model to have used its own deconstruction, in order to give rise to worldly, trans-religious instances, precisely by combining the idea of an omnipotent divine/sovereign with the recognition of its increasing impotence, mystified as part of a divine *oikonomia*.

The issue of hierarchy provides a further point. One of the pillars of Marcel Gauchet's theory whereby all 'great religions' lead to secularisation is that, historically, the articulation of a hierarchical structure among humans as much as between humans and their gods – with only very few individuals acting in the name of the gods – destabilised the relation between the instituting invisible *arche* and the instituted norm since the social foundation's otherness was hence incorporated inside the social tie (thus, authority became questionable). Yet if we pay attention to the specific manner in which this process took place within each theo-political tradition, we note the absence, outside of Western Christianism, and specifically in Judaism, Islam and Eastern Christianity (to which we limit ourselves), of anything that would be akin to the elaborate model of the Catholic Church and its hierarchy which, most agree, served as the blueprint for modern states.[4] The same historicised comparative method reveals pivotal differences between the ways in which the duo 'glorious' absolute sovereignty versus mundane, exception-riddled administration/*oikonomia* were perceived and dealt with. Whereas in the trajectories of other empires, notably in Byzantium, all unitary sovereignty was continuously threatened to dissolve into administration and *oikonomia* under the effect of the incurably problematic light that they threw on its deficiencies in coping with the Empire's day-to-day mess, what prevailed in the occidental empire was, on the contrary, an (initially theologically buttressed, cf. the Filioque) presumption of a perpetual, unquestionable 'dialectic' 'relation' (oscillation, see-saw) between sovereignty on the one hand – always-already legitimate, title-holding, irreducibly glorious (yet at the same time, often effectively impotent), and, on the other hand, the continuously expanding, yet ever-vilified, diffuse and often illegitimate powers of fact, which, having played their influential but subterraneous part infamously and even namelessly for centuries, have finally been ennobled (courtesy of insightful historians and sociologists) by receiving names, such as governmentality, managementality, etc. It is this 'see-saw'-like distribution that we identify as the occidental postulate that is – or so we claim – as original, unquestionable, undisputable, as any foundational postulate including, for instance, the idea of a chosen people awaiting the Messiah. Yet – and here resides the objective, the structuring Eurocentric dissymmetry – this occidental postulate is the only one that finds itself in a relationship of effective mutual presupposition with contemporary conditions, setting, structurally and worldwide, the stage on which we are meant to replay every day the artful comedy in which democracy and/or the rule of law continue to be the name of the game humankind is supposed to play, when what really happens, as we know by heart, is that, far below these high aspirations, everyone is busy just merely managing, as well as possible.

In sum, what working at the present study has taught us is the surprisingly parochial quality of occidental political theology both inside, and in relation to, the wider monotheist scene. Putting into tentative use a new method, 'comparative historical political theology', which tries to combine social anthropology and the history of religion (without, as far as possible, cumulating their respective blind spots), the hypothesis that we tested is that the very effort of attributing legitimacy to social orders, social blueprints, conceptions of social justice, etc., regularly offers (1) a textbook example of what historians call 'retrospective illusion' and (2) a textbook example of what consumer economists call 'patriotic preference'. High-flying aspirations to internal consistency were, of course, widespread among political orders well before modernity. Historically, however, gauging the discrepancy between the occidental language of the ambitious claims to validity/legitimacy, and the down-to-earth language used in the power games that fight them out, requires neither the suffering of a Shakespearian Shylock nor the insight of a Conan-Doylian Sherlock. Looking at their articulation without forgetting either side requires exposing oneself to a rare encounter of the geopolitical and the parochial.

This observation allows us to understand that the key legal and political theories of legitimate sovereignty remain instances of Eurocentric self-illusion, be it via euphoric commitment to the 'good cause', or the euphemistic glossing-over of its less presentable aspects; and that the resulting appraisals of legitimacy in and of the Western model of 'sovereign yet limited government' needs to be revised downward: instead of looking to locate it somewhere on the occidental-cum-universalistic axis, i.e. the axis of ideology/theology or of ideology/utopia, we can compare and contrast its ideological/theological inflexion by inscribing it on a map of occidental and other political theologies.

7.2

To summarise: if the instituted human person is the result of the polarity between two ideal types existing alongside each other, and in mutual presupposition, the legislator and the subject to law, the sovereign and the autonomous man; if this polarity has given rise, as to its historically most successful expression, to the occidental theme and deed of revolutions justified as progress, not against authority but by means of and in the name of authority – as well as, in its wake, ideas of limited government, subjective right and liberty; if, lastly, the occidental Christian/post-Christian subject is privileged to love the ruins of the economic-political theology of his erstwhile religion, which allows one to trust blindly in the all-encompassing quality of sovereignty imagined as the never-ending 'dialectic' of power and legitimacy: then we find ourselves in the presence of a group of implications that need to be recognised, of consequences that need to be drawn. First, a clean break between the modern and the mediaeval is no longer on the cards, whichever level of sense-making we are looking at, 'psychological' (subjects, consciousness, identities, genealogical continuities) or 'sociological' (social systems and their environments, communications, societal evolution, the rise of management, etc.). This is so because, since times immemorial – of which Byzantium has ever offered and still offers the modern West an unequalled instantiation – the structurally overlooked but primordial fact is that flatly efficient *oikonomia*, or management, has incomparably greater impact and 'steering power' than the imaginary sovereignty which, though 'glorious' in its subject-related principle, is also permanently on the brink of being revealed as powerless and must be protected against such compromising evidence (cf. once again Agamben's careful study of the topic). More specifically we might say that, to the extent to which 'sense' refers to the public instantiations of subjectivity and consciousness: the Byzantine Basileus, the Holy Roman Emperors, the popes, the absolutist kings, but also today's governments, all of them respectively enjoy/suffer a spectacular acclamation/disapproval that – insofar as 'sense', taken from a sociological angle, refers to communication – is perfectly at odds with the very limited character of their effective opportunities to intervene. This prompts the question of what it is that, ultimately, governments cannot ignore in order to remain legitimate? Public order as absolute safety? *Salus populi* as complete well-being? Michael Oakeshott was not merely being sarcastic when he stated that contemporary rulers and power-holders are perhaps best understood as:

> [so many] therapeutae [i.e.] the directors of a sanatorium from which no patient may discharge himself by choice of his own ... [The] outstanding fact of modern times is ... universal neurosis ... a [modern] state should be understood as an association of human beings undergoing treatment.[5]

If in the course of the second Christian millennium the Occident has applied the verdict 'glorious, but powerless' exclusively to Byzantium, we are now entitled to ask whether this is because the former avails of and the latter lacks a political theology allowing for a compassing culture of justification, which is needed in order to make-believe that a gloriously sovereign decision structure topples 'mere' *oikonomia*, and the powerful and intelligible dialectic of 'rules and exceptions' 'masters' the intrinsic limitations of the household, even emancipates it from God's anarchic monarchy. Indeed, Eastern Christian/Byzantine political theology centre-stages an anarchic and mysterious *oikonomia* as part of a wider principle that does not justify rules/exceptions so much as mystify them.

You can accuse the Byzantine of many things (the number and longevity of these accusations seems to prove the immense need for a negative sense-making potential and the success in providing for itself an identity by way of contradistinction from its Byzantine other), yet there exists a small group of things that you cannot say; you cannot say, for instance, that the Byzantines were particularly prone to confuse ends and means, or mistake expediency for an imperative of reason or ethics. The stereotypes of occidental 'hypocrisy' and Levantine 'untrustworthiness' that prevail today, just as much as they have during the past ten or so centuries, make tons of sense, no matter whether you choose to consider the continuous east–west split according to the identitarian dimension of modern sense-as-consciousness, or according to the sociological preoccupation of accounting for the emergence of an impersonal new sense-as-communications between social systems. But the contemporary world, while not being substantially more 'multi-polar' than the world of a thousand years ago (Byzantine history is, among other things, a unique observatory of this geopolitical multi-polarity, most especially obviously the Christian–Islamic border-zones), is based on far more communications happening – not only irrespective of east–west distances but including especially the growing geopolitical involvement and presence of the south.

What is noteworthy in these conditions is the fact that the accusation of 'hypocrisy', an accusation that is levelled at the West so frequently and in so many contexts, continuously belies the notion that occidental political theology is based upon a differentiating trump card that enables first its Catholic, then its Protestant ethos to comprise dogmatism with flexibility and to synthesise law and revolution, passing one off for the other. Because the late mediaeval Occident combined – unlike Byzantium – legalism with *oikonomia* (in the sense of offering 'justified exceptions' to established law), whereas for the Byzantines *oikonomia* was – as Agamben insists is the still the case, if in an unacknowledged form – an anarchic silence of the law; because it created such principles as immortal sovereignty, 'dualism in authority' and 'unity in diversity'; for these reasons the mediaeval Occident needs to be understood as offering its own take on the high-flying ambition of an *oikos* inscribed in the universalism of God/

Man; the latter was thence imagined, not after the idea of a Janus-faced limit or border, or of the two-headed eagle of the Byzantine rule symbol, but after the equally sublime ideal of a compassing constitution of political entities boasting the titles 'Empire' and 'Roman' – and 'Holy' to boot; whereas Byzantium was a powerful, centralised state with a legitimacy deficit, the ever threatening deficit that, in the West, the glorious legitimacy concocted for the new 'Holy Roman' Empire – later painfully inherited by the EU – had been erected to cope with the very prosaic and real weaknesses of Western imperial institutions, that resulted from its straddling proto-nationalisms.[6]

Furthermore, the fact that the mediaeval Catholic Church was given the chance of establishing itself as a feudal court 'for the world at large', as a consequence of the feudal law on its own had not been able to master the new situation emerging from assertive and corporate early individualism among the wealthy, literate, landed nobility of Western Europe,[7] is not unrelated to the contemporary, undecided role of *primus inter pares* that the West, militantly implicitly and silently assigns itself today, a role that non-Westerners either laugh off as a delusional grandeur in the face of growing world influence of non-European nations, or seek to counter in rather more prosaic, sometimes violent ways. It is in the context of this occidental version of Christian economic-political theology that we must read the full implications of the Catholic appropriation of Roman law, as well as its best-known product: the idea of immortal corporate sovereignty. The same move that gave us the dignity of the office of the sovereign as distinct from his person gave us the idea of sovereignty, guaranteed by an immeasurable overkill of potential, but thereby eminently capable of staging its everyday appearance as an effective jurisdiction even without power; the same move that gave us individualism with liberty – whereas Byzantium knew only individualism – replaced the Roman (including 'Byzantine') imperial expression *dominus mundi* with the abstract and impersonal *dominium mundi*; this led to the idea that, not the imperial West, but what is called 'humanity' – a word that functions today as a secularised synonym of the word *ecclesia* – is now the master-word of the world-as-*oikos*, the matrix of 'world interior politics'. Thus, the stage has been set for the millennial phase of Western-led globalisation-cum-managementalisation, which has recently shown its self-adapting abilities by compensating for its loss of sovereign power – through a cunning rehabilitation of the status of *primus inter pares*, based upon the over-appraisal of constant 'learning-by-experience' in the field of government. Tony Blair in his well-paid role as a global democracy 'advisor' and Middle East 'peace broker' is a caricature of this status that the West assigns itself, since, officially speaking, the title of 'master' of the world is no longer an option.

Without taking into account these unofficial, but highly symptomatic aspects of the functioning of the Western power machinery, all that can be offered to explain the success of Christianism in sustaining Western imperialism is some generalising conflation of its history with that of an easily conjured 'universal history of religion' in which, per Gauchet or Nancy, 'all' religions and their political theologies always surely lead to the 'singular' path of secularisation as 'progress' – and the biased presupposition that the Jews, or the Eastern Christians, or the Muslims, in order to stay within the so-called 'monotheist model of social organisation',[8] exited historical time as soon as they gave in to perpetual theological disagreements and civil wars, instead of following the West in replacing their religions with the new 'anti-religious' or 'civil-religious' model of religion and roadmap of how to successfully 'deal with' religious matters. In our view, by contrast, the image that best captures this process is of a Western-led path-of-progress (which is becoming ever wider, to the point of encompassing even the heart of the Amazon forest) on which 'the rest' have either been brought willy-nilly or joined for fear of ending one's journey as a particularly regrettable case of collateral damage (as we have seen, for certain Zionists, the choice is formulated as between being Westernised and – literally – annihilated). For us, however, the point is, as already hinted, that there is, and that there can be, no 'progress' without collateral damage. In this regard some among us find it harder than others to say 'stuff happens, let's move on'. One case in point, but there are many, is the modern religion of Zionist Judaism, which can almost be described as 'kind of a crusading Christianism with a kippa'. 'Stuff happens' regularly in Israel – mostly to

Arabs and occasionally also to Israelis. We saw, however, that for some people the whole conception underlying this is unacceptable; for example, the members of Neturei Karta inculcate in their children a different Jewish ethos, a different political theology. Yet it is undeniable not only that these are now in ruins but that in the new global *oikos* they can serve, at best, as exotic decor. We also saw how a few atheists born in Palestine before the state's foundation refused to become citizens by virtue of the 'Law of Return', thus also refusing the logic of the modern religion of Zionism, which dictates – like all modern nationalist movements that built identities through homogenising processes that were ostensibly liberating, even at the cost of death ('freedom or death!') – that 'bad stuff happens' and that we Jews – secular or not – 'must now all help consolidate' the ethno-religious nation's progress. Despite their honest, persistent refusal to join in, individuals like Professor Uzzy Ornan could not in the end defy their inclusion in the 'family' of nation states: in fact, having given up the cause of a secular 'Hebrew' state, he has eventually accepted that Israel is here to stay and started an NGO called 'I am Israeli', which promotes no more than a common-sense secularist agenda: to classify all citizens as Israelis rather than by religion.

We insisted on the Christian/post-Christian peculiarity among the great religions, especially in its occidental version, in order to describe the current state of modernity and the specific theological remainders or ruins that it must continuously leave behind in order to assure the reproduction of its processual existence. The first particularity relates to Trinitarian theology – the common stock of the large and successful churches both in Constantinople and the Vatican, as well as the seats of later 'national churches' – in which the idea of God as a living being in whose image man has been created, but also, as an economic relation of his hypostases, commands more respect than either God alone or man alone, and in which, by analogy, sovereignty is imagined as more glorious than either immanent law/politics or transcendent religion. The (postulated) 'unity as irreducible relationality' of both poles of this see-saw-like relationship is distinguished in that it results in a balanced spring corresponding functionally to that which assures the homogeneous movement of a Swiss watch. The Trinitarian God is distinguished from others, in Agamben's words, inasmuch as His being is that of a unified difference of 'persons' or hypostases; a God who always-already contains every possible difference stands for the crossing point of the one and the multiple, including the difference of a created 'exterior' world.[9] This theological imagination both contains and consists of (i.e. is nothing other than) a toolbox of distinctions, such as sacred/temporal, religion/civil religion, transcendence and immanence:

> [T]he only content of the transcendent order is the immanent order, but the meaning of the immanent order is nothing other than the relation to the transcendent end. 'Ordo ad finem' and 'ordo ad invicem' refer back to one another and reciprocally provide foundations, by themselves mutually taking each other as their ground. The Christian God is this circle in which two orders continuously penetrate each other.[10]

7.3

While the news of this (as any) genealogy rarely reveals itself to those whose world, life, mind, habits it continues to form, the most recent innovative turn that the occidental political language has undergone has left undeniable marks in certain sub-fields of semantic evolution. One example is the multiplication of words ending in '-tion', denoting 'activity in the making' (the present tense), to be put in perspective with a stagnation of words ending in '-ism', denoting doctrines, practices or habits or anything having its formative period in its past (the past tense or, in older lingo, the 'perfect'). There is a hint here that the current years are qualified by the fact that the perspective of perfection has been superseded, or wrapped up, by the perspective of 'the making' of a world that, in its transitory openness, has been integrated into a state of process, performance, operation. The terminology of Latin *actio, operatio*, and pseudo-Latin *secularisatio*, even *deconstructio*, reflect this shift in meaning, which has quietly and symptomatically taken possession of and thereby transformed the world in which politics, ethics, existence, had been unfolding throughout the Old European era, and transformed them into exhibits of a museum of geo-*oikonomia*, a site of looked-after ingredients within a new order, in which being and time are integrated. Yet from the occidental perspective, this is a matter not only to be understood as 'work-in-progress' but also one to be entrusted as progress; and submission to this blind trust in continuous 'work as progress' subordinates conceptual construction work at large to theology, all over again.

Secularisation, to take this example, comes in one out of two different forms. There is the dramatic or 'hands-on' form: religion understood as 'imperfection', secularisation understood as the consciousness of this 'imperfection' and the 'work' it needs. This is the form replete with denial, or alternatively of emphasis, where causality and identity, inheritance and disinheritance of religious influence and, therefore, identity crisis and drama are directly at stake. It is also what Schmitt is talking about, or is understood to be talking about. Here, the secular remains, potentially at least, in the power and control of a religious start position which, never deleted but only reduced to its 'zero degree', remains in place, even if it is subject to continuous shrinking. The second conception of secularisation forestages the awareness that what we are dealing with (coping with/managing/administering), is a state of things whose 'start position', lost in the immemorial past, has left no effective trace of a presence: the core Western Christian tradition whereby *oikonomia* is present as if basking in the glory of something transcendent, is, in this second conception of secularisation not so much 'disinherited' as it is ignored. The equivalent would be, for example, to see in the ruins of classical Greece not the 'glory that was Greece' – which secretly suggests the need to relive such glory – but pieces or fragments of a game called by names such as archaeological tourism and coming under UNESCO's cultural heritage protection programmes. Under this second conception – which, we stressed, is not the only one and certainly not the one that helps individuals and groups such as nations to make glorious identity statements – the secularisation process has completed its cycle, reached its end, achieved its perfection. It has given rise to true oblivion by means of avoiding (or ignoring, or more precisely forgetting) the 'zero degree', so that there is nothing left to secularise.

It is true that this point could coincide with the advent of a new wholly different religion, especially a religion that, having never gone through the peripety of secularisation, has never been asked to pay the price for it. Notably, however, it is the first sense of secularisation that is prevalent in both Western and 'anti-Western', secular and counter-secular, consciousness and discourses, namely the two poles of a noematic continuum where a reference to secularisation stands in for the notion of a forever imperfect emancipation from religious roots – meaning that we shall forever be unable to cleanse traces and ghosts. Here belongs Schmitt's conception of politics as a secular displacement – or more simply a secularised version – of the theologically defined moral duty of a Christian subject not only to manage as an *oikonomos* but also to acclaim/glorify the absent lord or master. Only if placed under the theological heading does the planetary takeover of politics by management appear either as a breach of identity, an abandonment of its 'innate' commitment or, conversely, as a matter of insuperable irredentism. If the Western consciousness is obsessed by the Christian 'degree zero' of global management, while the non-Western consciousness on the contrary ignores it, systems theory, with its theoretical take on society as rooted in social autopoiesis, and its 'disciplined' – as it were – silence over the psychic, offers itself as a non-anxious, perhaps zen-like, Western response to the question of how social order is possible.[11] This detachment, of course, presupposes that one focuses on impersonal communications taking place between systems, ignoring sense and sense-making as taking place between identity-craving consciousness, individual or collective. This, however, allows us to understand what it allows us to understand; it is not a panacea. It is not even forthcoming: the enjoyment of identity, power, integrity and the timeless project of the 'integration of society into nature'[12] are all taking place on the premises of subjectivity. Social systems coexist with them; they do not touch them; social systems theory offers no hint that any of those are going to stop asking their due.

As Quentin Meillassoux has convincingly argued, secularisation is inseparable from a symmetrically opposed campaign, which he calls religionising ('enreligement').[13] A slant towards religionising, understood as 'the opposite of progressive rationalisation', is effectively noteworthy, the result of a dynamic in which the successful critique or self-critique of metaphysics has resulted in an emptying out of institutional trustworthiness that can only give rise to a wild growth of personal religion: a religion that is merely personal, a personal choice, a subjective self-affirmation, an individual right. It follows that any interest in matters religious should be connected to an inquiry into the genesis of the secular as a telos and of the religion-indifferent, post-religious or trans-religious modern Western principles of public order, which in turn should include the problem of the name in which these principles have been successful, which under conditions of secularisation is the religious status quo ante or prehistory of the secular institutions. Institutions, unlike truths, whether 'religious' or 'secular', are, it has been observed, eminently those that we can understand;[14] institutions are, moreover, those that we cannot help understanding.

Let us come back to religion and its Other, science. We find at work an investigation and deconstruction of what one author, Joseph Glanvill, himself a clergyman, called in a famous title *The Vanity of Dogmatizing* (1661), and the dazzling effect of the polemic of which it is a symptom: namely the neutralisation of hitherto unquestionable postulates and the growing disrepute of the sacred in particular and the holy in general. The point here is that no matter what answer one gives them, the horizon of sense-making that is relevant to these questions – which have so powerfully shaped the political and socio-historic landscape – is no longer in place today. What the modern debate, counter-opposing free-thinking and religion, focused on was a relation of truth, of faith and knowledge, and of their entanglement or disentanglement. Yet these disputes are all but deserted in 2016, apart from a genre of prime-time pedagogically ecumenical TV discussions. The present time situates itself at a point that comes after the neutralisation of these postulates, after the rejection of their relevance. The polarity of 'managing' or 'coping with', as opposed to the ambition of sticking to the unmanageably political, has displaced the argument about principles.[15]

In a long series of *Leçons*, Pierre Legendre, a Sorbonne-based public law and religious science professor, has enquired into the question of the fate of civil law cultures of Central and Western Europe, once the various religious, epistemic and political claims that have hidden the imperialist nature of the occidental meta-claim to humankind–universal leadership encounter major difficulties. Instead of referring to post-religious or more generally post-enchanted or disenchanted forms of what he calls bare institutionality – based exclusively upon the functioning of result-producing mechanisms: the market of capitalism, the legal order of the positivist union of primary and secondary rules, the 'soft' empire of management – Legendre rejects the very notion of a post-religious or indeed post-dogmatic age as some form of exaggerated misunderstanding of human plasticity, no matter whether it is presented as 'optimistic' or as 'pessimistic'. Instead, he launches himself into an enterprise of rehabilitating 'dogma' against what he identifies as the obscurantist element deeply embedded in the Western Enlightenment. He does so by interpreting the latter's dogmatic anti-dogmatism as a continuation rather than a break with respect to religion and religiously sustained power, but also, and perhaps more importantly, by following his disbelief in any programme built upon the assumption that the subjection of the human being can be 'overcome'. As an alternative, he suggests a return to the historically concretised tension, confrontation, and correspondence between transmitted, normative textual bodies, concretely the biblical canon, on the one hand, and what he calls 'the 'West's second Bible' – mediaeval Roman, more precisely Roman-plus-canon law – on the other. This commitment does not suffer from his professional knowledge of textual criticism – Legendre, if anyone, is perfectly aware that the transmission of textual bodies is a merely factual, contingent matter.[16] Legendre, whose critical awareness of management and managementalisation dates back to the 1960s and 1970s, well before the Reagan–Thatcher era of the official takeover of neo-liberalism,[17] considered the polarity between legal texts, which he understands as bodies (or, as he says, 'monuments') of normative authority as well as techniques of management, partly anticipating Agamben's dichotomy of glory versus *oikonomia*, though with a different, and game-changing, plea in favour of law. The 'relation' between a glorious legal or political sovereignty and a mundane *oikonomia* or administration, like the one inherited by Europe and once (yet arguably no longer) sanctified by the Christian Holy, continues to be a *matter of cult worship or idolatry*, no matter the percentage of subjects who experience the related legal and constitutional rituals as 'empty'. This shows, not only the inversion of the relation of sanctity and authority (whose significance remains untouched by that inversion), but also, specifically, the extent to which the Christian/post-Christian theo-political model – comprising the idea of an omnipotent divine sovereign together with the recognition of its increasing impotence (interpreted as an invincible ground of the need of 'management' as part of a divine *oikonomia*) – still performs a mystifying function inside the disenchanted world that it made possible.

Evolutionary advances set new problems, but the disenchantment that followed the Enlightenment and the emergence of modern science has led, we contend, to a point of no return: the implosion of law and politics in a sea of managerialism has so far only been dealt with in terms of a rather blind, if not hypocritical trust in the binary 'relations' of religion to law/politics and of law/politics to management that are the result of centuries of synergy between Greek and Christian metaphysics. Indeed, as can be shown through an endless list of historical instances, knowledge – at least power-relevant, and in that sense 'ultimate' knowledge – has always been a matter of such blind/hypocritical trust in unquestionable formulas (*logoi*) and in this sense it has been 'sacred'. In most traditional cultures such truths were left unquestioned, their validity being a matter of liturgical certification, where they were grasped only in an embodied, numinous way. The anthropologist Rappaport to whose work we have referred earlier, speaks here of ritually certified 'ultimate sacred postulates'. Such would be the idea of One Triune God with no inherent material significations (in such a way that an unlimited spectre of significations can be and has been attached to it). Such 'ultimate Knowledges' were traditionally opposed to mundane knowledge which, though generally regarded as interesting and important, was taken to be obvious, transient, low in or devoid of sanctity, and contingent (or 'instrumental') rather than fundamental. Thus, for example, the Greek Fathers have left us two kinds of knowledge: their sublime theological writings, for which they are still famous; and their lesser known contributions, devoted to the long-standing enterprise of establishing a Byzantine 'mirror of princes', including a digest of advice about how to govern, which they sourced primarily from the pagan classics. By contrast, the theories of knowledge proliferating throughout disenchanted modernity, synthesise and subsume a homogeneous mass of equally proliferating 'facts', thus offering no other certainty except their own transient character and limited scope. Indeed, from a 'post-foundational' vantage point, we are requested to learn to love and get used to the uncertainty that comes with a type of knowledge that remains fragmentary compared to the overwhelming certainty that subjects have been allowed to take as true under the regime of the old *doxa*. And yet despite the fact that today 'nothing is sacred' (except perhaps the maxim 'nothing is sacred'), two 'values' are still not relativised enough and are even elevated to general organising principles as if they avail of an (albeit precisely godless) sanctity: legal/political collective sovereignty and individual quasi-sovereignty manifest in private economic rationality – *idia phronesis*. Indeed the bourgeois and post-bourgeois fiction of the supreme Will of *homo economicus* – capitalist or communist – is treated as certain regardless of the wealth of everyday repeated evidence to the contrary: its very survival is witness that it is gifted with some type of counter-factual resistance.[18] The question that needs to be posed, however, does not have the form of official melancholy often to be heard, which boils down to:

> The *homo oeconomicus* would be fine, alas what else should we aspire to be in the world as it presents itself today; but there must also be limits; what we need to do is to stop people from becoming total embodiments of the *homo oeconomicus*.

Instead, we need to argue just the opposite, namely something like:

> *Homo oeconomicus*? Fine with us! But then, let us apply the model consequently: for starters, why can this perfectly rational *homo oeconomicus* not dispense with 'empty' legal or political constitutional rituals, say voting or raising a

revolutionary fist in a demo? Why should we at the same time be subject to the imperatives of soulless economic rationality and in addition to the hopes, aspirations, and busy-body activities which the very homo *oeconomicus* model legitimately does away with?

7.4

We can now turn to the so-called 'post-secular' literature. Take, for example, Simon Critchley's *The Faith of the Faithless*.[19] The central thesis is that modernity is driven by a religious drive not to see the religious dimension in politics ('secularism, which denies the truth of religion, is a religious myth'[20]). Modernity is nothing but 'a series of metamorphoses of sacralization'.[21] This means that any modern political form(ation) makes use of something sacral, of a belief in divine sovereignty – be it popular ('God the monarch becomes God the people'[22]) or anonymous (e.g. 'the markets are not satisfied') – in its rituals (such as parliamentary elections), in the constitution,[23] in the 'magic'[24] of political representation,[25] etc. All this leads Critchley to claim that 'in the realm of politics, law and religion there are only fictions'.[26] 'Is politics practicable without religion? . . . I do not think so'.[27] Thus far we entirely agree; in whatever connection, to say that politics is limited, no matter by what argumentative means one says it, is not a small thing; it goes against the grain of a certain ever-unacknowledged if omnipresent duty, or debt, of making the required step beyond religion – in which we see a remake of the duty, of any Christian subject, to be a believer in the message of salvation that constitutes it. Interventions in political theology debates, of Critchley's kind, form part of the civil religion tradition that the positivists so prematurely declared over and done with. They forcefully recalled Machiavelli's assertion that, in ensuring social order, religion takes precedence over arms while, in turn, good arms take precedence over good laws.[28] Moreover, the emphasis on the fictional, unverifiable character of religious postulates – which is to say, by implication, also of politics and law – is a welcome correction of the tendency of modern state idolaters to see religion as having a kernel of universal reason. For Hegel, only humans have religion because they are reasonable and this is expressed plurally throughout history, culminating in Christianity's doctrine of incarnation and in post-Christianity's apotheosis of the immanent God-man who will soon mutate into a venerated Man-God. However, Critchley is not content to stop here. Like many and most other career-respecting Christian/post-Christian academics requiring love (and fees) in exchange for offering the good news no matter whether religious or secular, by means of an edifying discourse, capable, 'like some machine' (*tamquam machina quaedam*), to use the words of Saint Augustin, of 'making rise the structure of social love' (*per quam structura caritatis adsurgat*),[29] he proceeds to argue for the emancipatory political potential of faith in 'a fiction that we know to be a fiction, yet one in which we still believe'.[30] Our times, in other words, are so dark for the reason that modern politics has been a gigantic misunderstanding of its own fictitious nature. This is why 'these fictions need to be exposed for what they are'[31] – say: 'popular sovereignty is a lie'[32] – and 'the philosophical analysis of politics' becomes 'a labor of demythologization'.[33] Against this background, Critchley argues that we need a new conception of the stuff that makes political communities stick together, a new conception of the fictitious 'religious dimension, which is found in the life of every people'.[34] This is why the main 'concern of [his] book is with the nature of faith'.[35] Its nature is fictitious but linked to a 'rigorous activity of a subject'.[36] These two – the theory of political fictions (faith) and subjective ethical activism – are the elements of an 'ethical neo-anarchism'.[37] The recent return to Paul already indicated a 'vision of faith and existential commitment that might begin to . . . face down the slackening existence under . . . liberal democracy . . . motivated by political disappointment'.[38] The problem with this is that, despite its worthy motives, it leads to 'a politics of abstraction', forgetting the real world, i.e. to another kind of religion (for example Critchley attacks Žižek for defending an all-or-nothing-politics, which represents the 'general subjective structure that holds us captive'[39]).

Critchley's thesis, we stress, entails, inter alia, a peculiar reading of Levinas. As far as we understand him, Levinas insisted on delinking the category of the Holy that he associated with the 'infinite' and 'anarchic' ethical responsibility of opening up to the empirical other as being the absolute Other (*religare*), from the category of the Sacred, as present in established religions, to which political/legal duties which are 'parasitic' on the Holy and ethics correspond.[40] Hence Levinas' characterisation of the ethical subject is as 'obsessed' with infinite responsibility and as 'radically passive' and 'hostage'. We think that with this dramatic gesture Levinas sought to invert the usual model we presented earlier in which the sovereign subject must be presupposed as the 'pivot' that allows for the structured see-saw or pendulum oscillation between particularist religion and universal law/ politics. We wish to retain the reference to Levinas' drama as well as the see-saw comedy, because they alone, taken together, prevent us from 'processing' the 'idea of infinity' until it becomes a principle of legal or political justice applicable, as a category, class or genus, to some subordinate level. The idea of infinity has no significance for Levinas. It is experienced as an excess of affectivity and responsibility over knowable and calculable duty in the onerous, indeed unaffordable proximity to the face of my neighbour who, in terms of my ethical responsibility, comes complete with the claim of having to be approached as if absolutely unique and as if, therefore, 'higher', rather than as just another member of the genus to which she or he might belong. The idea of infinity as a sign of such godless transcendence experienced in the flesh is central to Levinas' ethics of proximity, based as it is on obsessively dedicating oneself to the other, who is approached as if s/he was absolutely Other. Thus, sociality is the result of an infinite ethical command: open up to the stranger! While 'opening up' is certainly not the same thing as 'binding together', thus, as that *religare* to which, according to one of the canonic auto-etymologies, religion considers itself as belonging, it is also undeniable that Levinas' suggestion, by offering a different gesture, offers an attempt to find the essence of the ethical message of the revelation in one definable gesture. It is important to stress that infinity, the only idea that is not produced by the subject but signifies a meaningless yet irreducible exteriority, concerns us at a pre-reflexive level. Levinas' ethics, in other words, sets us on a road in which whatever we make of it, for example seeing it as a march of progress, is irrelevant.

Critchley, however, finds this useless drama less than edifying and argues that in order for the subject not to be 'paralysed' by too much guilt – even for occupying a place under the sun and, *ipso facto*, marginalising another, per Levinas – it must, with poetic licence, channel ethical responsibility into universal political projects by still believing, nonetheless, in what it knows full well to be fiction: that a power sufficient to exercise an unlimited effect, a power capable to steer the world in a different, 'better' direction, actually exists. According to Critchley, this role is taken up by poetry. It has the 'critical task . . . to show that the world is what you make of it',[41] and that there can always be a 'work of collective self-creation',[42] and there can always be emancipation. For Marx, it was science that generated emancipatory knowledge of the world: for Critchley, it is rather art and poetry. Here he sides with thinkers who argue for a fundamental interrelation of aesthetics and politics, such as J. Rancière.[43] In sum, his 'ethical neo-anarchism' relies on the faith that the world can be changed 'for the better' if we find something unlimited in it and if we accept and assume the 'weakness' of having nothing at our disposal but fictions. Thereby, the weakness becomes 'a possible strength',[44] a 'powerless power'[45] that enables the 'fictitious constitution'[46] of a political collective endowed with an 'openness to the possibility'[47] of always newly finding something unlimited in the situation. A procedure that is immanently infinite – structured by an 'infinite demand'[48] – can never ever be realised once and for all. This ethics of 'overload'[49] implies a 'guilty heroism',[50] which accepts that 'the imperfect is our paradise',[51] i.e. leads to accepting that no fulfilment is ever truly fulfilling, as the very idea of fulfilment is a constitutive fiction.

Now, as Critchley's reviewer, Frank Ruda, first asks:[52]

why does this art, of creating self-conscious fictions, not still follow a religious structure in Marx' sense? Why do we not over and over again create the fiction that the world is what we make of it, *because* we know it will remain the same and the fiction is precisely what prevents change from happening? How to avoid the risk that the 'supreme fiction' (23, 81, 91, 93) is no other than the fiction of willed change for the better – one that we believe in only because we know it to be a fiction? Might not the danger of such 'Christianity without God' (as in Badiou) be that the fiction of change turns change itself into nothing but fiction?

Our own question goes a step further: what if emancipatory change through the 'work of collective self-creation'[53] is itself the perfectly correct way of expressing the supreme fiction spanning the millennia of the Christian/post-Christian West? What if Christianity with or without God has long been a misnomer for a cult of high politics in which political theology obfuscates economic theology and the sovereignty of creation obfuscates the non-teleological processes of *oikonomia*/administration of beings and things – even beings as things – inside a world which, behind the ambitious polis that it is imagined to be, is but a modest *oikos*?[54]

Ruda's second question to Critchley concerns the latter's argument that a self-conscious collective fiction can lead to collectively created 'interstices', namely spaces for political association and self-determination that work 'within the state against the state'.[55] These interstices are timely manifestations of something unlimited that has been created through political articulation, the exercise of what Laclau calls hegemony. They may be lost, but when they are, an 'infinite demand' soon demands the generation of new ones. And the fictions we believe in encourage us to believe this must be possible. In *Infinitely Demanding*[56] and elsewhere, Critchley discusses various examples: from indigenous rights movements in Mexico and Australia to Bolivia's Evo Morales ('who is directly answerable to genuine social movements'), and Brazil's *movimento sem terra*, to the movement in favour of the *sans papiers* and the *sans abri* in France, the movement for an alternative globalisation and anti-war movement or the current struggle about the question of immigration in North America and Europe through to various forms of direct action, civil society groups and NGOs. Although Critchley depicts these as 'creations', relying on demands that are impossible to fulfil once and for all, Ruda rightly wonders how to distinguish this practice from a less inspiring yet not dissimilar case, one that equally relies on limitlessness and lack of fulfilment: is not the unlimited expansion of the possible a key feature of the contemporary market? How can we avoid a position that copies the idea that 'nothing is impossible' – the commercial slogan of Nike® – and the threat of what Badiou once called a 'disaster of the unlimited'? Does one not come dangerously close to the very operation of capital?

Again, our criticism goes further. Are these 'interstices' 'new creations' in the sense of fashion? Are they subversive of state sovereignty – and its 'mythical violence', to quote Benjamin – or are they the result of adaptation to an imperialist social order centring on the cult of sovereignty and 'high politics' that obfuscates the empire of management and *oikonomia* in the environment of a Westernised, post-state-sovereignty world society? Žižek, for one, does have a point in suspecting these movements, which Critchley sees as articulating the possibility of a new poetic language of civil disobedience, for their complicity with power and their complacency about what he calls 'structural violence'. If for Marx religion was a means to leave the world as it is, for Critchley it becomes a means to change it. But information about more precise measurements of the distance between such an assertion and a mere play on words would be welcome. In the remaining residual notion of 'change', there is so little left of what is usually associated with this word that we are getting close to some degree of disingenuity (one could also say that Critchley most determined not to let go of the master-word 'change' in our own Kiplingian jungle, and sticks to it without any good reason for doing so, other than trying to be more loved by the left than he is). The distance taken from Marx – by dubbing religion a medium of change rather than an institution of no change – is insubstantial. To get things right, a first fundamental step would be to take leave of the whole crawling attempt of establishing a duality. How about, for instance, casting the situation in the following words: adaptive social orders persevere precisely because they are always subject to some degree of change; it is religion – such as the religion of the perennial 'Good News', to start with – that allows us to experience the resulting disorder with a sense of order.

We have not criticised Critchley's poetry just in order to certify that another way of turning Levinas' speculation into a programme of change-as-progress is possible. When in *Totality and Infinity*,[57] Levinas relaunched the term 'religion'

– one of whose etymological ramifications leads back, as we have already hinted, to the Latin verb *religare*, to connect – he did so as part of his ethical opposition to the (Kantian, Hegelian or other) philosophical view of totality. The core of his suggested godless 'religion' is the metaphysical idea of infinity, which 'is transcendence itself',[58] in the sense that it is an idea that cannot be produced by the subject but is experienced in the encounter with the other as wholly Other. In this sense, bringing together the Same and the Other without constituting a totality, '[R]eligion, where relationship subsists between the same and the other despite the impossibility of the Whole . . . is the ultimate structure'.[59] This strange 'relation' is not in fact a relation, however, as Levinas hints paradoxically, writing of what he calls a 'relation without relation'. What Levinas tries to do is to launch a 'religion of alterity' that evades the totalising duo private/traditional religion versus civic religion. At its centre lies the 'disincarnate Face', which concerns us not as meaning or representation, but as signification without meaning, as present in anyone's, any stranger's appeal, demand, or summons. In other words, 'the face to face remains an ultimate situation', because 'inevitably across my idea of the infinite the other faces me'.[60] With reference to Agamben's insights about the historical success of the Christian idea of government thanks to its apolitical-managerial economic theology (which, as he argues, continues to over-determine the political element in the Western legal and political imagination), we would like to suggest that Levinas' view of the idea of infinity, on which rests the independence of the anarchic right to be unbound from the *religare* exercised by legal or political duty and established religion, namely from sense as self-same consciousness, has at all times been subjected and over-determined in public discourse by a Christian/post-Christian political theology, central to which is precisely the postulate of a Triune God – the 'one' that is, as is the case for any all-encompassing relationality, subject to an *oikonomia* (which, cf. Agamben's inquiries, theologians do not often wish to own up to, any more than do politicising crits). While as we saw, Levinas describes the relation of ethical conscience to philosophy and religion, jurisprudence and politics with some deliberate ambiguity – subtly sabotaging, as it were, its drive towards closure and synthesis – it is precisely the hallmark of Western economic-political theology to identify autonomy and sovereignty with the relation of transcendence to immanence, and so to 'capture' ethics in the very process that manages the contingency produced in the 'relation', just as it 'captures' the indeterminacy and freedom of what Agamben calls the infinite 'forms of life' of the linguistic animal in the distinction between *zoe* and *bios*. If Agamben shows the capture of human inoperability in the trap of a tradition that combines the opposed strands of Greek philosophical metaphysics with the Stoic Logos – which 'structures' both the dualism *zoe/bios* (and *dunamis/energeia*), and Christian/post-Christian political theology – it can be argued, in the same tradition and by the same token, that Levinas' Face, and his 'Otherwise than being/non-being' were captured in the secularised postulates of the non-being that is the relation of the logos of God-cum-Sovereign, who consists of the relation of His different hypostases, and that of His incarnated Son, Jesus-the-*oikonomos*-cum-self-government, who manages the contingency that is produced in this 'relation'. By analogy it can be said that in secular Western liberal thought, individual and collective autonomy defines the 'human' and the commonwealth, and emerges in the 'relation' and distinction of 'negative' and 'positive' freedom. Thus, autonomy is a procedural principle, and not an ontological or substantive feature of the subject: it delimits the 'necessary' condition for the enactment of the ethics of freedom. Likewise, 'in the relationship between ruler and ruled, sovereignty belongs to neither but to the relationship itself'.[61]

8

Deeds without Words

8.1

One thing we have been careful to always keep in mind over the preceding pages is the blindness that is the price to be paid in exchange for the prowess of applying to matters social a scientific method, carried by the implicit infallibility of its objectivist and intellectual claims. Our Lacanians also tell us that we are even relieved or happy to pay it. Surely, but be this as it may, the point is that the intellectual or objectivist understanding of major social phenomena has flawed and compromised our sense-making potential. Too much of the social world, including issues of origin, identity, certainty, love, is written in an affective grammar and vocabulary, not in an intellectual one. Religions, we have argued, do satisfy this exigency of overflowing meaning, since identification with its images and participation in ritual acts by themselves construct and maintain the sense of the world in accordance with a holy, not a conceptual sense. This is why, although our age is defined by declining religiosity in the sense of belief and far more, participation in scientific acts of observation and analysis of the world in terms of scientific epistemology, the stuff of particular religious 'cultures' – postulates and cosmological axioms embedded in images, rituals and formulaic imaginations – continue to be desired or repressed as objects of 'blind' trust or mistrust. We have already mentioned a number of legal cases regarding the presence of the cross in Italian schools, in which the European Court of Human Rights (ECtHR) trusts as a symbol of universal values, as opposed to minarets in Switzerland or the burqa in France, which the ECtHR sees as active symbols of a tribal religion. Critics see in these decisions the validation, or influence, of Carl Schmitt's claim, in *The Concept of the Political* that the unity of a people – in this case the people of 'Europe' – derives from a decision about friends and enemies based upon a presumed substantial sameness and equality between the members of a polity.[1] As Hans Kelsen noted, however, tongue-in-cheek, it 'is more than doubtful whether the members of a polity can identify any set of qualities, moral or otherwise, which univocally and uncontroversially defines them as a political unity'.[2] Like Kelsen, we do not believe that such substantive, inert qualities exist. Yet things like crosses and minarets do exist, as do mental images of the world; for example, in Christianity, the image of the world as humanity's common household, resulting from creation plus redemption and given to the care of its human managers for the benefit of its human dwellers; or, in Islamic cultures, the image of two rival households – one of peace and submission to God's law (Arabic: *dar as-salaam*) and the other of war and insubordination (Arabic: *dar-al-harb*).

Likewise, there are religious, or religiously inflected, rituals with a long history that have survived multiple disenchantments, and whose entire gamut of widely varied conceptual meaning discharges the same function as before: endowing their participants with an inter-subjective, but a proximate and group-preferential 'clannish' sense of certainty and order that alleviates the experience of disorder that comes with inevitable, constant changes; changes that, in human, especially religious or political, history are never integral, but always: (1) largely 'collateral', and (2) multigenerational. In Byzantium, for example, the Christian Roman emperor passed from being acclaimed as *dominus* to being acclaimed as God's *oikonomos*; and yet neither this Christian rendering of imperial power as 'precarious', nor the presence of popular assemblies, makes a 'republic' of Byzantium;[3] for, whenever people meet, as they did in Byzantium but also in our day, under the condition that, short of disrupting the civic peace, they must acclaim a sovereign who guarantees their unity and common purpose, then, politically speaking, this has more to do with theology than with Athenian-style democratic deliberation, where participation and disagreement was of itself the highest value. Agamben shows the further transformation of acclamation in occidental political modernity even in relation to participating in modern 'consensus making' procedures which, apart from their variable conceptual content, are structurally analogous to mediaeval doxological/acclamatory rituals. Athenian-style democratic deliberation is by no means a synonym of contemporary 'public opinion'.

Today, we realise that much of professional politics and semi-professional activism constitute a (mass-media mediated) show bereft of actual capacity to keep promises; yet, for some of us more than for others, this is a show that 'must go on' fundamentally, we have argued, because some of us are motivated to identify with, or participate in, such icons and rituals as elections or protest movements, notwithstanding that, intellectually, we find them to be 'empty;' some of us, therefore, are comforted by performatively validating/certifying as a 'true social fact' the conjoined 'relations' of 'constituent/constituted power', of democracy and the rule of law, of revolution and constitutional settlement, namely the pillars of occidental political and legal identity throughout the past millennium. That some of us do this even as we realise that administrative rationalities prevail over both legal and political ones may be explicable for no other reason than that, without these procedures or liturgies, we would feel 'ideologically' naked before the reality of contingent change at this stage of globalisation – 'stripped', as it were, of our Christian theologico-political constitutional imagination. Our reward is to see our imaginary sense of certainty and trust pampered despite hard times, or in certain cases even our self-awarded honour of being the vanguard of political and legal modernity 'still in charge', acting out a moral duty to raise politics or the law on to a sovereign pedestal. The price we pay for this is a double one. First, we remain blind to the fact that what remains of the triadic conception that constituted the Western human – *zoon politikon, homo juridicus* and *homo economicus* – by now belongs, mostly, to the last one; for the Trinitarian Christian God, who had held this triad open, is now missing to most of 'us' Westerners (while it is questionable whether it has ever been alive to any subject of a non-Western culture). Second, we distinguish ourselves as the 'West', the privileged and parochial inheritors of a political theology from which sprang – effectively if unspectacularly and certainly unintentionally and largely without even being noticed – what today constitutes the de facto global Western legacy, at once for better and for worse: a functionally differentiated globalising society based on choice and management.

If indeed human 'bare life' is never quite bare or 'naked' as long as it avails itself of language and consciousness – if, in other words, our ideologies always correlate to a stage of adapting ourselves to core unfalsifiable, unquestionable 'sacred postulates' – then, consequently, there is little doubt that Reason – whether 'classical' Athenian, mediaeval and Franciscan, modern and enlightened, or post-modern, or marked by the 'return of the religious' – is burdened by a modicum of ideological imagination. With regard to their affective identification with a world, or more recently a 'Europe', that is committed to the militant pursuit of Universalist equality, legal as well as political, the writers of the Enlightenment, still influential today, appear to have identified performatively ('icon-omically' and 'experientially') with metaphysical postulates that they would conceptually reject and are embedded in icons and rituals that the Greeks and the Romans – at least pre-Constantine – ignored; one good candidate for such an icon would be a recognition of the cross as a sign of both failure and glory, one by means of the other. In the very gesture of disavowing the tradition that, for millennia, has been affectively seducing the Western subject through its symbols (starting from the cross, the symbol of universal salvation through martyrdom and resurrection) and rituals (e.g. those that mark the Pentecostal miracle, which allows the 'Good News' to be known equally by all), the thinkers of the Enlightenment took up this very tradition while carefully travestying it. In diverse versions, this has been trumpeted by a handful of twentieth-century authors, yet it is still usually forgotten or pushed aside, simply because people succeed so well in persuading themselves, or each other, that conceptual meaning is 'independent' of ideology, fantasy and affect – separated by some safe 'epistemological' barrier, or/and guaranteed by the sheer fees of 'top-ranking' universities. In fact, the 'boundary' between knowledge and the affective today is largely in the same state as it was between intellect and Will in mediaeval theology: an open building site. 'Theology', to be sure, has ever played and still plays a lead role.

Kant and Hegel understood Socrates' reasons for critique; but what has been far more decisive is their very un-Socratic, even un-Platonic, identification with the uniquely Christian Western duty to announce to 'the world' some 'Good News', to evangelise. According to this secular instalment of evangelism, universal morality can be found in both guises: in the categorical imperative and its exercise, but also in speculation about the necessary next step required by the 'historical process'. Common to both is the Western confidence that the Christian/post-Christian meta-religion still holds true, indeed is truer than ever: the determinable yet universal Reason underlying it could not (in the past), but can now (in the present) be manifested, having 'outgrown' its religious 'cloak' and shackles, such as faith, imagery, liturgy. The point is, however, that rather than to Reason 'itself', these world-mobilising claims refer to a particular tradition: that of Western Christianity/post-Christianism, a tradition that not everyone on this planet grew into (and many of those who succeeded in doing so, did so only as a result of violence that destroyed or marginalised gods other than Paul's Jesus). This prompts us to ask whether we have not reached the point at which Western thinking would be best advised to clarify its specific relationship to universalism. Whence the need of statements to/about all, when talking to/about someone or some group of people in particular? Is it just in order to underscore the overriding importance or urgency of what is being said? Or is it in order to prevent anyone else taking up the Universalist stance? Is it not the case that the universal problems of humans have always only been experienced in particular ways? And is not, in particular, everyone who has grown up and been schooled within the globally privileged Western framework unjustly enriched by an advantage, both competitive and affective, in conceiving and communicating the message of universality? Does not the non-European, in order to receive – in equality – the European-cum-universal message, first have to repress the iconomic and experiential meaning of her particular tradition? Is the minimal price in suffering, cognitive dissonance – so well described in Derrida's *Circumfessions* (1999), where we read of his family saying 'baptism' instead of 'bar mitzvah' and 'communion' instead of 'circumcision' – not already too much for anyone to be required to pay it? And what is gained by the Westerner in continuing to carry this privileging proximity to the Christian theo-political tradition while carefully silencing this 'burden' (to call it with its Kipling-ian justifying name) – except perhaps a secularising confirmation of this inequality of opportunities? Would the point not rather be to own up to the inadmissible and to spell out without reserve and condescendence that which cannot be justified?

Turning to current theories of legal or/and political constitutionalism, which their authors want to be 'scientific', the fundamental questions are barely different. Constitutionalists have to answer for their presupposition that sovereignty exists, or 'must' at least be postulated. Also, it might be asked in this context, is it really sufficient to simply talk of 'constitutional paradoxes'?[4] Is the more pressing question not how the institutional addressees of these paradoxes cope with the resulting uncertainty? Whereas, venturing to make a particular sacred order 'last', religious liturgies as well as post-religious 'empty rituals' give rise to social bonds both infallibly and without difficulty, scientific social theories can be spectacularly insightful, and, even so (or rather because of this), they fail to correspond to the desperate or, in any case impatient, need for the subject, placed on whatever side of the distinction, to be met with uplifting promises. Systems theory might offer by far the best example here, but, more generally, it is to be expected that, for every hundred insightful social theories, there will be at best only one or two very popular ones whose success will arguably be owed not to their insight or explanatory power regarding what is happening now but, rather, to the populist choice of meanings, familiar and community-related, iconic and (either explicitly or implicitly) experiential, that are selectively invoked and played out. It is their art of satisfying identities and giving rise to 'group formation', their preference for proximity underlying these meanings, not their instructiveness, that provide them with a society-wide and media-fostered echo. The 'show' of politics plus law 'must go on' for those enamoured with it, for the audience that identifies with the drama's characters; for those who don't appreciate it, the 'show' is unidentifiable – not unlike what occurs in the theatre of the absurd. In dealing with the crisis of legitimacy in the public sphere Jürgen Habermas proved able to analyse connections of this kind, but less so in his communicative-ethical writing where he neglects to enquire after how only some cope with the resulting uncertainty (cf. on this, Agamben's view of consensuality as functionally equivalent to early and mediaeval Christian acclamation). Žižek, at a different level, might confront us with a similar issue here, one that has less to do with his always brilliant insights than with his performative capacity of producing in his followers – notably in the West – a feeling of comradeship and solidaristic agency. What makes this thinker stand out from the crowd is his ability to take up a topic that is usually dealt with by some often nameless professional, politician, judge, or teacher, and repoliticise it in his own way. It is true that the use of this 'technique' might not be located too far from the 'charismatic professors' accused of dishonesty in Max Weber's famous *Science as a Vocation*. But Weber's comments were, after all, carried by a campaign of conserving, even boosting, the competences of the university, which, for him, was perhaps the institution or at least one of the two institutions (*ex aequo* with those of political life), that deserved to be helped, cared for, defended in the midst of the German rubble after the First World War; before applying Weber's standards to those of the post-Bologna European University of our times, some relevant calibration would impose itself. What needs to be said, however, is that even if the 'charismatic professors', lambasted by Weber, prove able, using their arsenal of charismatic comradeship, to sustain the hope of resurrecting democracy or the rule of law, they prove wanting in another respect, not being charismatic enough to satisfy the insatiable need for religious consolation in a post-religious world that is common both to their publics and those who have never heard and will never hear of them. By contrast it is this need that the openly liturgical traditions of religions, properly speaking, have far more means, routines and experience to deal with. This is the context into which we need to evaluate the 'post-secular turn'; e.g. the previously discussed cunning invocation, by evangelists of the 'event' of 'revolution', such as Žižek and Badiou, of the iconic figure of Saint Paul, the protagonist of the sudden 'Damascene conversion' story; or Habermas' much more gradual admission that traditional religion does have, after all, a place in public deliberation.[5] And this is also, we would like to suggest, why Agamben describes the Western theo-political tradition as still taking a dominant place, even today within the space of a disenchanted world – so that, for instance, most of us performatively embrace the traditional formulas that structure the 'relation' of religion to logos and of politics/law to *oikonomia* in binary terms, quite some time since these binaries have been conceptually discredited.

<h2 style="text-align:center">8.2</h2>

Christianism, as a religion and as the economic-political theology of glory that colonises and structures public space, has fallen victim, first, to the negative political theology enshrined in the manifold arguments and suggestions of theological *oikonomia* or management offered by the Eastern Church Fathers (second to sixth century CE); and second, half a millennium later, to the division and the ensuing juridification of the Occidental Church, which – programmed by the legal-revolutionary popes from the eleventh century onward – lasted throughout the Western Christian (Holy Roman) Empire and up to the sovereign states of early modernity.[6] From the glorious cult of an exhilaratingly generous creator, the Western Christian religion has turned into an instructive, action-guiding, administration-enabling art of coming to grips, by means of truth and power, with an ever more threatening limitedness of governability. Max Weber was right in theologising economy, but less so in all but discarding from his scope Byzantium, the long Middle Ages, and especially the theologian-economists of the first millennium who economised theology. Considering the deep roots of Christian economic theology and the Westernisation of the world, it is highly plausible that the 'human environment' (the domain of sense as identity and consciousness) with which globalised impersonal social systems have to cope (as analysed, if only sociologically, by social systems theory) is unduly crowded by the European, Christian and post-Christian consciousness and imagination that centre on glorious immortal sovereignty coupled with *oikonomia*. In this regard we have noted attempts to disinherit the European tradition,[7] while noticing that one should not overlook the limits of this laudable enterprise. Taking up again the suggestion that sense, at the level of human consciousness, far from being concerned exclusively with the actuality of what is happening now (or with the landscape of potential risks and hopes to which it gives rise), is, in addition to being a medium of communication and also a totem or a monument of identity (even and in particular if it is a ruined monument) the project of disinheriting tradition appears a double-edged knife, at least as long as social systems must operate in a human, consciousness-related, psychically motivated environment; it is one thing to unsubscribe from a tradition claiming undue universal rank, another thing to unsubscribe from any tradition excluding right away any claim that pretenders to some different inheritance might have about how to fill the void.

There are of course many 'alternative' candidates essentially vying to occupy – but not displace – the Eurocentric/ Universalist place/self: e.g. the new, modern religions/ no-longer-religions of post-Jewish religious Zionism or post-Islamic fundamentalist Islamism. There are also those who, considering that humanity persists in its subjection to consciousness, pin their hopes to the development of a new universal consciousness; one, for instance, based on the syncretistic and hybrid identities churned out by the hybrid identity-manufacturing processes of 'multiculturalism'. Yet insofar as the formation of hybrid identities is happening here and now, it is a phenomenon that belongs to society, social evolution and the communication (and commodity exchanges) that sustain them – and not to the human environment where psychic systems are, on the contrary, concerned with continuity, inheritance and identity. This observation puts the problems of failing integration and multiculturalism in a new light: hybrid identities are indeed born and used all the time; the burkini-wearing beach-goer provides an adequate example here (while its prohibition on French beaches provides an even more striking one of the helplessness of the *bon sens républicain*); the way in which these emerging identities are managed, however – in fact anarchically, yet officially 'under the auspices' of the sovereign state of law – satisfies in particular the psychic needs of the Christian/ post-Christian European subject; for the latter avails of (and is unlikely to give up) a long tradition of acclaiming mastery and sovereignty while being subjected to the state of lawlessness, or anomia, which is the core of any regime of *oikonomia*, and in which exceptions-to-the-rule can increase to the point of taking up the function of the rule.

Let us state it differently: Sense as 'consciousness' is both conceptual and affective. The conceptual components of the sense of limited-yet-sovereign government according to Western, Christian/post-Christian imagination – whereby legally or politically defined sovereignty are acclaimed even as they prove both vacuous and continuously overridden by managerial necessities – are by now globalised almost evenly (so that, for example, between England and Greece and between Egypt and Turkey sovereignty enjoys much the same infatuation, be it in the form of popular power, party power, police power, military power, etc.) However, the affective binding of the global subject to this paradigm is far from being assured. The cross, despite its putative status as a 'passive symbol' (sic!) of universal values, remains an object of love for the Christian and post-Christian subject and so does its embedded message: triumph coincides with impotence; the embrace of absolute principles and fundamental rules must coexist with consensual discourses and pragmatic discounts. Agamben shows how, in the Western imagination, the simultaneous loud acclamation of the imaginary God-cum-sovereign's glorious supreme power and the tolerance of the effective dismantling of the ruler's legitimacy, first, and exposure of his impotence, second, are two sides of a coin. This coin, in circulation in the West for millennia, has been in use for a considerably shorter time elsewhere. The revenge, or 'unfriendly takeover', taken by the managemental vice-master, or *major domus*, against the ruler, is structurally programmed in this paradigm – it is emphatically 'in the nature of the beast'. But what about those for whom the cross commands no love (or even commands hatred, as for example, a symbol of the crusades)? When, for example, a Syrian Muslim refugee seeks refuge in Europe on the basis of his intellectual knowledge that people of this continent swear by their allegiance to universal human rights (for 'there is no Jew or gentile', nor Christian or Muslim), but is turned away (e.g. forcibly sent back to a third country like Turkey, with which EU leaders reached a deal that defies the Geneva Convention), it is unlikely that s/he will not feel anger at the perceived European 'hypocrisy'. For in Islam's *dar-as-salaam* (house of peace, i.e. the realm of Allah's believers) universal religious rules and principles must always be defended – to the point of death – not too differently from those early Christian martyrs, who died before Christianity's economic theology was in place.

It is perhaps not wise, we submit, in light of the foregoing, to entirely disconnect the mode of operation of modern society's functionally differentiated systems from their Western Christian and European Christian background; impersonal communicative systems remain well adapted to procedural requirements, yet are powerless in terms of official (spectacular, imaginary) attributions of glorious hierarchical power. Have the polarising tendencies of the past few years not delivered lesson after lesson about the noisy, disruptive and indeed violent grasp of identitarian consciousness over silently and effectively self-regulating social systems? In this regard, enquiries into Trinitarian and Christological theology and its ruins, as the totem of the modern Western constitutional imagination (summed up by the great enthusiasm that attaches to revolutions and the scepticism that is directed at the subsequent constitutional settlements) have precious elements to contribute. They allow us a fresh look at: (1) the contemporary, almost directly *oikonomia*-governed, phase of the Western Christian missionary/'civilising' activity, which after having cast its worldwide action first under the *officium* of religious mission, then as governmental (political, economic, civilisational) colonialism, is finally conquering the world under the flag of management; (2) the various ways in which the contemporary humiliation of state power by management is experienced unevenly, with European consciousness proving more adept at handling the resulting performative contradiction whereby one acclaims and embraces either liberal or socialist versions of democracy, while being constantly confronted with their poverty, even meaninglessness. The new leases of life achieved for the benefit of the occidental privilege of delivering planet-encompassing standards keep diminishing and become increasingly expensive, triggering movements and genuine counter-offensives that tend to de-globalise, relocalise and provincialise the Northern/Western and, most specifically, European con- tributions. These movements make clear that management has gone global faster than any of the far more recognis- able preceding Christian exportation goods.[8] Moreover, if we are right that those who highlight the emergence of fluid, hybrid identities and plastic materialities[9] ultimately invoke the arts of mastery through management, then, despite their apparent secularism, they also need to be understood as deeply anchored in Western Christian economic theology. It is difficult to appraise this at the level of its real impor- tance; Agamben, based on materials that go back to the first centuries of the transformation of this Hellenistic Jewish sect into a 'universal religion', finds most innovativeness in the economic element. In this regard we will probably go out on a limb in openly pointing out that non-Westerners who advocate liberal or socialist reinterpretations of non-Western traditions mostly do so by addressing the public in places where the cross – and its embedded message that dogmatism is combinable with flexibility – is unquestioned. Thence the question: is management the most solidly encrypted way of distributing the Christian message worldwide? Is the cross its earliest symbol?

If we look for an early episode in Western history that exemplifies the winning occidental combination of glorious, pre-Christian, Roman-style mastery over contingency together with a humble admission that contingency persists and needs management, remembering Constantine the Great can be of help. His genius was to be the first emperor who commissioned statues of himself not looking like a stern Roman soldier looking you menacingly in the eye but, rather gazing upwards to the heavens; Constantine's main legitimis- ing myth, preserved by his bishop and biographer Eusebius, was of a cross miraculously appearing in the sky bearing the inscription 'by this symbol you will conquer'. Now, religions, and most specifically what have been called – not for very long[10] or quite accurately[11]– monotheist religions, are barely prepared to share the world with non-believers' silence or irrelevant 'noise' over their distinctive innovations; and yet their persistent exposure to other religions and non-believers has provoked the build-up of modes of coexistence, ways of 'living with' the silence/noise of other religions. We understand modern, functionally differentiated, managerial- or business-as-usual-centred world society – in which the business of religion and of managing the religion/secular binary 'relationship' forms an important part – not as a post-religious formation but as a case of successful Christian latency. Now, if we take up once more the medium sense not only as an enabling device present in impersonal social system-constituting communications, but also within consciousness and individual or collective identities, then it pays to ask in more detail the question of how much the consciousness of the Christian latency behind and within the operations of modern society is a matter of genuine indifference – rather than, on the contrary, a question of denial and anxiety. On the one hand, civilisations lacking genealogical roots in the monotheistic 'tradition' – especially such Asian civilisations as are located, seen from the West, behind Huntingtonian 'clash'-civilisational borders – seem genuinely indifferent to the intricacies of Christian latency or zero degree, managing to fully accept it as part of the world as it is, and to include it without reserve in their routines. It can perhaps be assumed that within civilisations that are not rooted, consciously or unconsciously, in any form of Western Christian genealogy (or if they are, explicitly deny it), the religious dimension in the managemental use of power is covered within a lasting and reliable latency, perceived as a perfectly secular, hardcore mode of regulating the public domain, and nothing else. If so, one would have to conclude that the managerial model or blueprint is functionally enhanced by the absence of any genealogical relationship – even by the absence of 'identity'. The model is taken over as such, as part of the world, unburdened from any duty of self-justification, while the memory of its origin plays a facultative role comparable to the Christian or Christian-resembling wedding ceremony frequently chosen by non-Christian Japanese couples.

In the absence of an identitary or genealogical relationship, a consciousness-related investment is neither possible nor necessary: the systemic functioning of society can thus be understood as a matter of mere instrumentality. This may of course be overlaid with the imperatives of a non-Western cultural and especially religious system, even if – or rather, precisely because – it is unrelated to the one that has produced it. Buying ourselves, for the occasion, into a much-questioned yet still celebrated and inspiring theory,[12] we suggest that, if the presence of Protestant ethics had been a good thing for capitalism emerging; it is its absence that might turn out to be an even better thing for capitalism to continue. On the other hand, things are different for the non-Western inmates of the Western situation – typically subjects instituted in other monotheist religions but living in or under the direct influence of Western values. Occasionally, the split between modern society's impersonal and strictly event-based dimension and the second-order sense that it carries as a product of its genesis from the Western Christian tradition leaves its latency and shows. It then appears, however, from very different angles, according to the subject perspectives involved. The double investment of (1) the promise of public order ensuring the arts of governmentality or managementality, and (2) loyalty to an absolute, ethical calling to devote one's life to (e.g. political engagement, or even 'marching' towards progress) is revealed symptomatically by the tension between those who find it compelling to subscribe to the notion that the process of history as work-in-progress must be given the shape of a working-for-progress (even as the latter's meaningfulness is doubted), and those who don't.

In turn, Westerners are frequently surprised that some of their global neighbours do not seem to see value in the art of managing difference rather than conflict. What we note, apart from the theoretical vantage points of secular Western consciousness in debates on the so-called return of religion, 're-religioning',[13] political theology, new secularism and post-secularism, is the denial and anxiety appearing as soon as this split shows or is addressed, and how quickly it can turn into conflict in turn. Thus, while the 'business' generated by the religion/secular controversy (notably the security 'business') today feeds managerial activities over the globe, the religion–secular relationship acquires an 'identitarian' dimension for those placed at the extremes of the polarity – the Christian/post-Christian individual or collective, and population groups identifying themselves as its 'enemies' (i.e. Islamists).

Further, with or without 'enemies' for Western minds in

particular, the possibility that the West's developing secular modernity should be understood as a means to continue its religious history (a hypothesis after all that was put to use a century ago in Max Weber's work on capitalism), is today exceptionally anxiety-provoking. Non-Westerners, who candidly take this questionable secularity at face value, are freer to use it openly as a mere technical appliance, an instrumental device or 'dispositive'. Jihadists usually see no problem about considering the questionably secular as perfectly compatible with their most traditional and unreformed and least problematised religious or cultural institutions. This is not to say that globalised modernity and functional differentiation are endangered by disaffected carriers of identity more than at any time in the past – disaffection and other states of consciousness, whether in non-occidental or occidental subjects, even in the case of those inhabitants of the UK who revert to their national identity, having received few if any of the benefits of globalisation, are not carrying relevant information for social systems. The unique world system that consists of 'empire' on the one hand and its equally unique justification –'universalism' – on the other, continuously provides Westernised humankind with the tension, controversy and crisis that are required by the pursuit of management/ manageability. This entails that some of those deprived of 'relevance', inside and outside the geographical limits of the West, will, as a collateral consequence, be sidelined or 'wasted', akin to the backgammon pieces accumulated beside the board. This vulnerability, this possibility of being wasted, pushes the material towards the ideological. It is also generalised and tends to be present on all fronts. Islamist fundamentalists and religious Zionists 'waste' their endo-religious rivals successfully, on the implicit argument that only they, not their secular-contaminated antagonists, are modern enough to seek to play backgammon with a West that keeps distinguishing itself from the 'rest'.

8.3

By now, the grand occidental promise that a better world is possible – equally for all – by means of an appropriate art of interplay between, on the one hand, political sovereignty/constituting power/revolution and, on the other hand, legal sovereignty/constituted power/constitutional settlement, sounds as hollow as the throne of the god of Christian onto-theology appears to be after the god of revelation has been killed. Insofar as we still act as if this promise is valid, however, this hollowness inflates to an absurd dimension. If we allow ourselves to set aside the immense direct human cost of such murderous incidents as the attack on 14 July 2016 in Nice, France, we are confronted with the mass murder of people celebrating the storming of the Bastille at a time when there is no central power to storm, by a person who wanted an 'Islamic' state led by a 'Caliph' (who would bear much more similitude to a 'divine right' type of premodern European sovereign than a premodern Islamic Caliph). As the title of a play written with the goal of capturing this condition, resulting from the stalemate between the world-conquering and world-saving Western missions of old, and the current evidence of the helpless abandonment of humankind by a recoiling West and Europe, we would suggest: *Antigone waiting for Godot*. The disaffected Muslim Tunisian-French perpetrator could not appreciate such theatre of the absurd and wished violently to turn it into a tragedy with himself as protagonist. To be sure this attitude is held by many the world over and exploited and echoed by populists. Not even the price to be paid for overwriting Sophocles' name on Beckett's is one that can be equally or predictably shared.

The promise of progress in the direction of 'more' or of 'better', most brilliantly epitomised in the concept of surplus value, Marx's top conceptual creation, is clearly present in all political promises that can realistically aspire to be received as trustworthy; this is no less true of the right-wing suggestions favoured by Carl Schmitt than of those of Schmitt's liberal or left-wing opponents. Such promises constitute the daily bread of politics and remote control as a see-saw of escalation and de-escalation (with Schmitt and too many politicians of his time – again, by no means only those from the right-wing – firmly on the side of escalation). The point here is about time. Once all is said and done, when the ballot papers have been counted and the Brexit result jumps out of the boxes, we are left with the need to manage the resulting mess and ten-sions. Promises – the forms of utterance upon which repose the political game in its entirety – come complete with daring guesses about alternatives and future evolution; they are, in this sense, performative utterances. Sadly, they are, as a rule, performed before publics who, on account of their regrettably imperfect understanding of the theory of performative utterances, tend to mistake them for information, a mix-up that gives rise, on a daily basis, to quantities of painful misunderstandings that sculpt the capital and capitalism of our information society. We suggest in fact that this 'mistake' invokes a blind trust not in the content of the promise but in its form: in the game of promises, 'certainty' derives from promise making itself. For now, it suffices to say that the 'mistaking' of performative utterances for actual information is a not easily deciphered, yet as such it is an unmistakable sign of the identity of Christian/post-Christian culture. The 'bridged' distance between performativity and information, the surplus obtained by passing the first off for the second, in fact the cunning move of counter-distinguishing both, has been put to use through the long prehistory of the mass-mediatised, industrialised ways of relating to truth. Again, however, there is no escaping that the Christian/post-Christian subject has a particular way of relating to promises. In *Opus Dei: An Archaeology of Duty* (a follow-up to *The Kingdom and the Glory*, drawing on an extension of Nietzsche's genealogy of morals and a reworking of Heidegger's history of being, but most specifically a contribution to the study of liturgy and the secular/non-secular double life of duty/*officium*), Agamben continues his study of Western political structures begun in *Homo Sacer* by investigating the roots of the moral concept of duty in the theory and practice of Christian liturgy:

> [T]he liturgical mystery is not limited to representing the passion of Christ, but in representing it, it realises its effects so that one can say that the presence of Christ in the liturgy coincides with its effectiveness. But this implies . . . a transformation of ontology, in which substantiality and effectiveness will seem to be identified.[14]

The main legitimating feature of political promises, their official scenario, as it were, is based on centre-staging political will and decision; their aftermath, on the other hand, is in the evidence of 'after-sale product support', i.e. coping with the consequences, dealing with the resulting outcomes, or in short: management. That said, we are conscious of the fact that there is no point in thinking of a definitive weaning of political discourse from the promissory form. The promise needs to be recognised as the vitally required central spring of politics within the type of society in which we find ourselves. Sociologist Niklas Luhmann[15] has repeatedly pointed to the slightly inflationary slant of political discourse as being a distinctive feature of the politics that is possible and required within modern society. In our own low-key analytical terminology: political discourse thrives on a moderately exaggerated portrayal of its possibilities, successfully conveying the sense that the hopes it tries to give rise to will not be entirely frustrated (or in any case not now, at the moment of promising). The term 'modern' is of course itself engrossed with problems. Luhmann uses it to refer to the type of post-sovereign, horizontal or flat, functionally differentiated society that is marked by rapid historical temporality, which reflects the evolution of social structures in the industrialised northern and western parts of the world. There are many different, sometimes contradictory, current uses of the word 'modern'; academic language has no power to restrain, define or protect the conditions of use of its vocabulary; in addition, when we are looking into matters of the contemporary relationship of decisionism and managerialism, political theology and the multiple processes it agentifies, it is not just 'modernity' in the industrial/post-industrial sense that needs to be summoned. Although our question is clearly inseparable from the topic and name of society's modernity, we need to make sure that, with all respect, the reality we address does not entirely coincide with Luhmann's self-referentially understated (deflationary) sociological-theoretical level of analysis and use of the term. Indeed, we are, by dint of our own concern, far from giving exclusive attention to his main topic, the historical emergence of social systems or system–environment differentiation.

Instead, our inquiry has been placed in the culturalist/ normativist horizon, which alone could allow us to approach, albeit in a new perspective that tries to avoid some of the pitfalls and truisms of the hidden mono-story of Western Christianism/Western secularism – the pitfalls and truisms that have not always been avoided by dignified Western-patriotic studies of 'the West', or the creation of the West/East conflict. In order to achieve this, we had to commit ourselves to a somewhat daring step – that of weakening and even partly deconstructing the watertight borders separating the Western and more exactly the long and incomparably well-documented European past from its present ('modern') state, and of heeding the long-term legacies and connections, rather than to the passion for a firm separation between 'periods'. *Pace* certain pages in Foucault (admittedly in connection with topics, objects and interrogations of a very different type than ours), we would argue – paraphrasing Ockham – that discontinuities should not be unnecessarily multiplied.[16] We read the affluence of recent publications on Western/Northern secularism and its paradoxical but momentous effects,[17] especially upon eastern and/or southern parts of the world, as an indicator of a structural particularity that we understand as an anomaly in religious history, a coincidence of opposites between Christianism and Secularism, which has been for-mulated, in allegiance to Hegel and Weber, with the famously precise but terribly simplifying formula: 'Christianism is the religion of the way out of religion.' What was at stake for us here was how to determine the articulation that constitutes the identity of most of the bi-millennial Western Christian episode.

It is in relation to mundane management that we can begin to speak of a truly continuous Western tradition. The managemental or vice-master position, variously yet always blissfully transfigured (and cognitively obscured) by glori-ous mastery and/or decisionist promises, plays the lead role. The sovereign/decisionist approach, basing itself on authori-tarian premises of doubtful historical credibility, signals the presence of an un-dethroned, 'fatherly' mastery within the European political family novel.[18] It is this supposed mastery that Schmitt's followers, even and in particular those who define their own position as 'leftist plus psychoanalysis inspired', have taken up as a political ideal or transferential object. But mastery, no matter the terms in which it is con-strued, is among the victims of the history of the twentieth century; it cannot realise itself otherwise than in the form of a farcical repetition, or perhaps less amusingly as the afterlife of a deceased and haunting original. The phenomenon of misguided nostalgia, giving rise to a series of both mythologised and radicalised remakes, has accompanied the evolution of modern society throughout as its anti-modernist twin; it is at work already in sixteenth/seventeenth-century absolutism (a secularising remake of the mediaeval doctrine of *potentia absoluta dei* in which the sovereign 'replaces' God) and again in twentieth-century fascism. It has always been a paradoxical mastery that is resurrected, a mysterious phoenix mastery reborn from ashes, or a seed that only springs after it dies, to refer to the already quoted pericope from Paul's First Epistle to the Corinthians. In this regard the current post-Lacanian investment in the notion of the 'need' for the subject to 'have a master' is, with all due respect, not so different from the equally often asserted and older 'need' for the political community to have a Leviathan, despite the difference of sophistication that distinguishes these two 'uncertainty absorption devices' (in social system theory lingo). Needless to point out in so many words that we are talking about the most amazingly telling case of epigenesis; sculpting its God as a sovereign, later its sovereign as a god, the Western history of political theology has indeed turned a page, and the phantasy of mastery – following certain Schmitt-cognoscenti, the phantasy especially of German male mastery – has suffered a serious setback in trust. This, however, opens the door to noting the epigenetic success history of the very motive of 'turning a page' – pointing back to the origins of this motive, which are clearly religious and neo-testamentary: the incarnation of the Lord: Christianity, or the turning of a page within the fundamental constitution of Judaism. Like Jesus with respect to the religion of the Pharisees, modernity has circulated the claim that it amounts to the opening of a totally separate and radically different 'new' time (or after-time), the time of the overcoming of the era of theology, giving way to an unending and humanity-encompassing process–progress – the process of the inclusion of all humankind within the history of Christian post-Christian progress.

Whether we are with, against, or beyond Schmitt, at stake is an addictive, happy-ending-bound progress narrative.

Work-in-progress is cast as work for progress. In order to gauge the present capacities to continue to trust in this narrative structure – in and beyond the geographical West – it is easy to identify it as the occidental, be it Catholic or Protestant, version of this narrative in which we find proudly centre-staged the glorious but invisible mastery and its power-wielding vice-master's decision. We did not need to look too far away from Western Europe to find elements that relativise the trust in this narrative; in Eastern Christianism, the 'happy ending' remains a secret part of an explicitly anarchic divine *oikonomia*, in which humans play a non-decisive role. This non-decisive human role underlies all Byzantine political history; it was dispensation from the law, not legislation. If anything, it was the self-restraint of the decision-making power-holder, rather than the use of the means of power used in view of goals, that was comparable to the basic axiom of sovereignty: the sovereign *placet* wielded without any duty of accompanying it with justifications or reasons.

The ruins of mediaeval/late mediaeval occidental political theology, as the totem of Western consciousness, continue to add their fictional, identity-enhancing, continuity-promising, glorious surplus sense to the purely effective, non-fictional, present-related sense offered us by systems theory, which deliberately limits itself to impersonal management and self-management – to the merely endless, inglorious, *oikonomical* loop of 'coping', 'dealing', 'communicating'. The discovery of a non-secular layer among the conditions of society's self-continuation, indispensable to the resilient subjective trust in this *oikonomia* (beyond the merely functional trust to which Luhmann has devoted a sociological study[19]), locates the unseen role of Christian imagination among reproduction that is often understood as exclusively and intrinsically secular.[20]

We are aware that suggestions of the sort we have made are sometimes considered as philological niceties, if not as 'merely academic'. This view overlooks an entire field of study: and one of some importance in terms of social evolution and strategy. We would refer to this as to the science of microphysics, which has come out of secular Western Christianism. Secular Western Christianity has produced, not only an archaeology of ruins, but also an art or procedure turning on the possibility of persistence under negation, also called 'zero degree'. In a dense treatise at once Hegelian and post-Hegelian, dispersed among several studies, Agamben starts by drawing an inventory of existing ventures relating to the zero degree. After epitomising, in *The Time that Remains*, the Pauline theme of deactivation and *désoeuvrement*, as well as the biblical theme of the Sabbath (both of which were to be given an increasing role in his subsequent work), he confronts, referring to linguistic, philosophical, historical inquiries, the issue of an absence that nonetheless lends itself, under given structural and contextual conditions, to being understood as a presence – a 'zero presence'. This zero presence, or zero degree, is, in our view, second to none as an enlightening concept that triggers understanding in this or perhaps any author in recent years. Agamben starts by developing said 'zero presence' in reference to Hegel's Aufhebung, Jakobson's and Trubetzkoy's phonological zero value, and Derrida's ontology of the trace. But further forms can be added *ad libitum*, e.g. in relation to the enterprise of modern law, such as Hart's secondary rules or Kelsen's Grundnorm; both of these act exactly as 'zero degrees', mere triggering devices, enabling the pyramid-shaped edifice of the normative order to gain (or rather conserve) its own 'integrity and dignity', which allows for their make-belief purchase and relevance over actual cases. In fact, legal positivism at large can be taken to act as Western law's function-enabling 'zero degree'; generally, notions like 'positivity' or 'validity' gain from being understood as paradigmatic 'zero degrees' or default regimes of law, insofar as they epitomise an absence, and sanction it as a condition for earlier created, yet still extant, law to extend its lease of validity. One needs to be conscious of the fact that, as soon as any such *arche*, model or principle is postulated within the real-time evolutionary experiments of history, a new burden arises: the burden of looking after the continuation of the initial *arche* in spite of its all-too-evident and embarrassing shortcomings. This, in a sense, is precisely how the problem of management, or, to use Heidegger's word, of care, besieges legal theorists. For Christian believers, of course, it is also the problem of the Church: let us only think of the excommunicated French dissident priest and scholar Alfred Loisy, saying, 'Christ has announced the Kingdom: what has come is the Church'. It brilliantly epitomises intra-religious epigenesis, or institutionalisation as the zero degree of a message. On a closer look, the potential that Loisy has aimed at can extend from the Christian Gospel to any and every religious and political (and so on) master-word that will trigger its social post-history. Even the straightest project of mastery exposes itself to the need to manage the challenges it introduces in order to grapple with the destabilising consequences of its own 'being-thrown-into-the-world', of its own 'being-in-the-world' (to use Heideggerian terminology here as shorthand). What we have in mind can be rendered by the image of a ship that capsizes as a result of the back-flow of its own waves (admittedly, a less optimistic example of 'feed-back' than those suggested by the pioneering cyberneticists[21]). Each new item, 'news', 'finding', 'discovery', etc., in order to transform the punctual event that it is into a lasting, referable and sustainable 'innovation', needs to develop a 'zero degree' in order to close its loop and remain there, unbothered by the silence of the rest of the world. In other words, if an invented object encounters silence, no reply, zero reply, then, in order to perdure, it must find in itself 'a way to live with that'.

8.4

Humans are a species that can only live in terms of meanings they fabricate for themselves in a world devoid of intrinsic meaning but subject to physical law. Meaning, moreover, is not only conceptual but also affective: icon-omic and experiential.[22] Indeed, for the social anthropologist trying to understand the institution of a human subject, the latter two are more fundamental than the conceptual kind. Taking these seriously leads us to yet another questionable point in the widespread ideas that are, if in a sublimated form, still identifiable in the arguments of Gauchet and Nancy, for whom the fact that the great religions unleashed critique remains 'paradoxical'. To the individual speaking animal, which depends on its parents longer than any other, meaning is not only a question of its production and critique but also of its performative transmission and reproduction: in every historical social order we find certain ideas that are incompatible with a negation or a zero, ideas often postulated long ago by ancestors who are 'sanctified' in the sense that they are performatively validated as true, or as irreversible social facts, even if they have no material significata, and they are therefore retained for purposes of non-critical, blind identification of/with a group or population: the phrase 'In God we trust', featuring on the US currency, indicates that in the US, like in other 'associations', inter-subjective trust can strictly speaking never be supposed; it remains conditional. Derrida thus spoke of the spectre of God undersigning the US declaration of independence insofar as its human signatories could not bring themselves to claim to act on the authority of the people they represented (as Arendt understood and lamented). Why? Because in our occidental legal and political imagination, as summarised by Hobbes, a people only comes into existence by the very act of declaring its sovereignty, whereas before it is nothing but 'a mob'. As is well known, this raises a famous contradiction, which, it seems, only the Christian/post-Christian subject has the means to fully appreciate. Yet in order to explain what divides us into the 'West' and 'the rest', should the correctly formulated question not be a slightly different one? Such as, is it possible that meanings fabricated in one generation are conceptually modified, even abandoned and yet performatively reproduced by a subsequent generation? We see, guided by the doctrine of the zero degree, especially in its application to 'secularisation', that it is perfectly possible for a political theology, in this case the occidental one, to persist after the belief in the conceptual truth of its parent religion has declined. Arguably, the signs of theological flourishing are even more favourable in periods of religious understatement, or decline. If ever more modern individuals turn away from the fabrications of our ancestors concerning our 'dependence' on non-human and super-natural gods, this emphatically does not rule out the possibility, even our freedom, to performatively validate such dependence, despite our 'constative' or simply declarative rejections.

Accordingly, when we ask whether religion still shapes our legal and political imagination, it is not enough to ask the question of belief, or even less, of faith. From this perspective, religion is not only, as it was for Marx, a manifestation of the 'drive not to know' (for Marx, creating gods equates creating the fiction of resolving real contradictions without actually resolving them). One might also say that religion functions as an enabler of consensus, and in particular as a means of alleviating the two consensus-endangering evils associated with language, the lie of course, but also the alternative, establishing the conditions of blind trust among participants. It is, we suggest, the indisputable key feature of Western religion that it economises idealism versus pragmatism, as utopia versus war binaries by turning their 'relation' into a loop or unending see-saw. The usual polemic between supporters of legal and those of political sovereignty can be examined from this perspective as well as their continuing purchase despite the emergence of systems theory-informed 'societal constitutionalism',[23] which focuses on contemporary, post-sovereignty governance without sovereign government, by an oligopoly of function systems; the latter owe, not their legitimacy (which for systemists is an internal problem of the political system), but the conditions of continuing each in its business, not to such overriding idealisations or generalisations as represented by the reference to legality (the rule of law, democracy, etc.) but to the continuous stream of their respective 'business' itself – to their 'communications', in Luhmann's understanding of this word. *Pace* many systems theorists today, we have suggested that it would be quite wrong to consider that humans, as 'psychic systems', are today condemned to be increasingly displaced and replaced by social systems,[24] in such a way that human involvement with matters of conscience becomes increasingly irrelevant. Closer to Luhmann's own discipline of non-totalisation, we have suggested that impersonal systems also operate in the environment of human sense-as-consciousness, where imaginary origins and identity do matter. What is difficult to deny is that such conscience-internal, and thus less conceptual and more affective sense, is relatively immune to critique. Hence the continuing purchase of such comprehensive 'fantasies' or ideologies as those postulating subjectively absolute, yet socially limited, social world-making power in theories that centre on either normative sovereignty or political supremacy. Insofar as both normative and political accounts presuppose an absolute, yet limited, power of self-constitution, they cannot entirely make good on their claims by logic alone.

We therefore suggest, as far as the speaking beings and their state of coexistence is concerned, that a long Western tradition of rationality has been entrusted to a shaky, non-rational, programmatic postulate: progress! Millennial hopes that matters of law or politics could, or will one day be built, solely upon objective knowledge and upon the safe immanence that springs from it, can no longer be endorsed except by means of such blind trust in the face of constant disappointment that progress brings with it a whole range of unintended consequences, and produces increasing amounts of human and non-human waste, all requiring more management, again in the name of progress. Studies in political theology contribute in rendering the discreet deficiency of Universalist programmes a little less discreet. They used to be seen as not fully secularised or 'deficiently immanent'; but this worked within a conception of power that belonged to a specifically occidental theosophical tradition based on the great achievement of mediaeval natural theology as a makeshift mediation meant to fuse transcendence and immanence. Indeed the most unsuspiciously secular distinctions, such as between power and law, or between the political and the purely legal understanding of state power (a power that would otherwise be limitless, absolute in essence and that is precisely therefore in need of being circumscribed in form), have been revealed, over the past three or four decades, as being plugged within a humanity-encompassing framework allowing for a fake 'civil war' between Huntingtonian and counter-Huntingtonian posturers – where, in reality, there is much more in common between today's populism on the right and the left, as well as between neo-nationalists and neo-globalists; militating in the name of a progress-entrusted sovereign power they jointly and unintentionally bring about, mostly a mess that needs swift management as well as extended states of emergency, in France, and even more so in Turkey. And as always, there is no need to add: someone pays.

A Western institutional and semantic hegemony has turned out to have been a global work of art – an 'art of governing', to use Foucault's uncannily fitting expression (although in his work it is applied, deliberately, only to Western history). The older distinction between God's *potentia absoluta* and His *potentia ordinata* – the distinction between what God can do if He forgets Himself, letting Himself become an instantiation of capricious sovereignty, and what He will do, being the ordered and self-disciplined God, the reliable and worthy subject in which our generation of secular Hegelians believes no less than their church-going ancestors did – turns out to have been an artful device that can in no way be taken for granted, as part of the furniture of humankind at large.

One wonders how it is that such binaries, such *distinguos*, if covered in appropriately fashionable and changing garb, still gain their authors, and the populist pastoralists who gloss them draw more devotional love than their exegetical power would in fact warrant. The metaphysical presuppositions underlying these distinctions are no longer with us and can barely be expected to revive; in this connection, systems theory is right to look past agency and sovereignty when explaining the fragmentary and impersonal constitution of contemporary society, deprived as it is of any preordained absolute power, any pre-established capacity to guarantee the conditions of its own continuation. This, however, cannot sideline or substitute the other dimension of sense-making and sense, that of slow-processed consciousness, as opposed to fast-breeding communication. Luhmann was always careful to resist this temptation: witness the role he attributes to the system/environment boundary (his real protagonist, far ahead of the system) and his unending musings on the equally unending divorce between consciousness and communications. Other observers of contemporary society, including some systems theorists, do not always resist the notion that, sooner or later, communication will 'win' against consciousness. In matters of tempo and half-life, the human psyche is conservative and erratic; it has little in common with the positivism-enhanced steady and statistical pace of communications enabling further communications. As a consequence, it has remained far closer to the ontology-centred framework, sticking to its landscape, temporality, flows, obstacles and attractors. This world of human consciousness and unconsciousness which, having lost its confidence that whatever happens in the visible, shared social world is under some control, has in no way disappeared, but continues its own evolutionary journey, accompanying the social evolution, even if it faces ever more difficulties in . . . communicating. Thus, a comprehensive metaphysical imagination, or fantasy, seems perfectly able to survive its deconstruction, uniting its spoils and fragments, just like the broken broomsticks in *The Sorcerer's Apprentice*; in fact, it can even spread and propel to ever more powerful, efficient, deleterious and uncheckable 'actions' which, instead of the intended outcome, make a mess that needs ever more management, housekeeping and side-lining of waste. Arguably, the notion that modern society is sustainable as a process of continuous differentiation *à la* Luhmann converts the tale of sorcery and collateral doom into a positively assumed programme, justified at best on the basis that we lack any equivalent of the order-loving and powerful master-sorcerer to come back at the end of the tale to put everything back as it was before the disaster-producing experiment; the apprentice and his broomsticks must thus find sustainable ways on their own, if not otherwise – and it is difficult to see how otherwise – then by means of even further social differentiation. In this sense, two perspectives need to be neatly distinguished – that of potentially action-guiding instructions, and that of well-founded fears. It is certainly a well-founded fear (and also a legitimate one, to the extent that fears can or need be legitimate), to think, with Jürgen Habermas, that human behaviour is motivated by subjective mental states.[25] Equally, Martin Loughlin is right to fear that legal constitutionalism may be but a fantasy legitimating extensive government;[26] so is Wendy Brown,[27] who identifies in contemporary democracy theory a continuous denial, in the form of 'averting our eyes' from forces that are immune to democratic scrutiny.

Those who today wish/vow/promise to repoliticise or conversely to re-juridify the fragmented social life-world that results from the modernity of functional differentiation – the modernity that Christianism, as an art of governing in Foucault's sense, first made possible with its emphasis on the individual – tend to cultivate an identity closer to that of Christian cult leaders than to that of political leaders or public intellectuals. Particularly telling are the efforts of 're-Christianising' the world by adapting Christian sacred postulates to today's disenchanted world: Slavoj Žižek, for one, openly speaks of the need to spread a new, godless, yet Christian,

Universalist 'heresy' at the expense of other traditional religions, which he confines to the realm of a particularity that is deemed dangerous. Now, even if one indulges the stupidity of supposing that any traditional religious particularity can be truly dangerous to modernity and the arbitrariness with which Christian and post-Christian fundamentalisms are declared as superior to others because they are singularly instrumental to efforts to effect radical, progressive change,[28] the really interesting question here is: will such efforts be met with similar counter-efforts on the part of non-Christian world-views? The most diverse considerations could be invoked here, starting from how to implement, in the name of its general desirability, a planet-wide regime of non-violence, and whether we may assume that a renewed Christian mission without God, and therefore arguably without omnipotence, would amount to a renunciation of violence.

Perhaps epitomising violence as a common negative denominator of everything else should itself be identified as part of the symptom rather than as part of an access to its understanding. But what are the chances (or risks) that an appropriately godless 'heretic' programme of Christian self-assertion will instigate the same type of move within other religions? There are none. Unlike political leaders such as Tayyip Erdogan or Narendra Modi, followers of non-Christianised traditions (including the anti-Zionist Jews we had been looking at), careful to avoid nationalistic or post-religious assertions of religion, are decidedly not tempted by the invitation to emulate the modern and post-modern Christian programmes. Among those who are tempted, Erdogan or Modi are perhaps the easiest to engage in our civil war, misrepresented as a 'clash of civilisations'. Less easy to recruit will be those who employ the technologies that the West invented – notably subjective right – in order to indulge in uncompromisingly and self-assertively mono-religious militancy, sometimes bloody, eminently media-covered (if with segments safely absent from the light of mass media perception), with the result that we know nothing of them, even and in particular when they are flourishing, and as long as they are. Nothing of this is new, least of all the double-sided growth of media selectivity and latency. With respect to the history of Islam, for example, there have also been geopolitically imposed factors of latency keeping Islamic movements *aggiornamento* for a long time and at a low level; these fell away, or were inverted into exacerbation, especially in the nineteenth and twentieth centuries, in favour of anti-colonial ethno-religious fundamentalism, or of the fundamentalism that sprang up in the aftermath of the Iraq war. But the decisive reasons why there is no equivalent drive to be found for religion-transcending or anti-religious messages in non-Christian cultures have little to do with these geopolitical contingencies. They have their roots in religion, or more precisely in the distance between the 'ultimate sacred postulates' underlying each of the civilisations at stake.

One level further, the Universalist problematic we are aiming at can be defined as a generalised desire to present a theoretically justified world view. Westerners/northerners and their emulators often interpret this desire as a universal human endowment and consequently perceive its absence as an astonishing lacuna. But whatever is deemed astonishing, or simply informative, must lie in the presence of a feature, not in its absence. To say it with Foucault (1977), it happened only within the Western-cum-Christian cultures – 'en occident' are his own understated words – that man has become a confessing beast (French: *une bête d'aveu*). The individual who is shaped as a truth-saying, truth-arguing, truth-exalting being is not part of divine creation: he is the product of a number of centuries of involvement in Western, secularising/secularised Christianity. What forms the actual content of the truth to be confessed is secondary to being attached to the image of a truth-exalting being; in this respect President Erdogan, to keep with this specimen of an occidentalised/Christianised Muslim, undoubtedly feels the need to deflect the accusation from Europe that he is engineering a 'démocrature', to use Le Monde's titular neologism. There is more: what is really at stake here is the Western institutional achievement par excellence, namely the possibility (art, or habit) of 'doing things with words' (with, as a cornerstone, the consensualist conception of marriage epitomised in the Western theological tradition from the mid-twelfth century onward, later to be relativised in this respect, but disseminated into a large spectre of other 'things' to be done with words). The fact of doing things with words has been essential – pastorally, politically, managerially – over centuries of Western evolution, and the extraordinary success, over sixty years, of its late theoretical recapitulation, known as speech–act theory, would have been unthinkable without its long and slow prologue.

Neo-Paulists, such as Badiou or Žižek, may be entitled, to an extent, to dream of yet another Western Christian heresy to rally us behind some sovereign who would fight against the structural social injustice of capitalism. The question is just how good are the chances that some such audacious sovereign, first, shows up and, more importantly, proves able to impose even a small fraction of the deeds promised/expected? Sadly, Prime Minister Tsipras – hurriedly dubbed the 'Thatcher of the left' – proved to be just an 'unwilling yet perfectly efficient' Thatcher with no money. That said, an even more fundamental question might be whether there is, outside of Arthurian legends, something that might be called, 'the age of the deed', and if so, whether it is not, as such, behind us; whether, that is, we have not changed regime from one based on deed to one premised on deals. As we have already hinted, decisive notions that inspire fear or hope, and that we might be able to mobilise, no longer come in the form of a deed, an accomplishment, an opus, an act, be it a speech–act, but in a strangely different form, that of an ongoing, unstopping process. If we are asked what constitutes the 'originality of our own present time', the winning candidate is not the deed. The decisive intervention has abandoned us, and with it 'true politics', starting with the Schmittian 'political', which decides on highest-intensity matters, as has Giambattista Vico's praised *verum factum*. We are left with managemental configurations – deals, arts of coping, successfully maintained routines. Agamben, following the traces of Foucault, identified governing and managing in common opposition to 'reigning'.

The notion of reigning, however, imposes an inquiry into what is entailed in the exercise of reigning. Brexit was swiftly succeeded by the disappearance of its arch-propagandist Nigel Farage, who resigned as leader of UKIP – even if he retained the post of Member of the European Parliament, the very forum he decries as meaningless. This particular embarrassment – of dreaming of a sovereign who is not just 'naked' in the sense of lacking legitimacy, but who is

not actually there – is certainly in the top ten of the embar-
rassments of our 'age of progress', and it is by no means
exhausted by its old-style constitutionalist ascription to the
king alone. Today's constitutional theorists cannot avoid this
embarrassment – even if they try hard, generally by theoris-
ing in myriad ways the so-called 'constitutional paradox' (the
fact that the holder of constituent power is, always-already
constituted). Doing theory also carries the heavy charge of
embodying one of the forms or exercises of this nameless
activity, reigning; the embarrassment thus touches the very
root of the sovereign exercise. The weak, embarrassing spot
in the midst of the most decisive is illustrated by hundreds of
anecdotes starting in antiquity. There are of course those who
are lucky (?) enough to be deaf to this – or perhaps any – form
of embarrassment. The others, however, know that what is
embarrassing is the cross-road of adulthood and infancy.
Infancy and 'glorious reign' coincide, and today it is simply
embarrassing to conceive of an adult person or a group of
them as sovereign (as endless Western Christian iconography
proves, the Christ-child did not encounter such a problem). It
now looks as if a basic disbelief endures in the notion that the
world, or anything within it – apart from some rare and well-
circumscribed islands in the meaningful world – offers itself
any longer to be reigned over. Also, trust in the present as
a moment or feature of perfection, which is not conceivable
otherwise than as the result of some reign (as opposed to governing, *oikonomia*, which is capable of producing viability) is
at a premium. As we noted above, the modern age favours
words ending in '-tion', denoting an activity in the making,
as opposed to words ending on '-ism', denoting doctrines,
practices or habits, or anything that has its formative period
in its past (and is, in this sense, 'perfect'). So, why do so many
still embarrassingly behave as if work-in-progress must be
undertaken, or as if there is a moral duty to bring about
progress? If theories, which presuppose blind trust in sovereignty, and progress without collateral damage – especially
the dissident and the political kind, which straddle the difference between science and militant cult – remain in circulation,
this is because they are perfectly commodifiable. They coexist
with their own commodified appearance. But the question
close to us – as academics – is this: do they have any purchase

on what is happening outside of the lecture theatre, or even the public square, where Indignados gather?

'[W]ords are deeds': the quest for the performative sense-giving exercise that Wittgenstein brought at its most concise and least wordy denominator is, regrettably, still far from receiving its due portion of historical, philosophical, and legal-religious attention. Foucault helps in this direction, following as he did the genealogical traces of speech–acts in the occidental paradigm of *world making by word making* – a relation that Christianity emphasises to the point of epitomising the *word* as the unique marker of the 'difference that makes a difference'. Wittgenstein's famous observation must then be read in conjunction with Foucault's insight about the unprecedented *value* that Western Christian history has tagged to the fact of 'saying it', of 'speaking it out'. We may call this the 'surplus value' of speaking out. Foucault was one of those gifted with a sense for the difference-construing adventure that Western Christian self-shaping has initiated, further transforming the speaking human animal as an outspoken animal, capable of a layer of otherwise unseen performances in matters of performativity (of 'doing things with words'). While there is no anthropological disposition that would bond either the truth-claiming or the truth-confessing animal of Foucault or the performative animal of Wittgenstein with the relationship of the living human to speech having only one particular historical shape (as demonstrated by diverse non-Western traditions, including that of a *koan* among zen-Buddhist monks, oscillating between word and deed), there is much to be said about the relentless Christian glorification of the word 'deed' as a reference of sacrificial participation in the world 'for the better', be it by way of a revolution on the part of militants, or of a permanent vigilance to reassert what has been achieved by the leadership of the political establishment.

The bond between deeds and words comes equally twofold, as the *parrhesiastic* ambition of 'saying it all', and as the duty of 'owning-up' (*aveu*) understood as *trust* in the value of the very fact of saying it, which works as an enabling or unfettering device; both are summarised in the anthropology of the occidental confessing animal. One instance is the paradigm suggested by the term *testament(um)* – the key, scissile and disseminating legal term that defines the Christian canon by locating it at the crossroads between two meanings, that of witnessing/testifying to someone (else's) words, and that related to the Roman law of succession, which qualifies the words of a testament as *ultimate* words. Moreover, Foucault's move to link the distinctive features of the Western-sculpted shape of man to the philosophical tradition asks what kind of animal the human is. This is what is captured by the notion of *aveu* – a term which, in present French, is an everyday technical term in criminal procedure and refers to the *account a human being gives of itself* (technically, in criminal law, *aveu* translates as 'confession'), but also a term that refers to earlier codes of honour, according to which an *homme sans aveu*, a 'man without *aveu*', designates a person undeserving of credit – distinct, but not remote, from the 'infamous man' elsewhere discussed by Foucault. Yet at the same time, *aveu* is but a side-form of the English word 'avowal', and similarly it refers to the Latin *votum*, consecrated by legendary deeds from archaic Roman history (cf. the self-sacrificial action of the Roman warrior who chooses to sacrifice himself as a *devotus* to help the victory of the Roman cause – the relevant material is analysed in Agamben's *Homo Sacer*). Likewise, in Western Christianity, *votum* means, for those who choose to make themselves subject to it, that they consent to doing away *with themselves* (cf. the doctrine of the 'civic death' incurred by the incumbent of a monastic order), and to *using* themselves and their own terrestrial life as the price of purchasing a higher, more worthy good. It formulates a conversion rate between life and words. One might thus surmise that for Foucault to call occidental man 'a beast of avowal' meant that occidental man had allowed his word, its formulated consent, to redefine the speaker as the pledge of her speech. Let us, however, also keep in mind that these resolute claims as to the position of discourse do not refer to the occidental human as a determined branch of humankind. Foucault is careful, on the contrary, to stick to a geographical-cum-historical indication, his terms being 'the human *within* the Occident' (French: *l'homme en occident*). He points to a *special feature* of the Western and Westernised subject: its duty of always and indefinitely exposing to each other words and deeds, the spoken and the speaker, charging one's own word with the care due to one's own life.

If we now look once again at Wittgenstein's phrase, 'words are deeds', it becomes clear that, while it is easily universalisable on the conceptual level, it can also be understood as a *particularly short formulation of the Christian message*. In fact, read together, Foucault's ethical duty of 'saying it all' (according to the Greek philosophical elite ideal of *parrhesia*), Foucault's foregrounding of a subjective duty of *confessing it all* (according to the interpretation of the occidental human as a *bête d'aveu*), and Wittgenstein's 'words are deeds', epitomise three closely related modes of identifying the distinctive feature of the Western Christian subject, according to which happenings count to the extent to which there are words, arguments, discourses, that finally endow them with reality. This is the site of the dialectical contradiction that a study of the Western/(post)Christian has to face. While the two poles, *relentless managerial world caring* and performative *(political or juridical) speech as world making* share common Western Christian roots, the exercise of the latter is, today, no longer plugged in the trajectory of the former. In this sense, the famous early nineteenth-century saying (by German revolutionary poet and dramatist, Georg Büchner), 'the revolution, like Saturn, devours its children', has emancipated itself from its first context, the French revolution, and now applies to the entire revolutionary matrix programmed by Western Christianism. To paraphrase Wittgenstein: we are no longer in the 'words are deeds' loop; rather, we are now dealing with deeds giving rise to other deeds without speech as a mediation. To use the term – employed significantly in both Luhmann's *Theory of Society* and Agamben's *Opus Dei* – there are but operations that generate further operations. In this connection, before once again elevating the usual suspect – the heedlessly inconsiderate banker – to the (dis)honour of providing the ultimate and exclusive embodiment of such an operation-totalism, we might as well think of other representatives of wordless efficiency, such as the young jihadist who blows himself and others up; or the equally young American recruit remote-piloting lethal drones, operating safely from behind his computer.

Notes

Chapter 1

1. For an example in the area of constitutionalism see J. Tully, 'The imperialism of modern constitutional democracy', in M. Loughlin, N. Walker (eds), *The Paradox of Constitutionalism*.
2. 'West', 'Western', 'occidental' – there is no denying that our decisive terminology is worn out in the extreme; our wager is that our untiring and multi-focused use of it will eventually succeed in endowing these rather vacuous identifying terms that we use strictly *faute de mieux* with an appropriate depth of focus.
3. Samera Esmeir, *Juridical Humanity: A Colonial History* (Stanford: Stanford University Press, 2012).
4. Alain Supiot, *Homo juridicus: Essai sur les fonctions anthropologiques du droit* (Paris: Seuil, 2005).
5. The term, (in)famously popularised by Carl Schmitt, has thankfully been appropriated by a large and growing body of non-fascist literature since. See Carl Schmitt, *Political Theology: Four Chapters on the Concept of Sovereignty* (ed. and tr. George Schwab; Chicago: University of Chicago Press, 2006 [Berlin 1922]); *Political Theology II: The Myth of the Closure of any Political Theology* (tr. M. Hoelzl and G. Ward; Cambridge, UK: Polity Press, 2008 [Berlin 1970]); *Roman Catholicism and Political Form* (tr. G. L. Ulmen; New York: Praeger, 1996 [1923]); Giorgio Agamben, *The Kingdom and the Glory: For a Theological Genealogy of Economy and Government* (Stanford: Stanford University Press, 2011); L. V. Kaplan and C. L. Cohen (eds), *Theology and the Soul of the Liberal State* (Lanham, MD: Lexington Books, 2010). The militant–millenarian theology of capitalism is described in E. Mensch, 'St Augustine, markets and the liberal polity', in H. de Vries and L. E. Sullivan (eds), *Political Theologies: Public Religions in a Post-Secular World* (New York: Fordham

University Press, 2006, pp. 121–60); C. Davis, J. Milbank and S. Žižek (eds), *Theology and the Political: The New Debate* (Durham: Duke University Press, 2005); P. Blond (ed.), *Post-Secular Philosophy: Between Philosophy and Theology* (New York: Routledge, 1998); James R. Martel, *Divine Violence: Walter Benjamin and the Eschatology of Sovereignty* (New York: Routledge, 2012); Talal Asad, *Formations of the Secular: Christianity, Islam, Modernity* (Stanford, CA: Stanford University Press, 2003); Gil Anidjar, 'Secularism', *Critical Inquiry* 33 (2006), pp. 52–77. See also M. Diamantides 'Constitutional theory and its limits: reflections on comparative political theologies', *Law, Culture and the Humanities* 11 (1), 2015; 'On and out of revolution: between public law and religion', *Law, Culture and the Humanities* 10 (3) 2014; 'God's political power in Western and Eastern Christianity in comparative perspective', in Anton Schütz and Massimiliano Traversino (eds), *The Theology of 'potentia dei' and the History of European Normativity* (115 Divus Thomas [2012]), 333–81; Anton Schütz, 'Legal modernity and mediaeval theology: the case of Duns Scotus, Ordinatio 1, D.44', in *The Theology of 'potentia dei'*, 418–52; 'A quandary concerning immanence', *Law and Critique* 22, 2 (2011), 189–203; 'Epigenesis, law, and the Medium Aevum as a medium', *Divus Thomas* 116 (2013), 15–36.

6. Pierre Legendre, *Dominium Mundi: L'Empire du Management* (Paris: Mille et une nuits, 2007), 26f.

7. E.g. Alexander Somek, 'Administration without sovereignty', in P. Dobner and M. Loughlin (eds), *The Twilight of Constitutionalism?* (Oxford: Oxford University Press, 2010), pp. 267–8.

8. Put in constitutionalist terms: 'We live today in an age simultaneously marked by the widespread adoption of the idea of constitutionalism, of ambiguity over its meaning, and about its continuing authority. Far from being an expression of limited government; constitutionalism is now to be viewed as an extremely powerful mode of legitimating extensive government. Where this form of constitutionalism positions itself on the ideology–utopia axis . . . has rarely been more indeterminate . . . notwithstanding the liberal gains . . . the significance of the idea of "the constitutional imagination" has never exhibited a great degree of uncertainty' (Martin Loughlin, 'The constitutional imagination', *Modern Law Review*, 78 (1) (2015), pp. 1–25 at 25). Alternatively: '[C]ontinued belief in political democracy as the realization

of human freedom depends upon literally averting our glance from powers immune to democratization, powers that also give the lie to the autonomy and primacy of the political upon which so much of the history and present of democratic theory has depended . . .': Wendy Brown, 'We are all democrats now . . .', in Amy Alen (ed.), *Democracy in what State?* (New York: Columbia University Press, 2011), p. 54; 'While weakening nation state sovereigns yoke their fate and legitimacy to God, Capital . . . becomes God-like: almighty, limitless, and uncontrollable. In what should be the final and complete triumph of secularism, there is only theology.' W. Brown, *Walled States, Waning Sovereignty* (New York: Zone Books, 2010), p. 66. Cf. In philosophical terms: 'Today, there is no legitimate power left anywhere on earth . . . The integral juridification and economization of the relations between humans and the confusion between what we can believe, hope, love, and that which we are required to do and not to do, to say and not to say [convicts] all the powerful of the world themselves of illegitimacy' (translated from G. Agamben, 'L'Église et le Royaume', in André Vingt-Trois (ed.), *Saint-Paul: Juif et apôtre des nations* (Paris: Paroles et Silence, 2009), pp. 27–36 at 35).

9. 'Widespread suspicion undermines trust in the courts and the law, even while it further entrenches the law by spurring in ever more legislation. Every new set of reforms opens doors for . . . more suspicion, and in return, more legislation.' Hussein Al Agrama, *Questioning Secularism: Islam, Sovereignty and the Rule of Law in Modern Egypt* (Chicago: University of Chicago Press, 2012), p. 141.

10. Giorgio Agamben, *Stasis: Civil War As a Political Paradigm* (Edinburgh: Edinburgh University Press, 2015)

Chapter 2

1. W. Brown, *Walled States, Waning Sovereignty* (New York: Zone Books, 2010), pp. 53–4.

2. The Byzantine patriarch Photius, for example, wrote: '*Oikonomia* means precisely the extraordinary and incomprehensible incarnation of the *Logos* . . . it means the occasional restriction or the suspension of the . . . rigor of the laws and the introduction of extenuating circumstances, which "economizes" the command of law in view of the weakness of those who must receive it.' Cited in Agamben, *The Kingdom and the Glory: For a Theological Genealogy of Economy*

and Government (Stanford: Stanford University Press, 2011), p. 49.

3. Ibid., p. 49.

4. For the discussion of our advanced stage in replacing law and politics by management in all but name see for example Somek, 'Administration without sovereignty', in P. Dobner and M. Loughlin (eds), *The Twilight of Constitutionalism?* (Oxford: Oxford University Press, 2010), pp. 267–87.

5. See title of Chapter 3 in Marcel Gauchet, *The Disenchantment of the World: A Political History of Religion*, tr. O. Burge, foreword by Charles Taylor (Princeton: Princeton University Press, 1999), p. 47.

6. Jean-Luc Nancy, *Dis-Enclosure: The Deconstruction of Christianity*, tr. Bettina Bergo, Gabriel Malenfant and Michael B. Smith (New York: Fordham University Press, 2008).

7. J. L. Nancy, 'Deconstruction of monotheism', *Postcolonial Studies: Culture, Politics, Economy* 6 (1) (2003), pp. 37–46.

8. We coin the term 'managementality' in order to continue the chain of 'psycho-political' puns on the theme of mentality, drawing attention to a certain shift from Foucault's 'governmentality' (and, incidentally, from the 'departmentality' observed by historians of Prussian state reforms under Frederick the Great). That the 'pre-eminence' attributed by Foucault to effective *governing* over sovereign ruling resolutely limits the distance from governmentality to managementality goes without saying.

9. See Agamben, *The Kingdom and the Glory*, esp. Chapters 4, 6 and appendix.

10. See Agamben *The Highest Poverty: Monastic Rules and Form-of-Life* (Stanford: Stanford University Press, 2013); also his *L'uso dei corpi* (Vicenza, Neri Pozza Editore, 2014); in English: Giorgio Agamben, *The Use of Bodies*, tr. A. Kotsko (Stanford: Stanford University Press, 2016).

11. For the interpretations of the conceptions of the relationship of Christianism and Empire, and the nature and motives of Constantine the Great's personal faith and conversion, cf. the provocative and suggestive new reading in Paul Veyne, *Quand notre monde est devenu chrétien: 312–394* (Paris: Librairie Générale Française, 2010).

12. In Western terminology, based on the notion of three 'persons', where Eastern terminology has the much less personal, yet more philosophical, three 'hypostases'.

13. The anti-intellectualism of campaigns directed against Trinitarian constructions, and their links to anti-institutionalist,

anti-Catholic (or anti-'pagano-papist') Enlightenment literature in politics and theology in England and the US, are unfolded in J. Z. Smith, *Drudgery Divine: On the Comparison of Early Christianities and the Religions of Late Antiquity* (London: School of Oriental and African Studies, 1990).

14. Agamben, *The Kingdom and the Glory*, pp. 50–1.
15. Agamben, *The Kingdom and the Glory*, pp. 255–6. Cf. Guy Debord, *The Society of the Spectacle*, tr. D. Nicholson-Smith (New York: Zone Books 1994).
16. Agamben, *The Kingdom and the Glory*, pp. 255–6.
17. Ibid., p. xii.
18. For a short introduction to the significance of the term in contemporary constitutional theory see M. Loughlin, *Foundations of Public Law* (Oxford UP, 2010), pp. 310–11. The debate on 'reflexive constitutionalism' centres, in abstract terms, on the need for permanent constitutional contestation and the revisability of constitutional norms through a permanent process of deliberation; it covers various theories of constitutional design understood in terms of *purely* bottom-up, deliberative democracy in *procedural* terms and avoids setting substantive norms; it stresses the law's role in providing the procedural framework to allow self-regulation by other sub-systems (politics, the economy, etc.). As Stijn Smismans notes in the context of analysing attempts to found a European Constitution, however, 'thinking normatively about ensuring bottom-up reflexive processes without reflecting on the substantive values of the constitutional design in which such processes have to operate is unlikely to deliver democratic governance'; this is, at best, an attempt to think constitutional design *'as if* such design could be neutral in substantive terms'; moreover, '[Law] has traditionally had a role in translating societal norms into substantive legal norms. As in no other subsystem, this process has been linked to democratic procedures. In reducing law to a procedural role, the definition of substantive norms will be left to subsystems that do not guarantee democratic processes.' See Smismans: 'European constitutionalism and the democratic design of European governance: rethinking directly deliberative polyarchy and reflexive constitutionalism', in K. Tuori and S. Sankari, *The Many Constitutions of Europe* (London: Routledge, 2010), Chapter 8, pp. 169–95 at 192 (emphasis added). We wish to draw from Smismans' critique that, so far, reflexive constitutionalism has not reflected enough on the role that Western law has histori-

cally played in both *promising and guaranteeing* a substantive meaning to democracy; Smismans' love of this guaranteed promise is itself too entrenched in Western consciousness to note the imbalance. See also below, Chapter 3.

19. G. Teubner, *Constitutional Fragments* (Oxford, Oxford University Press, 2013).

20. R. Rappaport, *Ritual and Religion in the Making of Humanity* (Cambridge: Cambridge University Press, 1999), p. 447.

21. J. Meyendorff, *Byzantine Theology: Historical Trends and Doctrinal Themes* (New York: Fordham University Press, 1979), p. 92. '[T]he Filioque dispute was not a discussion on words – for there was a sense in which both sides would agree to say that the Spirit proceeds "from the Son" – but on the issue of whether the hypostatic existence of the Persons of the Trinity could be reduced to their internal relations, as the post-Augustinian West would admit, or whether the primary Christian experience was that of a trinity of Persons, whose personal existence was irreducible to their common essence. The question was whether tri-personality or con-substantiality was the first . . ., basic content of Christian religious experience' (*Byzantine Theology*, p. 94).

22. Ibid., p. 183.

23. In the Old Testament the Lord had made clear that a true king, a king acceptable to Him as the King of kings, could only be one whom He, and not the people, had chosen. For as He said to the people through Moses: 'When thou shalt come unto the land which the Lord thy God shall choose, and shalt possess it, and shalt dwell therein, and shalt say, I will set a king over me, like as all the nations that are about me: thou shalt in any wise set him king over thee, whom the Lord thy God shall choose: one from among thy brethren shalt thou set king over thee: thou mayest not set a stranger over thee, which is not thy brother . . .' (Deuteronomy 17. 14–15).

24. After Max Planck, *Physikalische Abhandlungen und Vorträge*, vol. III, (Braunschweig: Vieweg & Sohn, 1958), p. 106 (author's translation).

25. Michael Sylwanowicz, *Contingent Causality and the Foundations of Duns Scotus' Metaphysics* (Leyden: Brill, 1996), p. 1. The Scotian, and more largely the Franciscan contribution to a political archaeology of the state of exception (which Agamben has some difficulty in admitting) has its roots in the before/after distinction and moreover in the unreserved attention with which these theologians subject themselves to

the biblical narrative. The bible-hermeneutic adjective 'post-lapsarian', meaning 'of the time that comes after the Fall and after the expulsion of the original couple from Paradise' is the paradigm of the numerous ways in which, especially yet not exclusively during the past fifty years, words carrying the 'post-' prefix have come to flourish; the term 'post-lapsarian' also had the strategically decisive merit of giving sufficient plausibility to the notion that the Franciscans had to mobilise all available potential in order to care for, govern and, wherever possible, act on (yet first of all: accept in principle!) such less engaging aspects of the created world as violence, repression, enrichment, law, serfdom, slavery, etc. Rather than eliciting any need for *theodicy*, the claim that *God*, when confronted with the human propensity to sin, *has revoked natural law in its original version*, the version that was intended for life in Paradise, replacing it with a new, tougher, 'heavy-duty' version of natural law, more appropriate for mankind after its fall, delivers the blueprint for a modern mankind defined by its passive capacities such as its manageability and governability, for example.

Chapter 3

1. See, among a rapidly growing literature, Momme von Sydow, *From Darwinian Metaphysics toward Understanding of the Evolution of Evolutionary Mechanisms* (Göttingen: Göttinger Universitätsverlag, 2012), p. 385, with reference to the work of Richard Dawkins.
2. Apart from the work of Niklas Luhmann, who was the artisan of a theory of modern society as a precarious set of problematic solutions (rather than as a progressive design that only needs to be taken for granted and pushed forward), another example of such advanced calculus is to be found in the work of media theory pioneer Friedrich Kittler.
3. Niklas Luhmann, *Risk: A Sociological Theory*, tr. Rhodes Barrett, with a new introduction by Nico Stehr and Gotthard Bechmann (New Brunswick: Transaction, 2002), p.34. Things are more complicated than is supposed by those readers of Nietzsche or Foucault who take genealogy to be part of a philosophical terminology invented by the first and continued by the second. The chances are that the genealogy of Jesus according to the Gospels of Matthew (I, 1–17) and Luke (III, 23–38), for example was decisive, among other sources, both for the son and grandson of Lutheran Pastors

in nineteenth-century Germany, and for the Jesuit-educated scion of the French provincial bourgeoisie in the twentieth century. The New Testament genealogy or filiation of Jesus gives a *causal* account of what and who Jesus is – but this is not the case for Nietzsche's or Foucault's somehow parodistic use of the term. What they call genealogy is a performance and has its site very precisely in the 'now' within which everything happens. Yet Luhmann's work, steeped in history, is evidence that the anti-causalist claim that 'everything that happens, happens *now*' is not an obstacle to doing history. His causality-critical (thus, in the word's older use, effectively 'agenealogical') method rests on the distinction of social systems and consciences (there is, in Luhmann's perspective, no such thing as 'psycho-social studies'). It excludes 'mentality' from the objects of sociological inquiry, but includes 'instrumentality' in dealing with matters of meaning.

4. S. Žižek, *The Sublime Object of Ideology* (New York: Verso, 1989).

5. See for Bateson's mantric definition of information, itself based upon Alfred A. Korzybski's distinction between map and territory, his *Steps for an Ecology of Mind* (Chicago: University of Chicago Press, 2000 [1972]), pp. 448–64.

6. Cf. Jean Clam, *Was heisst, sich an Differenz statt and Identität orientieren? Zur De-ontologisierung in Philosophie und Sozialwissenschaft* ('What it means to take one's orientation from difference rather than from identity: on de-ontologization in philosophy and the social sciences') (Konstanz: UVK, 2002).

7. The formula deliberately echoes German historian Fritz Fischer's standard-setting account (1961) of the German Reich's 'Grasping for world-power' in the First World War. The English translation is published as *Germany's Aims in the First World War* (London: Norton, 1967 [1961]).

8. Cf. André de Muralt, *L'enjeu de la philosophie médiévale: études thomistes, scotistes, occamistes, et grégoriennes* (New York: Brill, 1993). Cf. Diamantides. 'Constitutional theory and its limits: reflections on comparative political theologies', *Law, Culture and the Humanities* 11 (1), 2015.

9. 'Closure' is *not* to be understood in a normative sense; rather, the operational closure of function systems is spontaneous; it is also inevitable, as soon as a process specialising in certain types of operations takes off.

10. Cf. Steffen Roth and Anton Schütz, 'Ten systems: toward a

canon of function systems', *Cybernetics & Human Knowing: a journal of second-order cybernetics autopoiesis and cyber-semiotics* 22 (4) (2015), 11–31.

11. Cf. Luhmann, *Theory of Society I & II*, tr. R. Barrett, vols 1 and 2 (Stanford: Stanford University Press, 2012/13).
12. Cf. the otherwise rather well-informed introduction by Christian Borch, *Luhmann* (New York: Routledge, 2011) as one example of this attitude. Cf. also the lucid review article by Stephen Schecter, 'The turn toward Luhmann', *Canadian Journal of Sociology*, 36 (4) (2011), 389–94.
13. The inverted commas reflect the level at which we refer to the argument: contrary to what had been the case thirty or more years ago, the act of qualifying an argument or an attitude as 'neo-liberal' today refers more often than not to a consecrated gesture of taking one's distance, rather than to an interest in, or a concrete negation of any specific doctrine. As we are not investigating economic theory, all we refer to here concerns this level of merely value-laden judgement.
14. Cf Brenna Bhandar, Jonathan Goldberg-Hiller (eds), *Plastic Materialities: Politics, Legality, and Metamorphosis in the Work of Catherine Malabou* (Durham: Duke University Press, 2015).
15. Douglas R. Hofstadter, *Gödel, Escher, Bach: An Eternal Golden Braid* (New York: Basic Books, 1979), p. 686f.
16. Cf. for instance, Niklas Luhmann, *Social Systems* (Stanford: Stanford University Press, 1995); *Introduction to Systems Theory* (Cambridge, Polity Press, 2013).
17. Ps.-Aristote, *Oikonomika*, Book I, quoted after Agamben, *The Kingdom and the Glory: For a Theological Genealogy of Economy and Government* (Stanford: Stanford University Press, 2011), p. 57.
18. Martin Heidegger, *Sein und Zeit* (Tübingen: Niemeyer, 1927), p. 12.
19. Giorgio Agamben, *Homo Sacer: Sovereign Power and Bare Life* (Stanford: Stanford University Press, 1997).
20. The intense and relatively short evolutionary episode can be traced from early pioneering writing on the modern management phenomenon that goes back to the first half of the twentieth century, cf. James Burnham, *The Managerial Revolution: What is Happening in the World?* (New York: John Day, 1941), through Luhmann's work which, with the help of its strongly synthesising notion of system, describes the unfolding and refolding of this process in its numerous aspects, up to Agamben's *The Kingdom and the Glory*, which provides the decisive legal/religious clues to understand-

ing the managerial riddle. The key theme throughout is the decline/abandon of politics. It spans from Burnham's 1941 indifference about who would be victorious in the then ongoing Second World War (Burnham, writing in 1940/41, considers that the question whether 'Leninism-Stalinism . . . fascism-Nazism . . . or New Dealism' would be victorious to be inessential from the managerial viewpoint, alone decisive [*The Managerial Revolution*, p. 73f.]), through Luhmann's ironico-realist stance against Habermas in their celebrated and, in view of the intellectual history of the German Federal Republic, mentality-shaping controversy from 1970, to Agamben's rediscovery (2007) of the stratum of 'economical theology' and the massive incidence it had never stopped exercising over normative history, relativising Schmitt's campaign for political theology – and opening the gate, within Agamben's own writing, to what the Italian philosopher, differently and yet almost equally resistant to the call of traditional politics as the German sociologist, will later identify as 'destituent power'.

Chapter 4

1. Cf. for the notion of 'en-religioning', in a rather more restrained use than the one suggested here, see Quentin Meillassoux, *After Finitude: An essay on the necessity of contingency*, tr. Ray Brassier (London: Continuum, 2010), Chapter 2.
2. S. Mahmood, 'Religious reason and secular affect: an incommensurable divide?' *Critical Inquiry* 35 (4) (2009), 836–42, at 836.
3. Talal Asad, *Formations of the Secular: Christianity, Islam, Modernity* (Stanford, CA: Stanford University Press, 2003).
4. 'In the inevitable struggle over the issue as to whether the new power over nature should ultimately belong to the old manorial lords or to other classes as well, the Church turned the scales by establishing itself as a feudal court for the world at large.' E. Rosenstock-Huessy, *Out of Revolution: Autobiography of Western Man* (Providence/Oxford: Berg, 1993, p. 528). A convert to Christianity from Judaism, Rosenstock-Huessy celebrated the papal assumption of the role of unifier of the fragmented West European space as exemplifying what we need today in order to continue with the 'coming together' of humankind. Make no mistake: this was an expression of his Christian faith. As he topically

affirmed in *The Christian Future*: 'Today Orient and Occident are shaken by a cataclysm which shows the insufficiency of both in isolation. A new penetration of the Cross is required which shall draw together the hearts of men in East and West by showing that each has some essential ingredient of life which the other needs.' Eugen Rosenstock-Huessy, *The Christian Future or The Modern Mind Outrun* (New York: Harper and Row, 1966 [first edition: New York: Charles Scribner's Sons, 1947]), p. 174. 'Here he refers to the notion of the Cross as the context of humankind's unity. What Rosenstock-Huessy calls the *Cross of Reality* is fundamental to his social thought. While the life of humankind in time unfolds in response to a common destiny, that future is won – or lost – on the Cross of Reality.' M. D. Bryant, 'The grammar of the spirit: time, speech and society', in M. D. Bryant and H. R. Huessy (eds), *Eugen Rosenstock-Huessy: Studies in his Life and Thought* (Toronto: Edwin Mellen Press, 1986), pp. 233–61 at 249. Cf. Diamantides, 'On and out of revolution: between public law and religion', *Law, Culture and the Humanities* 10 (3) (2014).

5. See Diamantides, 'Constitutional theory and its limits'.
6. B. Bhandar, 'The ties that bind: multiculturalism and secularism reconsidered', *Journal of Law and Society* 34 (3) (2009), pp. 301–25.
7. Ibid., p. 301.
8. Ibid., p. 301.
9. S. Moyne, 'Hannah Arendt on the secular', *New German Critique* 105 (2008), 71–96 at 96.
10. Cf. Chapter 1, notes 5 and 6.
11. Simon Critchley, *The Faith of the Faithless: Experiments on Political Theology* (New York: Verso, 2012).
12. These radical neo-Hegelians reject much of Arendt's critique – in direct contrast to Arendt, the social question for them is the political question – but, mindful of the Lacanian idea that man has a 'passion not to know', they acknowledge the political usefulness of fiction, for example in radicalising Christian liberation theologies. Hence the turn towards Paulian theology, minus its liturgical 'packaging' and institutional history, e.g. in A Badiou, *Saint Paul: The Foundation of Universalism* (Stanford: Stanford University Press, 2003) or his *Philosophy for Militants* (New York: Verso 2012).
13. *Lautsi v Italy*; ECHR [2011] Eq LR 633, [2011] ECHR 2412, (2012) 54 EHRR 3, [2011] ELR 176, 30 BHRC 429.
14. E.g. *Leyla Sahin v Turkey*; ECHR 44774/98, [2004] ECHR

299, (2004) 44 EHRR 99. For a thoroughly scathing criticism of this and similar judgments from a libertarian point of view, see S. Mancini, 'The tempting of Europe, the political seduction of the Cross: a Schmittian reading of Christianity and Islam in European constitutionalism', in S. Mancini and M. Rosenfeld (eds), *Constitutional Secularism in an Age of Religious Revival* (Oxford: Oxford University Press, 2014), pp. 111–35. Cf. A. Vakulenko, '"Islamic headscarves" and the European Convention on Human Rights: an intersectional perspective', *Social and Legal Studies* 16 (2) (2007), pp. 183–99.

15. Rosenstock-Huessy, *The Christian Future.*
16. Cf. Jean-Luc Nancy, *Dis-Enclosure: The Deconstruction of Christianity*, tr. Bettina Bergo, Gabriel Malenfant and Michael B. Smith (New York: Fordham University Press, 2008).
17. Cf. P. Goodrich and P. Legendre, *Law and the Unconscious: A Legendre Reader* (London: Macmillan, 1997).
18. P. Legendre, *L'amour du censeur: essai sur l'ordre dogmatique* (Paris: Seuil, 1974); *Leçons*, especially vol. II, *L'empire de la vérité: Introduction aux espaces dogmatiques industriels* (Paris: Fayard 1983), and vol. VII, *Le Désir Politique de Dieu: étude sur les montages de l'État et du Droit* (Paris: Fayard 1988). For an introduction see A. Schütz, 'Sons of writ, sons of wrath: Pierre Legendre's critique of rational law-giving', *Cardozo Law Review* 16 (1994), 979–1019; also Goodrich and Legendre, *Law and the Unconscious; Oedipus Lex: Psychoanalysis, History, Law* (Berkeley: University of California Press, 1995).
19. Cf. Adam Tomkins, *Public Law* (Oxford: Oxford University Press, 2003), on the function of ritualistic features of the British constitution (oaths, etc.) which are anything but a bit of innocuous folklore.
20. As a reflection on the origins of these pitfalls, cf. Martin Buber, *Good and Evil* (New York: Pearson, 1980), who characterises as the two main sources of evil, the 'lie' and, more surprisingly perhaps, the 'alternative'.
21. On the need to distinguish between religion and metaphysics, as separate and, at particular junctures, perfectly antagonistic targets and locations of secularisation, on the prevalence given of the second, and on the consequences thereof, cf. Meillassoux, *After Finitude.*
22. As Jean-Claude Milner explains in *L'universel en éclats: Court traité politique 3* (Paris: Verdier, 2014), pp. 63–86, Michel Foucault's centre-staging of the 'hellenistic-cum-Roman-era', and generally his late yet inaugural gesture of moving

his research focus from modernity to antiquity, are not unrelated to the unspectacular and world-changing substitution of Alexander the Great's revolutionary cosmos-thinking and post-identity empire for the patriotic views of Alexander's friend and private teacher Aristotle and his Athenian-identity-based polis-thinking. Based on an important sample of scholarly work, Milner suggests that there are good reasons to date the foundation of universalism as we still know it to Alexander, as in the history of the 2.5 millennia to which modern politics traces its origins, he was the first to programmatically entrust his political project no longer upon a particular city or nation but upon a multi-nation entity, thereby becoming the harbinger of a new, 'globalising' Empire. In comparison to what the Macedonian Empire founder achieved, a few years before the inception of stoic philosophy properly speaking, the universalising role of Paul of Tarsus, three-and-a-half centuries later, appears as that of a belated follower, the proponent of some 'return-to-Alexander' (in Lacanian lingo); Paul also supplied a durable theologico-pastoral supplement of Alexander's short-lived Empire. Let us add that among the writers to whom Milner is indebted – as Foucault before him – we find the towering figure of André-Jean Festugière, the historian of Christian Platonism, cf. *La Révélation d'Hermès Trismégiste* (Paris: Les Belles Lettres, 1986 [1947]); II, p. 176ff.

23. The 'veil of ignorance' is, alongside the 'original position', a methodological device in John Rawls' work, allowing the reader to work out the morality of an issue. It is based upon the consideration that those who select the principles for the distribution of rights, positions and resources in the society in which they will live should be prevented from knowing who will receive which set of rights, positions and resources. John Rawls, *A Theory of Justice* (Harvard, Harvard University Press, 1999 [1971]), pp. 11, 17, 118–23.

24. A term coined by Étienne Balibar to connote the tension between the two ideals of modern democracy: *equality* (social rights and political representation) and *liberty* (the freedom citizens have to contest the social contract). He finds the tension between these different kinds of rights to be ingrained in the constitution of the modern nation state and the contemporary welfare state. We agree. We don't agree when Balibar seeks to keep rights discourse open, eschewing natural entitlements in favour of a de-territorialised citizenship that could be expanded and invented anew in the age of globalization;

we doubt that this strategy, based on Balibar's synthesizing concept of *equaliberty*, does not by itself constitute a sovereign gesture: far from synthesizing the two ideals the term offers a pedestal on which *any* suggestion as to how to temporarily structure the tension between these ideals can be put. Étienne Balibar, *Equaliberty* (Durham, Duke University Press, 2014).

25. See https://www.rt.com/viral/352863-sweden-muslim-handshake-lawsuit/, accessed 1 August 2016.
26. Cf. Loughlin, Walker (eds), *The Paradox of Constitutionalism* (Oxford: Oxford University Press, 2007).
27. S. Žižek, *The Sublime Object of Ideology* (New York: Verso, 1989); *The Plague of Fantasies* (New York: Verso, 1999).
28. Cf. Wendy Brown, *Walled States, Waning Sovereignty* (New York: Zone Books, 2010), p. 66.
29. J. Rancière, *Hatred of Democracy* (London: Verso, 2014).
30. In Badiou's work, for instance, subjectivity entails an escape from the otherwise determinist order of structuralism: the Party, which is needed, as the privileged subject of revolutionary struggle, in order to articulate, develop, represent, organise the revolts and unfold their implications by means of procedures that Badiou now terms 'interventions'. His faith in the Party results from its being the site of a concentration of particular imperatives for struggle. This concentration allows 'periodisation', by which is meant the passage to another historical stage.
31. S. Žižek 'The simple courage of decision: a leftist tribute to Thatcher', *New Statesman*, 17 April 2013 (accessed 1 August 2016 at: http://www.newstatesman.com/poli tics/politics/2013/04/simple-courage-decision-leftist-trib ute-thatcher).
32. A. Abeysakara, *The Politics of Post-secular Religion: Mourning Secular Futures* (New York: Columbia University Press, 2008), pp. 71–83 (at 82).
33. See below, Chapter 5, notes 12 to 14.
34. His work is called *Out of Revolution: Autobiography of Western Man*.
35. Marcel Gauchet, *The Disenchantment of the World: A Political History of Religion*, tr. O. Burge, foreword by Charles Taylor (Princeton: Princeton University Press, 1999).
36. Ibid.
37. Erik Peterson, 'Monotheism as a political problem', in *Theological Tractates* (Stanford: Stanford University Press, 2011 [1935]).
38. Despite the static meaning it acquired later (founding,

grounding . . .), the Greek word 'basis' is suggests 'march', as in *Anabasis* ('march upward') – the title of Xenophon's *chef d'oeuvre* recounting the military adventure of the 'Ten Thousand' into the Persian Empire.

39. For the strongest version of the claim to the presence of such a dynamic in each of the great European revolutionary sequences of the second millennium CE, see Eugen Rosenstock-Huessy, *Out of Revolution: Autobiography of Western Man* (Providence/Oxford: Berg, 1993).

40. As argued in A. Abeysakara, *The Politics of Post-secular Religion*. Cf. Amy Allen, *The End of Progress: Decolonising the Normative Foundations of Critical Theory* (Columbia: Columbia University Press, 2016), see especially pp. 1–10.

41. Agamben, *The Kingdom and the Glory: For a Theological Genealogy of Economy and Government* (Stanford: Stanford University Press, 2011), p. 1.

42. Ibid., p. 50.

43. Ibid., pp. 50–1.

44. Ibid., p. 51.

Chapter 5

1. The persistent silence observed by the two essential twentieth-century writers on political theology, Carl Schmitt and Ernst H. Kantorowicz, about each other's work upstages the one biographical feature they hold in common: an unambiguous commitment against the revolutionary left of the German post-First World War years. In Spring 1919, Kantorowicz joined the armed paramilitary militia forces, Schmitt's 1922 brochure volunteered intellectually, in painting its author as the paradigm of what the image of a 'right wing organic intellectual' would look like.

2. Cf. Jean-Claude Milner, in *L'universel en éclats: Court traité politique 3* (Paris: Verdier, 2014), pp. 87–114, suggests a bipartite overall narrative of the history of the university as an institution between the mediaeval times of its foundation and its present shape. Milner proceeds by centre-staging the *social substratum* of each. The original, mediaeval university is born from the need of the Western Church to find an 'organ of artificial reproduction' for its clergy. In the modern university he identifies, in the same way, an organ of self-reproduction for the world-wide bourgeoisie.

3. Cf. In Plato, 'theology' designates mythical accounts or poetic fictions dealing with the gods of the Greek pan-

theon; in Aristotle the word refers to the science of the separate substance, immobile and all-moving; and writers of Hellenistic times, most especially the stoics, conscious of their civic responsibility as pillars of public rituals, narratives and institutions, use the term in the connection with high-ranking offices and duties (all of which explains to some extent the Christian hesitations about adopting such a heavily charged term in dealing with its own matters). Hence we find in the work of Abelard no less than three titles, *Theologia summi boni* (1121), *Theologia Christiana* (1126?) and *Theologia scholarium* (1133–40), introducing his new science of the revealed God of the Christian message.

4. Periodising as an activity, periodisations as artefacts, by trying to locate the most appropriate moment to draw a line between two successive present periods, or realms or regimes of presence (dynastic succession might be the model here, but one that has ramifications far into the agenealogical space of social and cultural evolution), offers the most powerful expression of compossibility and continuation, and at once, of newness and discontinuity. Especially in the case of the birth of the modern mind at the time, for most interpreters, of Christopher Columbus or Niccolò Machiavelli, the focus on periodising is of obvious relevance to the way in which the present sees itself or wishes to be seen, the choices to which it feels bound, etc. In this sense, the divide between times 'theological' and times 'no-longer-theological', which is very much addressed and questioned by our argument, offers a case in point. Let us note, however, that there exists a different argument, directed, strangely enough and unlike ours, against periodising at large, which appears to extend the justified vigilance against misplaced and tendentious Western-centric uses of the divide between, say, the mediaeval and the modern period, to an appeal for the proscription of periodising as such. Cf. Kathleen Davis, *Periodization and Sovereignty: How Ideas of Feudalism and Secularisation Govern the Politics of Time* (Philadelphia: University of Pennsylvania Press, 2008).

5. Cf. Jacob Taubes, *The Political Theology of Paul*, tr. Dana Hollander (Stanford: Stanford University Press, 2003), p.103.

6. Though Schmitt's core insights, in *Political Theology: Four Chapters on the Concept of Sovereignty* (Chicago: University of Chicago Press, 2006), concern the close relationship linking metaphysics and politics, and is best formulated in his claim: 'the metaphysical image that a definite epoch forges

of the world has the same structure as a form of its political organization' (p. 46), his most successful mantra is a different one, namely: 'all significant concepts of the theory of the state are secularised theological concepts' (p. 36). This, however, is effectively just a mantra – an oracle, and one characterised by fundamental ambivalence. The word 'secularised' here can refer to an effective process of change; the trouble is that it can refer equally well to a swift gesture of passing off as 'different' an object that remains, in all but name or appearance, perfectly unchanged. It can refer to a transformation; yet it can also refer to a pseudo-change, a 'zero-degree transformation'. Accordingly, the phrase can be understood as meaning either of two extremely different things, and indeed as favouring two opposed (modernist, anti-modernist) theoretical readings of what happened during the past few centuries of Western history. Whether it is understood as pointing to a substantial, even a radical change, or to a case of upheld identity under the guise of a cosmetic change of appearance, depends on the *reader's input*, as what is seen in bi-stable image depends on the onlooker's input. To find her way out of the hypnotic trance – by making a . . . *decision* – the reader needs to ask a simple question: Are secularised theological concepts theological concepts? Yes, or no? Schmitt does not want to decide: wishing to serve all, he uses an argument equivalent to a Ponzi scheme. Whether the concepts underlying the modern theory of the state find in those of premodern theology (1) their genuine, if remote, point of departure, or (2) their exact spitting image, though covered by a paper-thin veneer – 'secularised' is a term that caters for both. Is 'secularisation' a world-changing, society-changing process? Or is it only a strategy of travestying an arid and unforgiving state of fact making it appear as a forward-looking and *manageable attitude*, by removing the religious effect from its confessional shrine, putting it instead into a redemptive future? The phrase owes the charm it exercises over a certain academic view of politics to a virtuoso compromise, an art of accrediting an undecidable equilibrium between two incompatible readings.

7. While other authors, such as his later adversary Hans Blumenberg and the declared Schmitt-sceptic Niklas Luhmann, had limited yet first-hand familiarity with late thirteenth-century doctrines on God's power, any such claim on behalf of Schmitt remains mere conjecture – which

is astonishing enough, as after all, it was Schmitt who first opened the path to political theology. The consistently unspecific level of his relevant utterances jars with their immense and unique success. Throughout the century following the publication of his study, an almost unquantifiable number of specialised historians have published studious and patient work, both editions of texts hitherto available only as manuscripts, and erudite comments dealing with the texts and themes that Schmitt refers to, if in the most vague and general terms. Today, nothing remains of the thin layer of ice upon which, back in 1922, the politico-theological prize-skater Schmitt produced his fast and elegant figures. Even so, it was his pioneering 180-degree turn that succeeded in announcing and, eventually, enforcing the end of the long glaciation period that had been imposed on late mediaeval philosophy by a powerful, multi-source anti-scholastic drive. The occasional volume on mediaeval Franciscan subtleties contributed earlier by one or the other dissenting (i.e. not neo-Thomist) Roman *monsignor* could barely interrupt a silencing campaign that started with the age of the humanists, outlived the Enlightenment and found its definitive expression in Carl von Prantl's four-volume indictment *Geschichte der Logik im Abendlande* ('History of Logic in the West') (Munich, 1855–70). The ice of indifference created by this long tradition of rejection thawed only gradually, starting with a few pioneering studies in 1930 and later giving rise to the ever-increasing explosion of monographs on late mediaeval philosophy/theology since 1970 and up to the present day.

8. In this perspective the 'All power to God!' of intellectuals of mendicant orders in the last quarter of the thirteenth century can be clearly seen as belonging to the same historical series that also includes, at its opposite end, the 'All power to the Soviets!' of Lenin's *Theses* of April 1917. It remains open to guess whether in matters of social governance the decisive bifurcations take place in the twentieth rather than in the thirteenth century. While Thomas of Aquinas' coining of *divine all-powerfulness* is based upon a daring reinterpretation of Book XII of Aristotle's *Metaphysics* – where God is presented as pure act *without any power* (on this cf. Gwenaëlle Aubry, '*Ousia energeia* and *actus purus essendi* from Aristotle to Aquinas: some groundwork for an archaeology of power', *Tijdschrift voor Filosofie* 77 (2015), 827–54), the Franciscan school's conception of divine power is built upon Will,

leading to a more rigorous definition of God's absolute/ ordinate power – in a distant but undeniable affinity to certain contemporaneous Muslim theologians of God's power, an affinity that still remains insufficiently investigated today.

9. Cf. Olivier Boulnois, *La puissance et son ombre: La toute-puissance divine de Pierre Lombard à Luther* (Paris: Aubier, 1994); A. B. Wolter, *Duns Scotus on the Will and Morality* (Washington, DC: Catholic University of America Press: 1986), with further references.

10. Cf. Michel Villey, *La formation de la pensée juridique moderne* (Paris: Presses Universitaires Françaises, 1968); Giovanni Tarello, 'Profili giuridici della question della povertà nel francescanesimo prima di Ockham', *Annali della Facoltà di Giurisprudenza dell'Università di Genova* III (1964), 338–448; Giorgio Agamben, *The Highest Poverty: Monastic Rules and Form-of-Life* (Stanford: Stanford University Press, 2013).

11. Kenan B. Osborne, *The History of Franciscan Theology* (St Bonaventure, NY: Franciscan Institute (St Bonaventure University), 1994).

12. Giacomo Todeschini, *Il prezzo della salvezza: Lessici mediaevali del pensiero economico* (Rome: NIS, 1994); Roberto Lambertini, *Apologia et crescità dell'identità francescana* (Rome: Istituto Storico Italiano per il Medioevo, 1990); 'La difesa dell'ordine francescano', in Alain Boureau, Sylvain Piron (eds), *Pierre de Jean Olivi (1248–98)* (Paris: Vrin, 1999), pp. 201 ff.

13. Cf. Luca Parisoli, *La philosophie normative de Duns Scot* (Rome: Antonianum, 2008).

14. Cf. the synthesis of Bernard Forthomme, *La pensée franciscaine, un seuil de la modernité* (Paris: Belles Lettres, 2014).

15. The motive of a religion that conceives of itself, in its own discourse, not as of the paradigmatic instantiation of the totality itself but as part of a larger compassing social totality, is generally understood as an indicator of that religion's capacity of functioning within a secular framework. If so, then the seeds of secularism go back, not to the thirteenth century (which, when considered as a date for the birth of the 'secular' is rejected by most specialists of the subject on account of its being far too early), but to the far earlier parable of the tribute penny (Matthew 17, 21–4): the time of the origins of Christianity.

16. Cf. Anton Schütz, 'Epigenesis, law, and the *Medium Aevum* as a medium', *Divus Thomas* 116 (2013).

17. Cf. Carl Schmitt, *Political Romanticism* (Cambridge, MA:

MIT Press, 1986 [first German edition, Berlin: Duncker & Humblot, 1919]).

18. The most-quoted example in this respect is the heavily philo-sophical-critical work of the Kurdish hanbali, Ibn Taymiyya, a Syrian contemporary of John Duns Scotus. Specifically, on his political theology, cf. Caterina Bori, 'Political theology and Islam: Ibn Taymiyya (d. 728/1328) and the Mamluk sultanate', *Revue de l'histoire des religions*, 1 (2007), accessed 24 August 2016, http://rhr.revues.org/5225, accessed 10 September 2016; Ovamir Anjum, *Reason and Politics in Medieval Islamic Thought: The Taymiyyan Moment* (Madison: University of Wisconsin Press, 2008).

19. Cf. Augustine who, somewhere in his *Confessions*, admits the perfectly realist possibility that he could have easily remained forever in his youthful Platonist mindset. Had he found a philosophical master worth his salt, the Church father tells his readership, he might never have started study-ing the Bible.

20. Cf. Schütz, 'Legal modernity and mediaeval theology: the case of Duns Scotus, Ordinatio 1, D.44', in *The Theology of 'potentia dei'*, 418–52.

21. For numerous worthwhile suggestions in view of Scotism as a prodrome of modern legal positivism, cf. Parisoli, *La philosophie normative de Duns Scot*.

22. This is probably the doctrine referred to by Lenin in his article from early 1917: 'The Military Programme of the Proletarian Revolution', when he mentions the 'reaction-ary Christian Socialists'. V. I. Lenin, *Collected Works*, vol. 23 (Moscow: Progress Publishers), pp. 77–87, at 80.

23. Martin Loughlin, 'The constitutional imagination', *Modern Law Review*, 78 (1) (2015). In sum, 'constitutional imagina-tion' refers to the way we have been able to conceive the relationship of thought, text and action in the constitution of modern political authority. Loughlin seeks to demonstrate how modern constitutional texts come to be invested with a 'world-making' capacity. The argument is advanced first by explaining how social contract thinkers have been able to set the parameters of the constitutional imagination (thought), then by showing that constitutions are agonistic documents and their interpretative method is determined by a dialectic of ideology and utopia (text), and finally by examining the degree to which constitutions have been able to colonise the political domain, thereby converting constitutional aspira-tion into political reality (action). It concludes by suggesting

that although we seem to be entering a constitutional age, this is an ambiguous achievement and whether the power of the constitutional imagination can still be sustained remains an open question.

24. See for example Somek, 'Administration without sovereignty', in P. Dobner and M. Loughlin (eds), *The Twilight of Constitutionalism?* (Oxford: Oxford University Press, 2010), pp. 267–8.

25. Cf. on this origin for a philosophical position, built on the groundwork of Derrida and far more daring and profound than other ventures coming from the same direction, see Serge Margel, *Superstition: l'anthropologie du religieux en terre de chrétienté* (Paris: Galilée, 2005).

26. The common eponymous reference exhausts itself at a merely nominal level – in other words, within a religious canon, a *name* is always carried and suffused by a meaning or ordered multiplicity of meanings, and the name 'Abraham' has, within each of the so-called 'Abrahamic religions', a meaning of its own, different from its meaning in the *other* 'Abrahamic religions'. Cf. Rémy Brague, *Du dieu des chrétiens ou d'un ou deux autres* (Paris: Flammarion, 2008).

27. For the kabbalist notion of Tsimtsum, God's self-contraction and increasing self-restraint in favour of man, cf. Isaac Luria (1534–72) and comments by Gershom Scholem, *Major Trends in Jewish Mysticism* (New York: Schocken, 1946); Moshé Idel, *Kabbalah: New Perspectives* (New Haven: Yale University Press, 1988); Charles Mopsik, *Cabbale et cabbalistes* (Paris: Albin Michel, 2003).

28. Cf. Pavel Lungin's film *Taxi Blues* (1990).

29. Cf. Jonathan Crary, *24/7: Late Capitalism and the Ends of Sleep* (London: Verso, 2014), who, however, painstakingly avoids any reference to 'religion'.

30. Cf. Margel, *Superstition*, pp. 63ff.

31. On the changed self-appraisal of those calling themselves 'secta', and 'religio' only since Tertullianus in the later second century – a change that has transformed them from *triton genos/tertium genus* – the 'third kind', as they were neither Greek (pagan) nor Jewish – to a religious movement, see Sachot, 'Comment le christianisme est-il devenu religio?', *Revue des Sciences Religieuses*, 59 (1985), 95–118.

32. Giorgio Agamben, *The Kingdom and the Glory: For a Theological Genealogy of Economy and Government* (Stanford: Stanford University Press, 2011), p. 162.

33. *Per* Gauchet all the great religions of the 'Axial Age' (the term

comes from the German philosopher Karl Jaspers), brought with them a three-fold 'dynamics of transcendence'. In sum: the 'sacred', previously dispersed and coextensive with something like 'nature', is concentrated in one omnipotent creator God who still sustains the world yet is increasingly withdrawn from it; subsequently, God's transcendence led man to abandon magical explanations for the phenomena that surrounded him; finally, as the new God was to be the God of all men, the idea of human universality under one God and his human vicar both legitimated and spread with political empires. These dynamics of transcendence result in a fascinating paradox: the more powerful God becomes, 'the more man is free' in the sense that man begins to reason for himself, to question the divine law, to embrace his freedom. Cf. Gauchet, *The Disenchantment of the World: A Political History of Religion*, tr. O. Burge, foreword by Charles Taylor (Princeton: Princeton University Press, 1999). Philosopher J. L. Nancy writes of the 'auto-deconstructive' tendencies of monotheisms to marginalise their myths in favour of narratives that relate directly to the needs and interests of man, including in relation to law and politics. J. L. Nancy 2003 'Deconstruction of monotheism', *Postcolonial Studies: Culture, Politics, Economy* 6 (1) (2003), pp. 37–46.

34. The arrangement of the three intellectuals as the original 'founding father' cloverleaf of modern, sovereignty-oriented state politics has invaded pedagogical, sometimes even scholarly accounts. However, apart from their common insistence on the political self-assertion of the mundane power-holder and his operations, and on his autonomy from transcending missions and offices – as the lieutenant, agent, heir, and debtor of the earlier theological addressee of these claims – the dearth of other common features should be kept in mind between Machiavelli, the Florentine historian and sage (1469–1525), Jean Bodin, the jurist and demonologist from Angers (1530–96), born two generations later, and Thomas Hobbes, the scientist and philosopher from Malmesbury (1588–1679), who was born two further generations after Bodin.

35. Yosef Hayim Yerushalmi, 'Postscript: reflections on forgetting', *Zakhor: Jewish History and Jewish Memory* (Seattle: University of Washington Press, second edition, 1996), p. 113.

36. In view of this rejection it is legitimate to speak of a certain persistent horror of 'Western democracy' in certain

Muslim circles today. What does remain misleading is not to report that the mediaeval triumph of Islamic theology over philosophy occurred in circumstances that were anything but conducive to a coherent Islamic political theology. The absence of a pyramidal 'Church'-type organisation, the fragmented nature of Islamic jurisprudence and the personal rather than territorial scope of Islamic law, etc., meant that there was no sustainable institutionalised benefit to power from theological sources – at least until the Ottoman Porte 'canonised' one out of the four Islamic law schools and started appointing *qadis* (jurisconsults) from that school throughout its territory; and certainly before the anti-colonial rise of political Islamism (which will covet, tragically, the mediaeval Western paradigm of a synchrony of divine and terrestrial sovereignty for the benefit of sovereignty). See M. Diamantides 'Towards a Western–Islamic conception of legalism', in L. Barshack, P. Goodrich and A. Schütz (eds), *Law, Text, Terror* (London: Glasshouse Press, 2006), pp. 95–118.

37. See 'Introduction', in M. Loughlin and N. Walker (eds), *The Paradox of Constitutionalism* (Oxford: Oxford University Press, 2007)

38. On this, in connection to Schmitt's later *Concept of the Political* (1927) and Leo Strauss' criticisms, see the indispensable study of H. Meier, *Carl Schmitt and Leo Strauss: The Hidden Dialogue* (Chicago: Chicago University Press, 1995).

39. See Schmitt, *Roman Catholicism and Political Form*, tr. G. L. Ulmen (New York: Praeger, 1996 [1923]).

40. It cannot be over-emphasised that the move towards the practice and doctrine of *oikonomia*, theological and otherwise, is a move away from the question of 'political theology' in the form in which it is dealt with by Schmitt and Peterson, and their many followers. There is no worse news for either economists or theologians than to be told of their *commonality*. The suggestion of a coupling between theology (religion) and politics casts over the universalist–oteriological message of glory and promise that they hold in common the shadow of a God who is at once an absolute guarantor of eschatological redemption (salvation, progress, emancipation, etc.) and an *oikonomos* asking us to 'hold on' and to 'bear with us' for the time being, like signs on construction sites that say 'Excuse any inconvenience – we are working for you'. For politics, as for theology (or religion), the idea of a proximity with *oikonomia* epitomises all symptoms of a

killjoy, as the very notion of the house concedes a portion of legitimacy of the particular, creating an obstacle for the enforcement of an abstract programme. Cf. Agamben, *The Kingdom and the Glory*.

41. For a new reading of European nationalism, one that contrasts with the usual assumption about its birth in the nineteenth century by tracing its roots to early modernity, cf. Caspar Hirschi, *The Origins of Nationalism: An Alternative History from Ancient Rome to Early Modern Germany* (Cambridge: Cambridge University Press, 2012).

42. Gregory VII's 'Dictatus Papae ... was a ... revolution and a decision of competent authority ... The first revolution of the Occident broke out in the breast of one man'. E. Rosenstock-Huessy, *Out of Revolution: Autobiography of Western Man* (Providence/Oxford: Berg, 1993), p. 539.

43. Harold Berman, *Law and Revolution: The Formation of the Western Legal Tradition* (Harvard: Harvard University Press, 2009), see especially Chapter 2, 'The origins of the Western legal tradition in the Papal Revolution', pp. 94–100.

44. Rosenstock-Huessy, *Out of Revolution*, p. 528.

45. Ibid., p. 529.

46. Ibid., p. 518.

47. Ibid., p. 536.

48. Wendy Brown, *Walled States, Waning Sovereignty* (New York: Zone Books, 2010), pp. 53–4.

49. Giorgio Agamben, *Stasis: Civil War as a Political Paradigm* (Edinburgh: Edinburgh University Press, 2015).

50. 'Hierarchy', not a word of classical Greek, is a neologism coined by famous yet unidentified Greek Christian writer Ps.-Dionysius Areopagita in the fifth/sixth centuries. It means 'the rule of the holy', and is used in two separate works to refer to the ruling personnel, here of the Church, there of the Heavens. In its modern and current use, the term refers to the verticality of any power structures with no relevance given to the notion of the Holy. The work of the Indianist and sociologist Louis Dumont offers a recent application of the term. Cf. his *Homo Hierarchicus: Essai sur le système des castes* (Paris: Gallimard, 1971); *Essais sur l'individualisme: une perspective anthropologique sur l'idéologie moderne* (Paris: Seuil, 1983).

51. Zygmunt Bauman, *Wasted Lives: Modernity and its Outcasts* (London: Polity Press, 2003).

52. Hence, even though the world should perish, God's Throne will remain; as such 'The throne is not a symbol of [finite]

regality but of [immortal] glory;' Giorgio Agamben, *The Kingdom and the Glory: For a Theological Genealogy of Economy and Government* (Stanford: Stanford University Press, 2011), p. 245. The embedded message is: The world presupposes sovereignty, rather than the other way around.

53. In the systems theory of Niklas Luhmann and his followers; for an example of its use see Clemens Mattheis 'The system theory of Niklas Luhmann and the constitutionalization of the World Society', *Goettingen Journal of International Law* 4 (2) (2012), 625–47.

54. Cf., for instance, Belgian philosopher and epistemologist Isabelle Stengers, 'Les généalogies de l'autoorganisation', *Cahiers du CREA* 8 (1985), addressing 'couplages à la place de causalité' and 'évènements couplés'. Niklas Luhmann – relevant entry: 'structural coupling' – has been focusing on the twilight of causality in the social sciences in countless articles and book-length studies since the early 1960s (cf. note 55 below). Earlier attempts to find a way out of all-powerful causal mastery include the post-Cartesian philosophers usually referred to as occasionalists (substituting *occasio* for *causa*) and their contemporary Leibniz, who centre-staged the issue in a work titled *Essays in Theodicy*. The decisive notion of Leibniz's version of immanentism is that of compossibility – a remote ancestor of the mid-twentieth-century neo-cyberneticist concept of heterarchy. Albeit with nuances, human mastery, succeeding upon divine mastery, appears as a dependent variable of its theological predecessor, as it is shown by numerous scholarly contributions to the genesis of the notions of state, state power and sovereignty in early modern European absolutism, but perfectly traceable to the history of mediaeval European theological doctrines of divine omnipotence and God's dual (i.e. absolute and ordered) power. Enquiring into the genealogy of power confronts the unsettling issue of where exactly to locate the superiority of a human-based over a God-based model of mastery. A reminder of Foucault's famously uncompromising way of dealing with this issue is in order here. For Foucault, the transition from divine-centred to human-centred humanities was a historical succession, not a discovery or a progress in knowledge. This is why he introduces the image of the waves leaving their trace on the beach, a likeness that incidentally can be encountered in kabbalist writing as well. Each wave draws its line on the sand, inscribes its signature, ceaselessly replaced by the

next. 'Humanism' has drawn a line on the beach; other faces preceded it; still others will follow.

55. Niklas Luhmann, 'Funktion und Kausalität', *Kölner Zeitschrift für Soziologie und Sozialpsychologie* 14 (1962), 617–44.

56. Its appointed Chair, Sir John Chilcot, described the inquiry's terms of reference as follows: 'Our terms of reference are very broad, but the essential points, as set out by the Prime Minister and agreed by the House of Commons, are that this is an Inquiry by a committee of Privy Counsellors. It will consider the period from the summer of 2001 to the end of July 2009, embracing the run-up to the conflict in Iraq, the military action and its aftermath. We will therefore be considering the UK's involvement in Iraq, including the way decisions were made and actions taken, to establish, as accurately as possible, what happened and to identify the lessons that can be learned. Those lessons will help ensure that, if we face similar situations in the future, the government of the day is best equipped to respond to those situations in the most effective manner in the best interests of the country.' The timing and nature of the Iraq War inquiry, decided by the then prime minister, was not expected to report back until after the 2010 General Election and in the end was delivered in 2016. It is apposite to remember that the Conservative party leader and later Prime Minister David Cameron dismissed the inquiry as 'an establishment stitch-up', and the Liberal Democrats threatened a boycott. In a parliamentary debate MPs from all the major parties criticised the government's selection of the inquiry team's members, drawing attention to the absence of anyone with first-hand military expertise, of members with acknowledged or proven inquisitorial skills, and of any elected representatives. Historian Sir Martin Gilbert's appointment to the inquiry was criticised on the basis that he had once compared George W. Bush and Tony Blair to Roosevelt and Churchill. Several MPs drew attention to the fact that Chilcot would be unable to receive evidence under oath. The criticism by the Liberal Democrats continued at the start of the public hearings, with party leader Nick Clegg accusing the government of 'suffocating' the inquiry, referring to the power given to government departments to veto sections of the final report. Meanwhile, a group of anti-war protestors staged a demonstration outside the conference centre.

57. Cf. the still today passionately disputed case of Austrian socialist writer and neo-Lamarckian biologist Paul Kammerer

(1880–1926). Invited to the Soviet Union and selected for a leading role in an important research institution in Moscow, Kammerer shot himself when he was accused of tampering with his research results. This is unlike the later case of Stalin's agro-biologist, the impostor Trofim Denisovitch Lysenko, who, though claiming to follow Darwin rather than Lamarck, was also utterly successful as an militant advocate of 'bettering nature', and upheld for decades the victory of Soviet scientific optimism over 'bourgeois' biological science, destroying with lasting effect, by systematically subjecting scientific experience to a preference for Party ideology, the very basis of a much-needed branch of research in the Soviet Union. Denounced since the 1960s, Lysenko – who, over the years of his rule over Soviet biology, managed to have numerous rivals and contradicting colleagues sent to the Gulag – himself successfully avoided any hardship, trial, etc., his biography showing that professional optimism, commitment to the cause of the proletariat, taking sides with 'progressive ideas', etc., can also optimise individual career chances, and even provide impunity. Cf. Dominique Lecourt, *Proletarian Science? The Case of Lysenko* (London: Humanities Press, 1977).

58. For a *philosophical* critique of the concept of *action* see the concluding volume of Agamben's *Homo Sacer* series, *The Use of Bodies*, tr. A. Kotsko (Stanford: Stanford University Press, 2016). There will be more on this topic in his forthcoming book (we quote the working title) *Karman e crimen: trattato sull'azione, la colpa e il gesto* ('Karman and crime: a treatise on action, guilt and gesture').

Chapter 6

1. See Aviezer Ravitzky, *Messianism, Zionism, and Jewish Religious Radicalism* (Chicago: Chicago University Press, 1996).
2. Moshe Halbertal, *Exile and Kingdom*, a review of Ravitzky, *Messianism, Zionism, and Jewish Religious Radicalism* (see previous note), available at https://newrepublic.com/article/70766/exile-and-the-kingdom, accessed 1 July 2016.
3. Ibid., n.p.
4. Ibid., n.p.
5. Ibid., n.p.
6. Ibid., n.p.
7. Ibid., n.p.
8. Tom Segev, *The First Israelis* (New York: Macmillan, 1986), p. 261.

9. Moshe Pearlman and David Ben-Gurion, *Ben-Gurion Looks Back in Talks with Moshe Pearlman* (London: Schocken Books, 1970), p. 221.
10. Segev, *The First Israelis*, p. 261.
11. Patricia J. Woods, *Judicial Power and National Politics: Courts and Gender in the Religious–Secular Conflict in Israel* (New York: SUNY Press, 2008), p. 72 and throughout.
12. Halbertal, *Exile and Kingdom* (n.p.).
13. Ibid. (n.p.).
14. Ibid. (n.p.).
15. Babylonian Talmud, treatise *Ketubot*, p. 111a.
16. *Berit* from *bara* (Hebrew: to choose, eat, cut; cf. *beria*, 'creation'). Such is the condition of the 'first appearance of a face in the undifferentiated chaos of the world . . . In contrast to the contract, before the alliance there is no name or particularity. This is not to circumscribe the problem of the "excluded third" (or to restate it). In Hebrew *berit* means both excision and creation. The creation of the world is an alliance in which the "absent" is neither a name for a creator God nor the world in relation to us but the very nature of alliance. God creates the world *through* alliance with humanity and so withdraws from Himself, takes leave of His Being like the womb, which opens and empties itself for the embryo. Absence is henceforth central in us and in God-for-us. Thus: the world is disappearance of the [meaning of] the world as indicated in the word *olam*. Not: absence in relation to my other but an absence in itself confronting which renders my other and the third visible.' In the covenant, 'all elements of contract are found united (process, negotiation, clarification of terms, presence of partners . . .) with the emphasis being on the act of alliance. The verb is not made out of the radicals of a noun; there is no object (in the accusative case). Making alliance is not part of an alliance; thus the act of making alliance does not contain its origin but refers to something else. One does not "ally" oneself to "an alliance" but one cuts it out (*kerot berit*, French: *la découpe*), or excises it (French: *la retranche*) since the same verb designates also the excommunication, the ostracism (*karet*).' S. Trigano, *Philosophie de la Loi: L'origine de la politique dans la Tora* (Paris: Cerf, 1991), p. 15.
17. 'The moment of the political is the moment of evasion, effacement, exit . . . The interpretation of the political from an immanent point of view alone, through a sociology of power for example, is all but condemned to miss the essence of the

phenomenon even if this immanence obliges us a threshold of transcendence. It is the "before" of power – power that is already "in power" – that determines our comprehension. Thus, democracy and theocracy are both confronted with one single common experience: that of posing the political, the necessary, prior to clarity (rational or traditional), and [forging] a myth of an origin, which remains forever outside investigation.' Ibid., p. 15.

18. Ibid., p. 15.
19. The paradigmatic way of creating and keeping bonds of alliance is directly related to the history of the complex object called a symbol. Friends – often acting for 'families' – broke a clay shard, called a *symbolon*, each keeping one of the two pieces – evidence that would, when and if necessary, testify to their alliance. Here, the anticipated annulment of the break as an act of memory was a condition of the efficacy of the pact. In general the *polis* was an exceptionally conservative society, all but outlawing legislation, as much as any other 'innovation', so 'new laws' were resorted to only sparsely and in exceptional situations, when 'memorable' law was not deemed expedient. Rebellion was not an option. In contrast, the growth of legislation in imperial Rome coincides with the increased social mobility that it sought to regulate.
20. Anthony Kaldellis, *The Byzantine Republic: People and Power in New Rome*, Harvard (Harvard: Harvard University Press, 2015).
21. M. Diamantides 'Glorious sovereignty – inglorious oikonomia; the political theology of managing humanity in a historicised comparative perspective', in P. Goodrich and M. Rosenfeld (eds) *Economies of Interpretation* (New York: Fordham University Press [forthcoming 2017]).
22. II Samuel [II Kings], VII: 8–16, Psalm 132 [131]:11.
23. Gilbert Dagron, *Emperor and Priest: The Imperial Office in Byzantium*, tr. Jean Birrell J. (Cambridge: Cambridge University Press, 2003), p. 313.
24. Ibid., p. 314.
25. Cf. reports from Western diplomats and travellers, including the early mediaeval Italian traveller and diplomat Liutprand of Cremona, whose account (to the Saxon Holy Roman Emperor Otto I) of his first embassy to Byzantium, and especially of the imperial audience granted him by the Basileus Constantinos Prophyrogenetos in 949/950, tells of a theatre stage-like scenography that included the theatrical gesture

of lifting the Emperor, who had until then been 'sitting only slightly elevated just over floor level', *on his throne* high up above the assembled subjects, close to the ceiling of the palace. To increase the baffling effect, this was done at the moment when the Italian ambassador had to put his head to the ground for the purpose of ceremonial *proskynesis* (the ritual of bowing completely down in front of the other person). Cf. Liutprand of Cremona, 'Antapodosis', VI/5, quoted after the ed. Paolo Chiesa, *Liudprandi Cremonensis Opera Omnia*, Corpus Christianorum, vol. 156 (Turnhout: Brepols, 1998), p. 147.

26. G. Dagron, *Emperor and Priest – The Imperial Office in Byzantium* (Cambridge: Cambridge University Press, 2003), p. 167.
27. Cf. Kaldellis, *The Byzantine Republic*.
28. Perfectly illustrated in the surprisingly detailed prescriptions of a fourteenth-century author, the Pseudo-Kodinos, in his *Traité des offices*, ed. Jean Verpeaux (Paris: Éditions du CNRS, 1976).
29. For the presence of this theme, however subordinate, also in the mediaeval West, see Stefan Kuttner, *Harmony from Dissonance: An interpretation of Medieval Canon Law* (Saint Vincent, Latrobe: Wimmer Lectures Series, 1960), with references to the early Greek Fathers and synods, yet unlike the situation in Byzantium, harnessed in a solid fabric of legalistic and administrative reason (which is not addressed by the author).
30. John A. McGuckin, *The Ascent of Christian Law: Patristic and Byzantine Formulations of a New Civilization* (New York: St Vladimir's Seminary Press, 2012), pp. 269–71.
31. Cf. Kuttner, *Harmony from Dissonance*.
32. Dagron, *Emperor and Priest*, p. 394.
33. Ibid., p. 191.
34. Cf. the celebrated article by Percy Ernst Schramm, then one of the foremost specialists in the field, whose title tells more than it perhaps wishes to about the comparative politico-theological significance of the east–west theme, 'Sacerdotium und Regnum im Austausch ihrer Vorrechte' ('Priesthood and kingship in the exchange of their prerogatives'), *Studi Gregoriani* 2 (1947), 403–57.
35. The tendency has ramifications at other moments of history: for example, one could examine whether Catholic conciliarism has not been far more influential in shaping the imagination of the modern state than the – stats-prone – classical Greek *demos*.

36. Treatise *Pirkei Avot* [1:6], available at http://www.torah.org/learning/pirkei-avos/#; accessed 3 August 2011.

37. The Hebrew verb *kneh* ('acquire') has the same root as the word for 'marriage'.

38. Cf. R. Cover, 'Obligation: A Jewish jurisprudence of the social order', *Journal of Law & Religion* 5 (1) (1987), 65–74.

39. D. Manderson, *Proximity, Levinas and the Soul of Law* (Montreal: McGill-Queen's University Press, 2007).

40. This idea came upon listening to J. Martel's lecture at Birkbeck School of Law in June 2011.

41. M. Diamantides, 'Levinasian ethics and the morality of law', in D. Manderson (ed.) *Essays on Levinas and Law: A mosaic* (London: Palgrave Macmillan, 2009), pp. 128–44; 'Levinas and critical legal thought', in M. Diamantidis (ed.) *Levinas, Law, Politics* (Abingdon and NY: Routledge/Cavendish, 2007), pp. 179–220. Understood as a hotbed of the potential subversion of established powers rather than as a disciplining ethical supplement of their exercise, ethical responsibility emphatically does *not* throw out the baby (politics) together with the bathwater (norms), as its critics would have it. Instead, it expresses a desire for freeing politics from the totalising effects of modern pragmatism in its duality, i.e. as politics of representation or as popular democracy. Removing the baby from both the cleansing water (the authority of norms) and indeed the bath tub (the authority of facts) has the effect of keeping the baby 'dirty' (in Levinas, for example, responsibility is infinite, thus the crucial issue is not that of equipping existing power structures with sustainable legitimacy by pseudo-cognitive 'why'-questions like: 'why is our community worthy to be upheld?', or: 'why this kind of community rather than that?', but to aporetic problem-questions such as: 'Is it at all righteous to be, to persist in being?'). Actions/decisions remain but cannot be redeemed as justified or duty-imposed. All they can do is to prove unjustified, bereft of an *arche*, thus 'useless' – if, that is, what is useful is understood as bolstering either the chances of some worthy identity (otherwise, i.e. if the identity is, on the contrary, oppressive, as giving rise to resistance against it). The desire to remain infinitely, gratuitously responsible is political insofar as it does not function as an enabling device to realise an objective goal, whether provisionally or definitively. I must answer/decide on the basis neither of an *arche*, nor of a 'principle' of

anarchy, as Reiner Schürmann suggested in a famous book of this title, but rather miserably, provisionally and sceptically conscious of not 'getting there' (of not realising any significant historical goal – even if, with some luck, I avoid some of what would be even worse). The attitude works against the assumption of the state institutional machinery as the repository of *Sittlichkeit* and its necessary context; it also defies materialist models of pseudo-plurality that purport to provide the appropriate answer for each and every one of a myriad of processes.

42. Cf. C. Douzinas, 'The many faces of humanitarianism' *Parrhesia* 2 (2) (2007), 1–28.
43. See https://www.opendemocracy.net/can-europe-make -it/slavoj-zizek-benjamin-ramm/slavoj-i-ek-on-brexit-cri sis-of-left-and-future-of-eur, accessed 10 October 2016.
44. Paul Veyne, *Quand notre monde est devenu chrétien (312–394)* (Paris: Albin Michel, 2007).
45. Diamantides, 'God's political power in Western and Eastern Christianity in comparative perspective', in Anton Schütz and Massimiliano Traversino (eds), *The Theology of 'potentia dei' and the History of European Normativity* (115 *Divus Thomas* [2012]), 333–81.
46. Justinian's *Digest*, § 1.4.1.
47. Justinian's *Digest*, § 1.3.31.
48. *Institutes*, § 2.17.8).
49. *Theophylactus, Historiae III*, ii, as translated by Edward Gibbon, *The History of the Decline and Fall of the Roman Empire* (London: Philipps, Sampson & Co, 1851), Part II, Chapter XLV, p. 311.
50. C. Thornhill, *A Sociology of Constitutions: Constitutions and State Legitimacy in Historical-Sociological Perspective* (Cambridge: University Press, 2011).
51. These are well summarised in D. Dyzenhaus, *The Constitution of Law: Legality in a Time of Emergency* (Cambridge: Cambridge University Press, 2006), pp. 35–53.
52. Carl Schmitt, *The Concept of the Political* (Chicago: University of Chicago Press, 1996).
53. E.g. C. Mouffe, *Agonistics: Thinking the World Politically* (London: Verso, 2013); 'Deliberative democracy or agonistic pluralism?', *Social Research* 66 (3) (Fall 1999), 745–58.
54. Cf. Diamantidis, 'Constitutional theory and its limits'.
55. Cf. Diamantidis, 'God's political power in Western and Eastern Christianity in comparative perspective', in Anton Schütz and Massimiliano Traversino (eds), *The Theology*

of *'potentia dei'* and the *History of European Normativity* (115 *Divus Thomas* [2012]).

56. See A. Laiou 'On just war in Byzantium' in John S. Langdon et al. (eds), *To Ellinikon: Studies in Honor of Speros Vryonis, Jr., vol. 1: Hellenic Antiquity and Byzantium* (New Rochelle NY: 1993), pp. 153–7.

Chapter 7

1. Cf. Marcel Gauchet, *The Disenchantment of the World: A Political History of Religion*, tr. O. Burge, foreword by Charles Taylor (Princeton: Princeton University Press, 1999).
2. Ibid., p. 36.
3. Ibid., p. 36.
4. Cf. Thornhill, *A Sociology of Constitutions: Constitutions and State Legitimacy in Historical-Sociological Perspective* (Cambridge: University Press, 2011).
5. Michael Oakeshott, *On Human Conduct* (London: Clarendon Press, 1975), p. 308.
6. Cf. Hirschi, *The Origins of Nationalism: An Alternative History from Ancient Rome to Early Modern Germany* (Cambridge: Cambridge University Press, 2012).
7. For example, C. Morris, *The Discovery of the Individual: 1050–200* (Toronto: Toronto University Press, 1972).
8. J. L. Nancy, 'Deconstruction of monotheism', *Postcolonial Studies: Culture, Politics, Economy* 6 (1) (2003).
9. Agamben, *The Kingdom and the Glory* (Stanford: Stanford University Press, 2011), p. 87.
10. Ibid., p. 87.
11. Niklas Luhmann, 'Wie ist soziale Ordnung möglich?', in *Gesellschaftsstruktur und Semantik: Studien zur Wissenssoziologie der modernen Gesellschaft*, vol. 2 (Frankfurt: Suhrkamp, 1981), pp. 195–285.
12. Henri Frankfort, *Kingship and the Gods* (Chicago: University of Chicago Press, 1948).
13. Cf. Q. Meillassoux, *After Finitude: An essay on the necessity of contingency*, tr. Ray Brassier (London: Continuum, 2010). The argument here springs from an inquiry into the special relationship between the process of self-rarefaction of metaphysics and the proliferation of personal religion this provokes – while the secularisation process itself had been triggered by the longstanding rarefaction of personal religion.
14. The observation is to be found in Heiner Müller's poem,

'Mommsen's Block' (concerning historian Theodor Mommsen's reluctance to finish his already Nobel Prize-crowned *Roman History* by writing the still outstanding fourth volume, the *History of the Emperors* – justifying himself with the mere 'court tittle-tattle' level of topic and sources), in W. Ernst (ed.), *Die Unschreibbarkeit von Imperien: Theodor Mommsens Römische Kaisergeschichte und Heiner Müllers Echo* ('Why empires cannot be written: Theodor Mommsen's *History of the Roman Emperors*, and Heiner Müller's echo') (Weimar: Verlag und Datenbank für Geisteswissenschaften, 1995), pp. 41–7.

15. First published in German in 1951, *Minima Moralia: Reflections from Damaged Life*, Theodor W. Adorno's patient explanation of why the moral maxim has stopped being an appropriate form, offers a *tour d'horizon philosophique* of immediate post-Second World War Germany, and fore-shadows, under the notion 'Kulturindustrie', at least one aspect of the takeover of managemental form.

16. Pierre Legendre, *L'autre Bible de l'Occident: le Monument romano-canonique. Étude sur l'architecture des sociétés (Leçons IX)* (Paris: Fayard, 2009).

17. Cf. P. Legendre., *Paroles poétiques échappées du texte: Leçons sur la communication industrielle* (Paris: Seuil, 1982); *L'Empire de la vérité: Introduction aux espaces dogmatiques industriels* (Paris: Fayard, 1983); but cf. already, *Jouir du pouvoir: Traité de la bureaucratie patriote* (Paris: Minuit, 1976).

18. For the methodological background, cf. N. Luhmann who, e.g. in *A Sociological Theory of Law* (London: Routledge, 1985), refers to counterfactual resistance/stability as the dis-tinguishing element between normative and cognitive ways of dealing with disappointing experiences. We either learn or behave normatively – in which case we stick, unbothered, to what we expected in the first place.

19. Simon Critchley, *The Faith of the Faithless: Experiments in Political Theology* (New York: Verso, 2012).

20. Ibid., p. 111.

21. Ibid., p. 10

22. Ibid., p. 55.

23. Ibid., p. 107.

24. Ibid., p. 85.

25. Ibid., p. 88.

26. Ibid., p. 91.

27. Ibid., p. 24.

28. Cf. N. Machiavelli, *The Discourses*, ed. Bernard Crick;

(Harmondsworth: Penguin, 1970), p. 141: *The Prince*, ed. Harvey C. Mansfield, Jr (Chicago: University of Chicago Press, 1985), p. 48.

29. Augustine, *Epistle 55*. Cf. B. Fischer, '"Tamquam machina quaedam": Ein Wort Augustinus' (Ep. 55.39) zum Ethos der Liturgiewissenschaft', *Miscellanea Liturgica in onore del Cardinale Giacomo Mercati*, vol. 2 (Rome/Paris: Desclée, 1967), pp. 85–93.

30. Critchley, *The Faith of the Faithless*, p. 10.
31. Ibid., p. 90.
32. Ibid., p. 86.
33. Ibid., p. 90.
34. Ibid., p. 68.
35. Ibid., p. 161.
36. Ibid., p. 18.
37. Ibid., p. 114.
38. Ibid., p. 157.
39. Ibid., p. 236.
40. E. Levinas, *Nine Talmudic Readings*, tr. A. Aronowicz (Bloomington, IN: Midland Books, 1990), p. 141.
41. Critchley, *The Faith of the Faithless*, p. 91.
42. Ibid., p. 4.
43. Cf. Jacques Rancière, 'Democracy, dissensus and the aesthetics of class struggle', *Historical Materialism* 13 (4) (2005), p. 294ff. Rancière began to theorise a new conception of revolution, in the manner in which aesthetics related to that concept, in his early work *The Nights of Labor: The Workers' Dream in Nineteenth-Century France*, translated by J. Drury, with an introduction by J. Reid (Philadelphia: Temple University Press, 1989), wherein he drew on his archival work on nineteenth-century workers' movements. Rancière's thesis was simple: workers were relegated to a certain position in society by means of a division of their time and space, and the forms of life appropriate to those positions. This meant working during the day (in, say, a factory), and sleeping at night, getting rest for the next day's work. Their revolutionary act was equally simple: the workers would no longer merely sleep at night, but use their time for something else – reading, writing, discussing, appropriating the language and literature of their 'superiors'. While Rancière's anarchism is hugely interesting, his version of universal revolution as being about purely present-day processes, unburdened by the legacy of the past and the fear of pure future, is open to criticism. Terry Eagleton, for one,

compellingly argues that there are severe limitations in the revolutionary potential of the self-creation and recreation of an autonomous aesthetic. For him, aesthetics equal ideology, but the possibility of the appropriation of the aesthetic by the 'universal victim' is less likely and effective than the reactionary and repressive potential of the creation of the autonomous aesthetic sphere by the particular ruling class. Eagleton's critique of the aesthetic category rehearses the Marxist notion of religion as the opiate of the masses, and art as substitute for religion. T. Eagleton, *After Theory* (London: Penguin, 2004), p. 47.

44. Critchley, *The Faith of the Faithless*, p. 91.
45. Ibid., p. 251.
46. Ibid., p. 40.
47. Ibid., p. 245.
48. Ibid., p. 117.
49. Ibid., p. 220.
50. Ibid., p. 243.
51. Ibid., p. 221.
52. See Frank Ruda, review of Simon Critchley, *The Faith of the Faithless*. Available at http://marxandphilosophy.org.uk/reviewofbooks/reviews/2012/593, accessed 10 October 2016.
53. Critchley, *The Faith of the Faithless*, p. 4.
54. The spectacular feature here, which underlies a certain Christian-apologetic position throughout, seems to be a propensity to shamefully hide away the reference to *oikonomia* under the fig leaf of a reference to higher-minded politics. The suspicion that this amounts almost to a professional arcanum of political theologians seems to be confirmed by an interview of G. Agamben with Gianluca Sacco about his first encounters with economic theology (8 March 2004). Agamben explains : 'I was working on the same theologians (the early apologetics, Justinius, Ignatius, and Tertullian) that Peterson analysed in his book on monotheism, in order to rediscover the origins of the political theology that he wanted to criticise. I realised that at the centre were not only and not so much the concepts of monarchy and political theology that Peterson wanted to reconstruct but another concept: oikonomia. It was a curious fact that every time this concept appeared Peterson interrupted the citation . . . I asked myself why this concept was being removed . . . I realised that the concept of oikonomia was central for [Peterson and Schmitt] and tried to construct a genealogy' (emphasis

added Cf. 'Intervista a Giorgio Agamben: Dalla teologia politica alla teologia economica (con Gianluca Sacco)', *Rivista della Scuola Superiore dell'economia e delle finanze/ Centro Ricerche Documentazione Economica e Finanziaria*, 2005. Available at http://rivista.ssef.it/site.php?page=200403081 84630627&edition=2005-05-01.

55. Critchley, *The Faith of the Faithless*, p. 233.
56. Simon Critchley, *Infinitely Demanding: Ethics of Commitment, Politics of Resistance* (London: Verso, 2013).
57. E. Levinas, *Totality and Infinity: An Essay on Exteriority*, tr. A. Lingis (Duquesne: Duquesne University Press, 1999).
58. Critchley, *The Faith of the Faithless*, p. 80.
59. Ibid., p. 80.
60. Ibid., p. 81.
61. M. Croce, cited in M. Loughlin, *The Idea of Public Law* (Oxford: Oxford University Press, 2003), p. 83.

Chapter 8

1. C. Schmitt *The Concept of the Political* (Chicago: University of Chicago Press, 1996).
2. As quoted by Hans Lindahl in 'Constituent power and reflexive identity: towards an ontology of collective self-hood', in M. Loughlin and N. Walker (eds), *The Paradoxes of Constitutionalism* (Oxford, Oxford University Press, 2007), p. 14. Kelsen's reasoning is that '[S]plit by national, religious and economic conflicts, that unity is ... more a bundle of groups than a coherent mass of one and the same aggregate state'. H. Kelsen, 'On the essence and value of democracy' in A. Jacobson and B. Schlink (eds), *Weimar: a jurisprudence of Crisis* (Berkeley, CA: University of California Press, 2000 [1927]), p. 89.
3. For the reasons for our disagreement with this thesis, defended by historian A. Kaldellis in *The Byzantine Republic: People and Power in New Rome* (Harvard: Harvard University Press, 2015), see Chapter 6.
4. Cf. Loughlin and Walker, *The Paradoxes of Constitutionalism*.
5. E.g. in J. Habermas, *Between Naturalism and Religion: Philosophical Essays* (London: Polity Press, 2008). Habermas' 'conversion' was gradual rather than sudden; in the 1980s a younger Habermas argued against religion, seeing it as an alienating reality; from the mid-1980s to the beginning of the twenty-first century he stopped discussing religion, relegating it to matters of private life; since the turn of the

century, Habermas has recognised the positive social role of religion.

6. In the intervening centuries, we encounter the explosion and golden age of the one dominant religion-founded power that appears to have consistently rejected, throughout many centuries of theology, the appeals of management and *oikonomia*. See Garth Fowden, *Before and after Muhammad: The First Millennium Refocused* (Princeton: Princeton University Press, 2014); also *Empire to Commonwealth: Consequences of Monotheism in Late Antiquity* (Princeton: Princeton University Press, 1993).

7. Cf. Dipesh Chakrabarty, *Provincializing Europe: Postcolonial Thought and Historical Difference* (Princeton: Princeton University Press, 2008); A. Abeysakara, *The Politics of Post-secular Religion: Mourning Secular Futures* (New York: Columbia University Press, 2008).

8. Cf. Pierre Legendre, *Dominium Mundi: L'Empire du Management* (Paris: Mille et une nuits, 2007), p. 26f.

9. See e.g. *Plastic Materialities: Politics, Legality, and Metamorphosis in the Work of Catherine Malabou* (Durham: Duke University Press, 2015).

10. As is well known, the term 'monotheism', albeit in its English version a seventeenth-century neologism, is in its current meaning not found before the religious and cultural science awakening at the end of the eighteenth and in the first years of the nineteenth century.

11. Cf. on this Rémy Brague, *Du dieu des chrétiens ou d'un ou deux autres* (Paris: Flammarion, 2008), cf. see Chapter 4, note 26.

12. Max Weber, *The Protestant Ethic and the Spirit of Capitalism* (London: Penguin, 2002).

13. Cf. for the notion of 'enreligioning', with rather more restrained use than the one suggested here, Q. Meillassoux, *After Finitude: An essay on the necessity of contingency*, tr. Ray Brassier (London: Continuum, 2010).

14. G. Agamben, *Opus Dei: An Archeology of Duty*, tr. A. Kotsko (Stanford: Stanford University Press, 2013), p. 40.

15. Cf. for instance, Niklas Luhmann, *Social Systems* (Stanford: Stanford University Press, 1995); *Introduction to Systems Theory* (Cambridge: Polity Press, 2013).

16. Cf. the article 'Philosophical archaeology', for Agamben's critique of 'discontinuism' – the exceptional event of an (early) Foucauldian choice *not* ratified by Agamben, in *The Signature of All Things: On Method* (Boston: MIT Press, 2009).

17. Such as, among many others, Talal Asad, Samera Esmeir, Serge Margel, Marcel Gauchet, Jean-Luc Nancy, Pierre Legendre, discussed above.
18. On this point see Nicolaus Sombart, *Die deutschen Männer und ihre Feinde: Carl Schmitt, ein deutsches Schicksal zwischen Männerbund und Matriarchatsmythos* ('German men and their enemies: Carl Schmitt, a German destiny between male alliance and matriarchal myth') (Munich: Hanser, 1991); let us signal a French translation published under the title *Les mâles vertus des Allemands: autour du syndrome de Carl Schmitt* (Paris: Cerf, 1999).
19. Cf. Niklas Luhmann, 'Trust', in *Trust and Power: Two Works* (Hoboken, NJ: Wiley, 1979).
20. Giorgio Agamben, *The Kingdom and the Glory* (Stanford: Stanford University Press, 2011); Marie-José Mondzain, *Image, Icon, Economy: The Byzantine Origins of the Contemporary Imaginary* (Stanford: Stanford University Press, 2005).
21. Cf. especially the Macy Conferences, starting from the 1940s, as documented e.g. in Jean-Pierre Dupuy, *On the Origin of Cognitive Science: The Mechanization of the Mind* (Boston: MIT Press, 2009).
22. ˮCf. Roy Rappaport, *Ritual and Religion in the Making of Humanity* (Cambridge: Cambridge University Press, 1999), pp. 70–4. For an instructive conceptual pun stressing the mutual presupposition of image (*ikon*) and household (*oikia*), 'ikonomia'/ikon-omia, cf. Marie-José Mondzain, *Image, Icon, Economy*.
23. Cf. G. Teubner, 'Societal constitutionalism: alternatives to state-centred constitutional theory?' in Christian Joerges, Inge-Johanne Sand and Gunther Teubner (eds), *Constitutionalism and Transnational Governance* (Oxford: Hart, 2004), pp. 3–28.
24. There is thus no such thing as a consistent dynamic leading to ever more of one kind and ever less of the other – here we disagree with Hans-Georg Möller's claim that we witness a movement leading 'from soul to systems'. Cf. Möller, *Luhmann Explained: From Souls to Systems* (Chicago: Open Court, 2006).
25. Jürgen Habermas, *The Future of Human Nature* (London: Polity Press, 2007) p. 16 ff.
26. 'We live today in an age simultaneously marked by the widespread adoption of the idea of constitutionalism, of ambiguity over its meaning, and about its continuing authority far from being an expression of limited govern-

ment; constitutionalism is now to be viewed as an extremely powerful mode of legitimating extensive government. Where this form of constitutionalism positions itself on the ideology-utopia axis . . . has rarely been more indeterminate . . . notwithstanding the liberal gains . . . the significance of the idea of the constitutional imagination has never exhibited a great degree of uncertainty.' Loughlin, 'The constitutional imagination', *Modern Law Review*, 78 (1) (2015), p. 25.

27. '[C]ontinued belief in political democracy as the realization of human freedom depends upon literally averting our glance from powers immune to democratization, powers that also give the lie to the autonomy and primacy of the political upon which so much of the history and present of democratic theory has depended' . . . 'While weakening nation state sovereigns yoke their fate and legitimacy to God, Capital . . . becomes God-like: almighty, limitless, and uncontrollable. In what should be the final and complete triumph of secularism, there is only theology.' The former quote is Brown, 'We are all democrats now . . .' in Amy Alen (ed.), *Democracy in what State?* (New York: Columbia University Press, 2011), p. 54. The latter is Brown: *Walled States, Waning Sovereignty* (New York: Zone Books, 2010), p. 66.

28. In one particularly stunning series of examples Žižek pushes his Christian-centric idyllism all the way to 'comparing' Eastern doctrines of non-involvement, e.g. that of the *Bhagavad Gita* (!), with Christian doctrines of concern and subjection, speaking of which he does not shrink from allusively drawing his readership's attention to the fact that Heinrich Himmler (the national-socialist dignitary in chief of the SS and the extermination camps, called by some historians today 'the murderer of the century') is said to have carried a copy of it *Bhagavad Gita* continuously in his pocket. Cf. S. Žižek, *The Puppet and the Dwarf: The Perverse Core of Christianity* (Boston: MIT Press, 2003), pp. 32–3.

Index

Index

Index